LAST TEAM STANDING

To Mom and Dad

Last Team Standing

How the Pittsburgh Steelers and the Philadelphia Eagles — "The Steagles" — Saved Pro Football During World War II

Matthew Algeo

Da Capo

Da Capo Press
A Member of the Perseus Books Group

Copyright © 2006 by Matthew Algeo

Designed by Mark Corsey

Grateful acknowledgment is made to David Meinert for permission to quote excerpts from the lyrics to "Candy Cigarette" by The Presidents of the United States of America.

Photo credits:
Jo Hanshaw (photo insert page 3, bottom photo)
Pro Football Hall of Fame/WireImage.com (photo insert page 6, both photos)
Temple University Libraries, Urban Archives, Philadelphia, PA (all other photos)

Cataloging-in-Publication data for this book is available from the Library of Congress.

First Da Capo Press hardcover edition 2006
First Da Capo Press paperback edition 2007
Hardcover: ISBN-10 0-306-81472-2; ISBN-13 978–0–306–81472-3
Paperback: ISBN-10 0-306-81576-1; ISBN-13 978–0–306–81576-8

Published by Da Capo Press
A Member of the Perseus Books Group
www.dacapopress.com

Da Capo Press books are available at special discounts for bulk purchases in the U.S. by corporations, institutions, and other organizations. For more information, please contact the Special Markets Department at the Perseus Books Group, 2300 Chestnut Street, Suite 200, Philadelphia, PA 19103, or call (800) 255-1514, or e-mail special.markets@perseusbooks.com.

1 2 3 4 5 6 7 8 9—10 09 08 07 06

Contents

∎ ❘ ❘ ❘ ∎

Roster

■ ı ı ı ı ■

1943 Phil-Pitt Steagles
(Players who appeared in five or more games)

Name	Position	Number	Height	Weight	Age
Bova, Tony*	E	85	6-1	190	26
Draft status: 4-F (eyesight)**					
Butler, Johnny*	HB	27	5-10	185	24
Draft status: 4-F (eyesight, knees)					
Cabrelli, Larry	E	84	5-11	194	26
Draft status: 4-F (knee)					
Canale, Rocco	G	75	5-11	240	26
Draft status: 1-A (active duty Army)					
Conti, Ed	G	67	5-11	205	30
Draft status: 3-A (father)					
Doyle, Ted*	T	72	6-2	224	29
Draft status: 3-A (father)					
Gauer, Charlie	FB	32	6-2	215	21
Draft status: 4-F (ulcers, knee)**					
Graves, Ray	C	52	6-1	205	24
Draft status: 4-F (hearing)**					
Hewitt, Bill	E	82	5-9	190	33
Draft status: 4-F (perforated eardrum)					

Name	Position	Number	Height	Weight	Age
Hinkle, Jack	HB	43	6-0	215	25
Draft status: 4-F (ulcers)**					
Kilroy, Frank "Bucko"	T	76	6-2	240	22
Draft status: 1-A (Merchant Marine)					
Kish, Ben	FB	44	6-0	200	26
Draft status: 4-F (head injury)**					
Michaels, Ed	G	60	5-11	210	28
Draft status: 4-F (hearing)					
Miller, Tom	E	89	6-2	198	25
Draft status: 4-F (head injury)**					
Paschka, Gordon	G	61	6-0	205	23
Draft status: 3-A (father)					
Schultz, Eberle "Elbie"*	G	71	6-4	252	25
Draft status: 3-A (father)					
Sears, Vic	T	79	6-3	223	25
Draft status: 4-F (ulcers)					
Sherman, Allie	QB	10	5-10	160	20
Draft status: 4-F (perforated eardrum)					
Steele, Ernie	HB	37	6-0	187	25
Draft status: 3-A (father)					
Steward, Dean*	HB	36	6-0	210	20
Draft status: 1-A (drafted in 1944)					
Thurbon, Bob*	HB	49	5-10	176	25
Draft status: 4-F (reason unknown)					
Wistert, Al	T	70	6-2	210	22
Draft status: 4-F (osteomyelitis)					
Wukits, Al*	C	50	6-3	190	25
Draft status: 4-F (hernia)					
Zimmerman, Roy	QB	7	6-2	200	25
Draft status: 3-C (father, farmer)					

* Property of the Pittsburgh Steelers. (All others property of the Philadelphia Eagles.)

** Honorably discharged from military service for physical reasons.

Preface: 1941

▮ ▯ ▯ ▯ ▮

IT WASN'T SUPPOSED TO BE a date that would live in infamy. That December day was just supposed to be Tuffy Leemans Day. After six seasons, Alphonse Emil Leemans, the New York Giants' burly halfback, was hanging up his spikes for good. Leemans was one of the toughest players in the National Football League—his nickname was not ironic—but he was also one of the most popular players, among teammates, fans, even opponents. He was self-effacing. He had a good sense of humor. After practice he liked to unwind by helping his wife make candlewick rugs.

Leemans had been discovered by Wellington Mara, the teenaged son of Giants owner Tim Mara. While visiting Washington, D.C., in the fall of 1935, the younger Mara saw Leemans lead George Washington College against mighty Alabama. GW got throttled, 39-0, but it wasn't Leemans' fault. But for him, the *Washington Star* reported, "the Buff and Blue might have yielded even more points." Especially impressive were Leemans' booming punts: twice he booted the ball more than 60 yards—from his own end zone. So taken was Wellington that, upon his return to New York, he practically begged his father to sign Leemans. Wisely, the old man took his son's advice: the Giants made Leemans their second pick in the first NFL draft the following spring. He proved to be more than just a great punter: He led the league in rushing his rookie season, carrying the ball for 830 yards. He also played excellent defense and returned kicks. He was an all-pro that season—and every season thereafter.

But now it was time for Leemans to move on to more lucrative pursuits—he had his eye on a duckpin bowling alley outside Washington—and the Giants wanted to give him a big sendoff before his final home game, at the Polo Grounds on December 7, 1941, against the Brooklyn Dodgers. (Professional football teams routinely "borrowed" the name of their local baseball franchise, much to posterity's confusion. There were even two different pro football teams called the New York Yankees in the 1940s.)

It was a perfect day for football, clear and cool, not a cloud in the sky. The massive stadium was packed with more than 55,000 fans, the league's biggest crowd of the season. Looking a little sheepish, Leemans accepted his parting gifts: a silver tray in the shape of a football and a small trophy, presented by Giants captain Mel Hein; a gold watch from his George Washington coach, Jim Pixlee; and $1,500 in defense bonds, presented by Jim Farley, New York State's Democratic boss, former Postmaster General—and ardent Giants fan.

Smiling, Leemans stepped up to the big microphone.

"Fans, teammates, my former coach, George Washington alumni, and"—sotto voce—"the Brooklyn Dodgers." The crowd roared with laughter. Leemans gave a brief, heartfelt speech in which, according to the *New York Times,* "he thanked every one for everything."

The rest of the day was sure to be anticlimactic: With a record of eight wins and two losses, the Giants had already clinched the Eastern Division title for 1941. They would play the Western Division winner for the league championship in two weeks, so today they would play hard—but not too hard.

With six wins and four losses, the Dodgers were playing for nothing but New York City bragging rights.

The game down in Washington that Sunday was meaningless, too. The Redskins were hosting the Philadelphia Eagles. Both teams had long been eliminated from playoff contention. The Redskins were ending their worst season since moving from Boston in 1937. The Eagles were guaranteed to finish with more losses than wins, just as they had every year since joining the league in 1933.

But the weather was spectacular in Washington, too, and the capital, weary of all the war talk and eager for outdoor diversions before the dreary Potomac winter took hold, turned out in force. Griffith Stadium, a dilapidated old battleship of a ballpark on Georgia Avenue NW, was nearly sold out. More than 27,000 fans filled the place, enabling the Redskins to set a new single-season attendance record: 194,450. Among the crowd were hundreds of servicemen, dapper in their long, double-breasted dress coats (soldiers in beige, sailors in dark blue), chatting, laughing, flirting with the girls working the concession stands, sipping hot cocoa or coffee (or maybe a little contraband whiskey). One of the servicemen at the game was a young naval officer named John F. Kennedy.

Not to be outdone by the Giants, Redskins owner George Preston Marshall orchestrated two "days" at Griffith Stadium that Sunday. One was for Bob Hoffman, a Redskin who was stricken with tuberculosis midway through the season. Hoffman was recovering nicely but was "believed to be under heavy expense." Collection boxes were placed throughout the stadium, the contents of which would be forwarded to the ailing player. It was also "Georgetown Day," to honor the four Hoyas taking part in the game: Clem Stralka of the Redskins and Lou Ghecas, Joe Frank, and Jim Castiglia of the Eagles. In a pregame ceremony each was presented a brand new suitcase by Al Blozis, a Georgetown senior and star tackle on the school's football team, who had the honor of representing the student body.

Of the three games that Sunday, the only one that really meant anything was at Comiskey Park in Chicago, where the

Cardinals were hosting their cross-town rivals, the Bears, before a crowd of 18,879. Usually the rivalry was phlegmatic—the Bears almost always won, and easily—but this game was different because there was a lot on the line. If the Bears won, they would tie the Green Bay Packers for first place in the Western Division, forcing the first divisional playoff game in league history. (The Packers had already finished their schedule, and many of them were in the stands to root the Cardinals on.) The Cardinals had something to play for as well. They were out to avenge a 53-7 whipping that the Bears had administered to them eight weeks earlier. There were no "days" at Comiskey that Sunday, only football.

The games in New York and Washington kicked off at 2:00 p.m., Eastern Time. The Chicago game began 30 minutes later.

At Griffith Stadium in D.C., the Eagles, who were 14-point underdogs, surprised everybody by quickly taking a 7-0 lead over the Redskins. Eagles halfback Jack Banta, who'd been cut by the Redskins earlier in the season, gained a measure of revenge on his old team by scoring the touchdown on a nice seven-yard run. Nick Basca, a rookie from Villanova, added the extra point. At the top of the stadium, in a rickety press box reeking of cigar smoke, the sportswriters, lined up behind their Underwoods and L.C. Smiths, kept one eye on the field and another on the Associated Press Teletype machine, which was spitting out reports from the other two games. In Chicago, the Cardinals were leading the Bears 7-0 in the first quarter. In New York, the Dodgers were beating the Giants by the same score early in the second quarter. It was shaping up to be a day of upsets.

Then, at around 2:45 p.m., the Teletype machine pounded out an enigmatic message: CUT FOOTBALL RUNNING.

Pat O'Brien, the AP man at the Eagles-Redskins game in D.C., turned to his friend from the *Washington Post*, Shirley Povich, and shrugged: Must be a problem with the wires.

But then came this: PEARL HARBOR BOMBED.

Then this: WAR ON.

The writers huddled close around the machine, silent and disbelieving. They were the only people in the stadium with any knowledge of the events unfolding, at that very moment, half a world away.

"For a few moments it was our exclusive secret," Povich later wrote. "And hard to grapple with was the stupefying news."

Jesse Jones—commerce secretary, presidential confidante, and one of the most powerful men in Washington—was enjoying the game from a box seat on the 50-yard line. An usher approached and handed him a note. Jones read it, got up, put on his coat and hat, and left the stadium in silence.

Another usher was dispatched to locate Edward A. Tamm, the assistant director of the FBI, and escort him to the stadium switchboard. Tamm was patched into a call with J. Edgar Hoover, who was in New York for the weekend, and Robert L. Shivers, the special agent in charge of the bureau's Honolulu office. Shivers held the phone out his office window. Tamm and Hoover could hear the explosions emanating from Pearl Harbor.

Soon Griffith Stadium echoed with cryptic announcements.

"Admiral W.H.O. Bland"—the head of the Navy's Bureau of Ordnance—"is asked to report to his office at once," the public address announcer solemnly intoned, the words bouncing around the stadium like a wayward punt.

"Mr. Joaquin Elizande"—the resident commissioner of the Philippines—"is asked to report to his office." The announcements grew more frequent, and urgent. Newspaper reporters and photographers were asked to report to their offices as well. The press box rapidly depopulated. By halftime, just a single photographer was on the sidelines.

But the big news—the outbreak of war—was never officially announced at Griffith Stadium.

"We don't want to contribute to any hysteria," the Redskins' general manager, Jack Espey, said at the time. Years later, though, Redskins owner George Preston Marshall gave a more prosaic explanation: "I didn't want to divert the fans' attention from the game." So, between the four-star pages, the PA announcer droned on with the usual announcements.

"Seymour hit off tackle and picked up about three yards."

"That pass, Baugh to Aguirre, was good for about eight yards."

But the crowd knew something was amiss.

"By the end of the half, there was a buzzing in the grandstands," the *Washington Post*'s Shirley Povich wrote. "Inevitably, shreds of the story began to ripple beyond the vicinity of the press box."

But those ripples never reached the players on the field.

"We didn't know what the hell was going on," Sammy Baugh, the Redskins' star passer remembered. "I had never heard that many announcements, one right after the other. We felt something was up, but we just kept playing."

Similar scenes unfolded in New York and Chicago: big shots were paged, the games went on, and the fans in the bleachers were oblivious. Perhaps it was just as well, considering the hard times ahead. For tens of thousands of Americans, a professional football game would be their last carefree diversion for many years. For some—including some on the field—it would be their last ever.

In the end, December 7, 1941, wasn't a day of upsets. The Redskins came from behind to beat the Eagles, 20-14. The Bears came back too, beating the Cardinals to force a playoff with the Packers. Only the Dodgers held their early lead, beating the Giants 21-7 and ruining Tuffy Leemans Day. Fans streaming out of the stadiums were greeted by newsboys hawking extra editions that confirmed the dreadful rumors: "U.S. AND JAPS AT WAR." More than 2,300 sailors, soldiers, and civilians at Pearl Harbor were dead.

The next day, President Roosevelt went before Congress and declared, "The American people in their righteous might will win through to absolute victory." Both chambers passed a declaration of war, with only one lawmaker—Montana Representative Jeanette Rankin—dissenting. Across the country, shock gave way to panic, and in San Francisco, air raid sirens wailed as dozens of "hostile planes" were sighted over the city. The planes weren't real, but the fear was.

Football was rendered utterly inconsequential. The day after Pearl Harbor, reporters asked Giants head coach Steve Owen what he thought about the upcoming playoff game between the Bears and the Packers. Owen, a rotund and usually jovial Oklahoman, answered gravely in his slow Southern drawl: "I don't know what is going to happen." He seemed so serious. It sounded as if he were talking about the war, not a football game.

Professional football players contributed mightily and often heroically to the war effort. Those who could fight, fought. Bob Hoffman, the tubercular Redskin, recovered well enough to serve four years in the military, not returning to the NFL until 1946. Each of the four Georgetown alums honored before the Eagles-Redskins game on Pearl Harbor Day also went off to war, as did Al Blozis, the Hoya football star who presented them with luggage. Blozis, however, never returned. After Georgetown, he played two seasons with the Giants. Then he enlisted in the Army, only to be killed on a battlefield in France. Nick Basca, the Eagles' rookie kicker that day, would meet a similar fate.

In all, 638 NFL players served in the military during World War II. It's an impressive number, especially considering the league only had about 330 total roster spots when the U.S. entered the conflict. Three hundred fifty-five NFL players were commissioned officers. Sixty-nine were decorated. Nineteen (including Al Blozis and Nick Basca) died for their country. Two—Jack Lummus of the Giants and Maurice Britt of the Detroit Lions—were awarded the Medal of Honor.

By the spring of 1943, with the war still raging and no end in sight, the 23-year-old National Football League was facing a crisis unimaginable today: a shortage of players. The Pittsburgh Steelers had just six under contract. The Dodgers had none. Front offices suffered, too. The owners of the Dodgers, the Eagles, the Bears, and the Cleveland Rams were on active duty. But the league persevered. Aging stars were lured out of retirement, and a few active servicemen managed to get leave for games—though not always through official channels.

But mostly the league subsisted on players who'd been deferred from the draft. Some had families to support. Others worked in essential war industries. The lion's share, though, were physically unfit for military service. They had ailments that precluded military careers but not football careers: ulcers, flat feet, partial blindness or deafness, perforated eardrums. It was these men—known, sometimes derisively, as 4-Fs (for their draft classification)—who really kept the NFL alive.

One team in particular emblematized the lengths to which the NFL was forced to go during World War II: the Phil-Pitt Steagles. Created by merging the Steelers and the Eagles, the Steagles were a wartime anomaly, like ration books and air-raid drills. The team's center was deaf in one ear, its top receiver was half-blind, and its best running back had ulcers. Yet, somehow, this woebegone group—including center Ray Graves, tackles Ted Doyle, Frank "Bucko" Kilroy, and Vic Sears, halfbacks Johnny Butler, Jack Hinkle, and Ernie Steele, and quarterbacks Allie Sherman and Roy Zimmerman—melded to form one of the finest pro football teams either Pittsburgh or Philadelphia had ever seen, and captured the hearts of sports fans nationwide. And they did it all while working full time in defense plants, and in spite of the fact that their two head coaches could not abide each other. Perhaps no team in NFL history has overcome more enormous and unusual obstacles and adversities than did the Steagles.

Professional football's 4-Fs didn't storm the beaches of Iwo Jima or Normandy. They couldn't. But they were, in smaller ways, heroic. In America's darkest hours, they gave the nation something to cheer about, and their accomplishments, often in the face of long odds, exemplified the spirit that won the war. They also saved professional football. Without them, today's NFL, its 32 franchises now worth a combined $26 billion, might not exist. They didn't know it, but they were pioneers. This is their story and the story of their times.

LAST TEAM STANDING

A Bad Break

AL WISTERT NEVER EVEN WANTED TO CARRY THE BALL. He was a tackle, for crying out loud. Halfbacks carry the ball. Fullbacks. Even quarterbacks sometimes. But not tackles. Tackles hunker down on the line of scrimmage. On offense, they make blocks. They give the quarterback time to pass. They clear a path for the real ball carriers. If a tackle touches the ball, something's gone horribly wrong: there's been a fumble. But Wistert's coach at the University of Michigan, the innovative and mercurial Herbert "Fritz" Crisler, thought, since nobody ever expects a tackle to run with the ball, why not have him run with the ball? It was the kind of contrarian brainstorm that Crisler loved. Wistert had his doubts, though. He'd never carried the ball in a real game. Ever. But who was he to question the legendary Coach Crisler?

So here he was now, lining up in his usual spot at left tackle, down in a three-point stance. It was October 18, 1941, a golden Saturday afternoon, and Michigan was in hostile territory, playing Northwestern at Dyche Stadium in Evanston, Illinois. It was a big game. Both teams were undefeated. The loser would be all but eliminated from the Big Ten Conference race. It was also the Wildcats' homecoming game and the stands were filled with 47,000 screaming fans. Wistert could barely hear halfback Tom

Kuzma shout, "Hut!" Center Don Ingalls snapped the ball back to Kuzma.

Next thing he knew, Wistert was in the backfield, running toward Kuzma's outstretched hand. Kuzma stuck the ball in his gut. Wistert wrapped his arms completely around it, almost hiding it—just as Crisler had told him to do. He put his head down and started running for his life. Northwestern tackle Alf Bauman saw him coming, but Bauman thought Wistert was going to block him. He stepped aside, not realizing Wistert was carrying the ball. Holy cow, Wistert thought, Coach Crisler was right! Another 40 yards or so and he'd score a touchdown. For an instant he imagined the sensation, crossing the goal line, casually placing the ball on the ground, being swarmed by gleeful teammates. He charged downfield toward the goalposts, a giant H rising tantalizingly from the back of the end zone.

Born to Lithuanian immigrants in Chicago on December 28, 1920, Wistert was the youngest of six children. His father, Kazimer Vistartius, was a mounted policeman in Chicago, and when Al was just five, Kazimer was shot while chasing a man suspected of holding up a taxicab. The bullet entered Kazimer's neck and lodged in his hip, and he died 11 months later. The killer was never caught.

"He was a great role model," Al said of his father. "He exercised every day. He never drank. He never smoked. And he was just a tremendous human being." One of Al's earliest memories is of hanging onto his father's belt while he did chin-ups.

When he was 13, Al saw his first professional football game. His oldest brother, Whitey, took him to see the Bears play the Giants at Wrigley Field. (Back then, pro football teams typically played in baseball parks.) It made quite an impression.

"As I'm sitting there watching that game, I'm dreaming that, hey, maybe someday I could play pro football. That's when I started dreaming about it." But his mother wouldn't let him play football in high school.

"Mother was a widow and she said, 'What if you get hurt? I

can't pay any doctor bills!' So she said that she preferred that we didn't play."

Wistert finally got his chance to play at Michigan.

Whitey had been an all-American tackle for the Wolverines in the early 1930s, so Al figured he'd play tackle at Michigan too. He even wore his brother's old number 11. (At the time, the NCAA wasn't picky about uniform numbers. Today, linemen usually must wear a number between 50 and 79.) But Al didn't have his brother's all-American aptitude—at least not at first.

"I must confess I never thought he'd make a football player," Fritz Crisler recalled. "When I first saw him Al was clumsy and didn't seem to have enough speed."

But he was big (six-two, 210 pounds), he was a quick study, he was tough, and he worked hard. He learned how to block and tackle. He learned how to cover punts and kickoffs. He became a starter his sophomore year, and he usually played all 60 minutes every game. He loved football, the contact, the "survival-of-the-fittest aspect," as he put it. For his bruising style his teammates nicknamed him "The Ox."

Michigan went 7-1 in Wistert's first year as a starter, losing only to eventual Big Ten champion Minnesota, 7-6. In his junior year, Wistert hoped to avenge that loss. But first the Wolverines had to beat Northwestern.

At the instant Wistert entertained visions of touchdown glory, Northwestern figured out what the hell was going on: The tackle had the ball! Before he knew it, a pack of purple-and-white-shirted defenders were breathing down Wistert's neck. He gained about seven yards before a half-dozen Wildcats jumped on his back.

"Down I went," Wistert remembered. "And I wanted to make sure I didn't fumble the ball, so I had both hands on the ball. And pretty soon I was diggin' a trough with my nose. And my left wrist somehow got caught underneath all that. And I broke the wrist. Broke the wrist and my nose." It was the last time Al Wistert ever carried the ball in a football game.

Michigan ended up beating Northwestern 14-7 but lost to Minnesota a week later, 7-0. Despite the injuries he'd sustained in his ill-fated rushing attempt, Wistert didn't miss a game in 1941. After the season ended, he was selected to play in the East-West Shrine Game, one of college football's all-star games, on January 3, 1942, in San Francisco. It was a memorable trip for Wistert: The day after the game, he married Marguerite Eleanor "Ellie" Koenig, his childhood sweetheart.

A few weeks later, Wistert had an operation on his injured wrist. His doctors had told him that the bones weren't fusing properly: they were misaligned, so surgery was necessary. But Wistert still played football the following fall, wearing a specially designed brace to protect his wrist. In 1942, his senior year, the Wolverines went 7-3 and Wistert's teammates voted him Michigan's most valuable player. He was also named an all-American—just like his brother Whitey.

But the spring of 1943 was a tumultuous time in Wistert's life. His injured wrist still hadn't healed and he had to have another operation. He graduated from Michigan and took a job at Ford's massive Willow Run plant near Ann Arbor, where 40,000 workers were turning out eight B-24 bombers each day. He and Ellie were expecting their first child. And he was drafted twice: once by the Philadelphia Eagles, and once by Uncle Sam.

Getting drafted by the Eagles was probably worse, Wistert remembered with a laugh.

"When I got the letter, I wondered who the Eagles were. That's how famous they were! They hadn't had a winning season yet—and they started in 1933! So they'd gone through ten years of football and never had a winning team."

In any event, the war took precedence. Wistert knew he'd be in a uniform come fall—and it wouldn't come with shoulder pads.

In June, Wistert learned he'd been selected by the nation's sportswriters to play in the *Chicago Tribune*'s college all-star game later that summer. The game annually pitted the country's best recent graduates against the reigning NFL champions. It was the brainchild of Chicago sports entrepreneur and *Tribune* sports editor Arch Ward, who also launched major league baseball's all-star game. In the first *Tribune* all-star game, in 1934, the college players had held the Chicago Bears to a scoreless draw. The collegians won two of the next four games in the series, but by 1943 the professionals had clearly established their supremacy, winning four in a row. (In time the defending NFL champs would come to dominate the series so thoroughly that fan interest evaporated, and the series was canceled after the 1976 game. The pros ended up winning 31 games in the series and losing just nine.)

The 1943 game would pit the collegians against passer extraordinaire Sammy Baugh and his Washington Redskins, who'd beaten the Bears 14-6 to win the NFL title the previous December. The game, usually played in Chicago's mammoth Soldier Field, was moved 16 miles north in 1943, to relatively cozy Dyche Stadium—the site of Wistert's disastrous rushing attempt. The Office of Defense Transportation had ordered the game be relocated to the smaller stadium to reduce attendance, thereby reducing fuel consumption and, more importantly, wear and tear on tires, a major concern now that Japan controlled most of the world's rubber plantations.

When practices for the all-star game began in early August, Wistert and Ellie moved into a tiny apartment above a garage in Chicago. A few days before the game, Ralph Brizzolara, the general manager of the Chicago Bears, stopped by out of the blue and asked Wistert if he'd like to play for the Bears in the fall. Wistert was interested but reminded Brizzolara that the Eagles had drafted him and still held his signing rights. Brizzolara said he'd work on that. In the meantime, he offered Wistert $3,000 to play for the Bears.

"And then you'd have the championship money," Brizzolara added, "since we're almost always in the championship game. So you'd go home with a nice tidy sum of money in your pocket."

Wistert said he'd think about it.

The next night, Harry Thayer, the Eagles' general manager, dropped in on the Wisterts. Thayer also offered a $3,000 contract—without any mention of championship bonuses.

"Three thousand dollars?" Wistert said in mock indignation. "That's peanuts! I wouldn't consider playing for that."

"How much money do you want?"

"Forty-five hundred dollars."

Thayer laughed. "Wistert, let me tell you something. You're a tackle, not a halfback. We pay our best backfield men in this league that kind of money—not tackles."

But Wistert wouldn't budge. Thayer told him he'd run the offer by Greasy Neale, the Eagles' head coach, and get back to him.

Thayer telephoned Coach Neale later that night. Neale took the call in his suite at the Hotel Philadelphian, where he was playing cards with several of his players. Training camp was almost under way and Neale was eager to get Wistert signed. He asked Thayer how much money Wistert wanted.

"Forty-five hundred dollars," Thayer said.

"Forty-five hundred!" repeated Neale, incredulous. He let out a long whistle.

"Well just get him in here," he instructed Thayer. "Get him signed and get him in here."

The players around the card table exchanged knowing glances. Forty-five hundred dollars would make Wistert the highest-paid player on the team. He was a rookie. Not only that: He was a tackle. Who did he think he was?

Wistert ended up signing with the Eagles for $3,800, though his teammates were under the impression he was getting $4,500.

In reality, the negotiations were probably pointless. As the Bears and the Eagles knew, Wistert was scheduled to report to his draft board in Chicago for his physical examination shortly after the all-star game.

The *Tribune* all-star game took place on the night of Wednesday, August 25. The attendance was 48,000, about half of what it would have been at Soldier Field, but there was no reduction in fanfare. War or no war, *Tribune* sports editor Arch Ward always pulled out all the stops. The pregame ceremonies featured a military drill team, marching bands, and a "pageant" of WACS, WAVES, and SPARS (the last being the Coast Guard's female reserve). At 8:30 p.m., the stadium lights were extinguished and each player was introduced under the dramatic glare of a single spotlight. Wistert, the all-star team's co-captain, got a special introduction.

The collegians not only upset the NFL champions, they buried them, 27-7. Sammy Baugh threw for 273 yards, but the all-stars completely shut down the Redskins' running game. The *Tribune* heaped praise on Wistert, "whose mighty line play had a lot to do with bottling up the Redskins' attack."

Wistert's play particularly impressed Tony Hinkle, one of the all-star team's assistant coaches. In peacetime Hinkle was the head football (and basketball and baseball) coach at Butler University in Indianapolis. For the time being, though, he was in the Navy, coaching the football team at the Great Lakes Naval Station near Chicago. Great Lakes was one of the country's most powerful service teams, with a schedule that included college titans like Michigan and Notre Dame. It was an all-star team in its own right, its roster dotted with all-Americans and NFL veterans, ostensibly sent to the base for naval training. Hinkle knew Wistert was due to be inducted and asked him if he wanted to play for Great Lakes. Wistert thought it sounded like a good idea, especially since his contract with the Eagles would be nullified if Uncle Sam did indeed come calling.

About a week after the all-star game, Wistert reported to a building in Chicago's Loop for his physical.

"I zoomed through it," Wistert remembered. "They hardly looked at me." But after the exam, Wistert was asked several questions about his medical history. One of them was: Have you ever had surgery?

"I told them about an appendectomy and the wrist being operated on. And they wanted to take some more x-rays of the wrist. And pretty soon they had half-a-dozen different doctors come in and look at those x-rays and everything and discuss whether they were gonna take me in the service or not."

The doctors told Wistert that his draft board would be in touch with him shortly.

While he waited, Wistert and Ellie packed up and moved again, this time to Philadelphia. On Sunday, September 5, 1943, Wistert reported to his first NFL training camp.

"I was there for a day or two before somebody told me that some of these guys are from Pittsburgh."

Wistert was floored. He had no idea that the Eagles and the Steelers had merged.

"I had heard nothing about it and I didn't know that we were combined with the Pittsburgh Steelers at all—this was something that was unknown to me."

Al Wistert had just found out that he was a Steagle.

■ | | | | ■

NEARLY THREE YEARS EARLIER, on October 29, 1940, on a stage in a crowded auditorium in Washington, Secretary of War Henry Stimson was blindfolded with a piece of cloth taken from a chair in Independence Hall. On a simple wooden table in front of Stimson sat an enormous glass bowl filled with 9,000 inch-long, cobalt-blue capsules. Inside each capsule was a tiny piece of paper with a number from one to 9,000 written on it. Stimson sunk his hand into the bowl, slowly withdrew a single capsule, and handed it to President Franklin Roosevelt.

The president, standing behind a large podium, broke open the capsule and removed the piece of paper. He leaned into the forest of microphones carrying the ceremony into anxious living rooms across the country and solemnly intoned, "1-5-8."

America's first peacetime draft was under way.

The historian George Q. Flynn writes, "The idea that all able-bodied men owe an obligation of military defense can be traced to the dark caves of prehistory." But it wasn't until the French Revolution that conscription was formally codified, the French National Assembly declaring, "Every citizen must be a soldier and every soldier a citizen or we shall never have a constitution." After

Napoléon I employed draftees to great effect, Britain and Germany adopted conscription as well.

The United States, though, had always viewed conscription with suspicion. Not until the Civil War did Congress authorize a nationwide draft, compelling males aged 20 to 45 to serve in the Union Army. The results were less than spectacular. The law permitted draftees to pay for substitutes, enabling the wealthy simply to buy their way out of service. The draft was so unpopular that in 1863 it triggered riots in New York City that claimed at least 20 lives. (The Confederacy implemented a national draft that was nearly as unpopular, if only because it utterly disregarded the principle of states' rights.) A draft put in place for World War I lasted less than two years and was abolished immediately after the armistice.

But with another global conflict looming, Franklin Roosevelt urged a return to compulsory military service. Not only was the army too small—it comprised fewer than 188,000 soldiers when Hitler invaded Poland on September 1, 1939—it was also woefully out of shape. After reviewing troops at Ogdensburg, New York, in August 1940, Roosevelt confided to a friend, "The men themselves were soft—fifteen miles a day was about all they could stand and many dropped out. Anybody who knows anything about the German methods of warfare would know that the army would have been licked by thoroughly trained and organized forces of a similar size within a day or two." As envisaged by Roosevelt, a draft would not only make the army bigger; by instituting stringent physical requirements for draftees, it would also make it healthier.

In the speech accepting his party's nomination to run for an unprecedented third term in 1940, Roosevelt said most Americans "are agreed that some form of selection by draft is necessary and fair today as it was in 1917 and 1918." However, many Americans were not agreed. Conscription was opposed by a diverse coalition, including organized labor, isolationists, pacifists, religious leaders, youth groups, African-American organizations, and, perhaps most poignantly, gold-star mothers who had lost their sons in the last war.

Their arguments were equally varied: the draft was unconstitutional and unfair, it would encourage war, it would stymie economic growth. So fervent were the opponents that Senator James F. Byrnes, a Democrat from South Carolina, declared that a draft bill didn't stand a "Chinaman's chance" of passing. But after France surrendered to Germany on June 21, 1940, the opposition began to wane. It all but vanished after Wendell Willkie, FDR's Republican opponent in the 1940 election, came out in favor of the draft on August 17.

On September 16, 1940, the draft became law. All men between the ages of 21 and 35 were required to serve one year in the armed forces. The draft was administered by the Selective Service System, so named because the draft was discriminate: Not every draftee was automatically inducted. Deferments could be granted if a draftee had dependents, was "necessary in his civilian activity," or was "physically, mentally, or morally unfit" to serve. The draft was discriminate in another way: African-Americans were banned from the Marine Corps and the Army Air Corps (later known as the Army Air Forces), while the Army and the Navy maintained segregated units.

A hallmark of Selective Service was decentralization. More than 6,000 local draft boards were established across the country, each composed of three "reputable, responsible men, familiar with local conditions." (Women were barred from serving on draft boards because members were occasionally required "to check registrants for physical defects." The ban was lifted in 1967.) Each draft board was more or less autonomous, free to determine, without interference from Washington, which draftees were to be deferred and which were to be inducted. Inevitably this decentralization led to idiosyncrasies: A draft board in Wisconsin, for instance, was far more likely than one in New York City to consider a cheese maker "necessary in his civilian activity."

On October 16, 1940, "R-Day," more than 16 million men registered with Selective Service. At courthouses and libraries, in church basements and elementary school gymnasiums, they completed forms that required them to disclose all sorts of intimate information. Each registrant was asked about his education, occupation, family, health, and criminal record. He was asked whether he conscientiously objected to war, whether he was an ordained minister (or studying to be one), or whether he was in the armed forces or a state legislature (all grounds for deferral). The boards then classified each registrant into categories ranging from 1-A (fit for general military service) to 4-F (unfit), and assigned each a serial number. A lottery would be held to determine the order in which registrants would be called.

Each draft board was limited to no more than 8,500 registrants. To be on the safe side, 9,000 capsules were put into the glass bowl from which Henry Stimson selected number 158. According to the *New York Times*, 6,175 men had been assigned that serial number by local draft boards nationwide. They would be the very first men inducted. In New York City alone, the *Times* reported, the 158s included "a Cody, a Chan, a Re and a Weisblum."

After the ceremonious first draw, the rest of the capsules in the glass bowl were randomly selected and opened by more ordinary bureaucrats. The next four numbers drawn were 192; 8,239; 6,620; and 6,685. The process lasted into the next morning.

ⵏⵏⵏⵏ **2** ⵏⵏⵏⵏ

Keystoners

I N 1794, WHEN GEORGE WASHINGTON WAS PRESIDENT, the Pennsylvania Assembly passed "an Act for the prevention of vice and immorality." Among other things, the act banned "disorderly sports" on Sundays. Pennsylvania was just one of many states with such "blue laws," so named either for the color of the paper on which they were originally printed or because "blue" was then a disparaging term for the puritanical.

In the early twentieth century, many states relaxed their blue laws to permit Sunday baseball. By 1920, teams in Chicago, Cincinnati, Cleveland, Detroit, New York, St. Louis, and Washington were all allowed to play on the Sabbath, but teams in Philadelphia and Pittsburgh were not. Connie Mack, the venerable owner and manager of the Philadelphia Athletics baseball team, bitterly opposed Pennsylvania's antediluvian blue laws, albeit on fiscal, not philosophical, grounds: "We cannot meet our payrolls playing on 77 weekdays at home," he complained.

In defiance of the blue laws, Mack scheduled a home game for Sunday, August 22, 1926. An "unusually subdued" crowd of 12,000 watched the A's play the Chicago White Sox at Shibe Park that afternoon. Mack's team won the game but he lost the ensuing court battle. In September 1927, the Pennsylvania Supreme Court upheld the state's blue laws by a vote of 7-2. The court ruled that Sunday baseball was an "unholy" form of "worldly employment."

The blue laws applied to professional football as well, which necessarily made it difficult for the National Football League to do business in Pennsylvania. Nonetheless, two teams tried. The Frankford Yellow Jackets, based in a neighborhood in Northeast Philadelphia, joined the league in 1924 and played their home games on Saturdays. The Pottsville Maroons joined the league in 1925. They often did play on Sundays, but there wasn't a cop or prosecutor in Schuylkill County with the temerity to tell the lager-fueled coal miners who filled Minersville Park that they couldn't watch football on their only day off.

The Yellow Jackets would go on to win the NFL championship in 1926, and Pottsville nearly won it the year before (but was suspended by the league for playing an exhibition game at Shibe Park, in violation of Frankford's territorial rights). Neither club was strong enough to whip the Great Depression, though, and by 1931 Pennsylvania was without an NFL franchise.

Connie Mack, meanwhile, took his campaign against the blue laws from the courtroom to the state capitol in Harrisburg. In 1931, he led a lobbying effort that resulted in the Pennsylvania House passing a bill legalizing Sunday sports. But the Senate soundly defeated the measure, prompting Mack to threaten to move his team across the Delaware River to Camden, New Jersey. Finally, in April 1933, both chambers passed a bill authorizing each community in the commonwealth to hold a referendum on the blue laws. The legislature was passing the buck: Each town could decide the matter for itself. Governor Gifford Pinchot gladly signed the measure into law; the local voting was scheduled for November 7. (A simultaneous effort to legalize the sale of beer at sporting events was less successful. Ballparks statewide would remain dry until the 1960s.)

Gambling that Pennsylvania's two largest communities would vote to lift the ban on Sabbath sports, the NFL immediately installed teams in Pittsburgh and Philadelphia. Not surprisingly, both franchises went to prominent local citizens with deep football roots. Art Rooney was awarded the Pittsburgh franchise, which he named the Pirates (an uninspired choice, he later conceded). The Philadelphia franchise went to Bert Bell, who dubbed the team the Eagles, after the symbol of FDR's newly created National Recovery Administration. Both Rooney and Bell paid a league entrance fee of $2,500.

ART ROONEY HAD GROWN UP in a poor Irish-Catholic neighborhood on Pittsburgh's north side. He made his money playing the horses in the days before pari-mutuel machines, when the odds were set by bookmakers at the track and savvy gamblers could make a killing. It's said Rooney once turned a $20 bet at Saratoga into a $380,000 payday. ("Racing's not the same now," Rooney said wistfully years later. "The romance is gone.")

Rooney was a minor league baseball player, an amateur boxer, a ward politician, and a shrewd investor. He was a football entrepreneur, too. In the early 1920s he organized a semipro team on the north side called Hope-Harvey. (Hope was the name of a fire station that the team used as a dressing room; Harvey was a doctor who cared for injured players without charge.) Rooney was the team's owner, coach, and halfback.

Rooney recruited several players from Hope-Harvey for the Pirates.

"I bought the franchise in '33," he said, "because I figured that it would be good to have a league schedule and that eventually professional football would be good."

Bert Bell played a little football, too, but not in an Irish ghetto. Bell was an Ivy Leaguer. Christened de Benneville Bell in honor of a French grandmother ("If I can lick the name de Benneville," he'd say, "I can handle anything"), Bell was a true-blue blueblood, the scion of a wealthy family from Philadelphia's moneyed Main Line. His father, John Cromwell Bell, was a prominent Philadelphia lawyer who served as Pennsylvania's attorney general from 1911 to 1915. The elder Bell had gone to the University of Pennsylvania and was determined to see his son go there as well.

14

"Bert will go to Penn or he'll go to hell," he liked to say.

Bert chose Penn. He played football for the Quakers from 1915 to 1919, with a year off for service in France during World War I. He was the team's starting quarterback in the 1917 Rose Bowl. After graduation, he coached at Penn and Temple. His family's fortune was nearly wiped out by the stock market crash of 1929, but when the NFL offered him the Philadelphia franchise four years later, Bell couldn't pass up the opportunity. He borrowed part of the franchise fee from the family of his wife, a former showgirl named Frances Upton. As part of the deal, he also agreed to pay off some of the debts of the now-defunct Frankford Yellow Jackets.

ON TUESDAY, NOVEMBER 7, 1933, voters in Philadelphia and Pittsburgh overwhelmingly approved measures legalizing professional sports in their cities on Sundays between 2:00 p.m. and 6:00 p.m. (Pending the votes, the Eagles and Pirates had played their home games on Wednesday nights.) On November 9, election officials in Philadelphia certified the results, and Bert Bell was issued Permit No. 1 for a game between his Eagles and the Chicago Bears the following Sunday, November 12, at Philadelphia's Baker Bowl. Nearly 18,000 fans filled the rickety old wooden ballpark that day, lured, as the *Philadelphia Inquirer* put it, "by the novelty of a Sabbath game." What they witnessed was indeed novel: The newborn Eagles held the reigning NFL champions to a 3-3 tie. It would be many years before the Eagles would come that close to beating the Bears again.

In Pittsburgh the wheels of bureaucracy turned more slowly. The election results still weren't certified when the Pirates hosted the Brooklyn Dodgers at Forbes Field the Sunday after the vote. A group of local ministers went looking for the superintendent of police, Franklin T. McQuade, to demand he put a stop to the technically illegal game, but they never found him—Art Rooney had invited McQuade to sit with him in the stands, in order to forestall such interference. With the city's top cop so disposed, the game went off without incident. The Pirates got hammered 32-0, but the attendance (12,000) was good and as the *Pittsburgh Post-Gazette* reported, "no sense of desecrating the Sabbath was experienced." Two days later, the Pittsburgh vote was finally certified. The National Football League was now permanently established in Pennsylvania.

Despite their vastly different backgrounds, Art Rooney and Bert Bell hit it off immediately. Maybe it was because they were the two new kids on the block. Maybe it was because they were both devout Catholics (as well as devout Republicans). In any case they became devoted friends, and along with George Halas and George Preston Marshall, they would exert a powerful influence on the NFL. But unlike Halas and Marshall, their teams were lousy. After seven seasons, Pittsburgh's record was 22-55-4, Philadelphia's 18-55-3. Both teams were losing money—lots of it. Rooney's losses totaled about $100,000, which must have acutely embarrassed a man renowned for his business acumen. Bell was not much better off. At one point he borrowed $5,000 from Rooney to keep the Eagles afloat.

Before the 1940 season, Rooney tried to improve his team's fortunes by renaming it the Steelers, in honor of Pittsburgh's principal industry. Around the same time, a sportswriter introduced Rooney to a young New York playboy named Alexis Thompson, triggering a convoluted sequence of events that football historians have dubbed the Pennsylvania Polka.

Lex Thompson's late father had made a fortune in steel. In 1930, when he was just 16, Lex inherited that fortune—an estimated $3.5 million. After graduating from Yale, Lex and three classmates started a successful drug company that sold a popular brand of eye drops called Eye-Gene, but Lex was interested in more pleasurable pursuits. Tall, handsome, and dashing, with wavy brown hair and a dimpled chin, he enjoyed gin martinis, beautiful women, and carousing. He even dated screen legend Lana Turner for a time. His drinking buddies included Clark Gable and William Holden.

Lex Thompson was also a passionate sportsman. At Yale he lettered in soccer and lacrosse. He bobsledded in St. Moritz, played jai alai in Florida, water-skied in Monte Carlo, and was a member of the U.S. field hockey team that competed in the 1936 Berlin Olympics. So, in the autumn of 1940, when he was 26 and had a little "spare time" on his hands, it was only natural that Thompson, in his words, "decided to look around for a sports hobby." He first considered buying a professional hockey team, but was dissuaded by the small crowd attending a game at Madison Square Garden one Saturday night. So he turned to football.

Throughout the 1940 season, Thompson tried to persuade Rooney to sell him the Steelers. Rooney was sorely tempted, but he resisted Thompson's generous offers, mainly because Thompson intended to move the team to Boston, which was much closer than Pittsburgh to Thompson's New York home. Rooney did not want to leave his hometown bereft of professional football.

Then, in early December, just before the league championship game, Rooney and Thompson held a series of secret meetings with Eagles owner Bert Bell in Philadelphia. On December 9— the day after the Bears destroyed the Redskins 73-0 for the title— the results of those meetings were announced to an indifferent world: Rooney was selling the Steelers to Thompson and buying a fifty-percent stake in the Eagles, becoming a co-owner with Bell.

"I certainly hated to give up the franchise in the old home town," Rooney said, "but it would have been poor business to refuse the proposition for a second-division ball club at the terms which were offered"—reportedly $160,000.

To further complicate matters, the two teams also pulled off a massive trade, with more than a dozen players changing hands. Rooney took many of his favorites from Pittsburgh to Philadelphia. Thompson picked up several Eagles in return.

What was not formally announced was Thompson's plan to relocate the Steelers to Boston after the 1941 season. But Pittsburgh would not be left without pro football. After the Steelers moved, Rooney and Bell intended to operate the Eagles as a statewide franchise that would split its home games between Philadelphia and Pittsburgh and be known as the Keystoners (taking its name from Pennsylvania, the Keystone State). Rooney and

Bell even considered asking the league for permission to play all the team's games as home games—half in one city, half in the other.

"Rooney and I have been working on a deal for some months," Bell revealed to a reporter. "We have agreed to the merger but don't know whether the league will okay the deal. Both of us feel, however, that consolidation is the real solution of our mutual problems, financial and otherwise."

But the plan was doomed from the start. When Washington Redskins owner George Preston Marshall caught wind of it he was furious. Marshall had moved his franchise out of Boston just three years before, claiming a lack of fan support. He saw no reason why the city should get another one.

"He can sell if he wants to," Marshall said of Rooney, "but I'll certainly vote to block any move to shift the Pittsburgh franchise to Boston or any other city. Nor will I stand idly by and permit a merger that would hurt pro football's standing in either Philadelphia or Pittsburgh."

Lex Thompson, just four years removed from Yale and new to the National Football League, was not inclined to antagonize the irascible Marshall. Neither, for that matter, were Rooney and Bell.

So, through the winter of 1940–41, Thompson owned the Steelers and Rooney and Bell owned the Eagles. Thompson announced he was renaming his team the Iron Men, and he hired a new head coach, Greasy Neale, a Yale assistant coach whom Thompson was familiar with from his college days. After that, though, Thompson did nothing. By the spring, he still hadn't even opened an office in Pittsburgh. Rooney called him to find out why. Thompson told Rooney he wasn't happy owning a team so far from home. Rooney told Thompson he wasn't crazy about running a team in Philadelphia.

"Then I got an idea," Rooney later explained. "I asked him how he'd like to make a switch and let me stay in Pittsburgh and take over the Philadelphia territory himself. That suited him because Philadelphia is so much closer to his New York headquarters, and that's how it was worked out."

On April 8, 1941, Rooney announced that he and Bell were the new owners of the Steelers and Thompson was the new owner of the Eagles. Basically the three men had traded franchises.

"I know we've gone around in circles," Rooney said, "but I guess we're settled now."

In the end, everybody was happy. Lex Thompson owned an NFL franchise close to New York, Rooney got to keep the Steelers (who never played a game as the Iron Men), and Rooney and Bell both got a much-needed cash infusion. Fans were bemused, though in 1941 the result of all the maneuvering was made clear: both teams still stank. The Eagles and Steelers won just three games between them—the same number they'd won the year before. Bell began the season as the Steelers' head coach. After losing the first two games, he asked Rooney, "What do you think we should do?"

"Bert," Rooney answered, "did you ever think about changing coaches?" Bell never coached another game.

New Priorities

ELMER LAYDEN HAD BEEN THE COMMISSIONER of the National Football League for less than a year when America went to war in 1941. In his younger days, Layden was one of Notre Dame's fabled Four Horseman, the backfield immortalized by the hyperbolic sportswriter Grantland Rice: "In dramatic lore they are known as famine, pestilence, destruction, and death. These are only aliases. Their real names are: Stuhldreher, Miller, Crowley, and Layden."

Layden was 37 and the head coach at Notre Dame when, in early 1941, the NFL hired him on the recommendation of the ubiquitous sports entrepreneur Arch Ward. The move from the Golden Dome to the pros must have been quite a shock to Layden. While college football in general—and Notre Dame in particular—was wildly popular, the professional game was held in considerably lower esteem. In those days, football was considered a pastime for college boys, not a respectable occupation. College coaches denigrated the pros relentlessly (conveniently ignoring their own financial interests in the game). Amos Alonzo Stagg, the legendary University of Chicago coach, called "Sunday professional football" a "serious menace." He pleaded with college players to eschew the NFL, telling them "a real man would never turn to professionalism."

Many listened, opting instead for more reputable (not to mention lucrative) careers. In 1936, the first player chosen in the first NFL draft, Heisman Trophy winner Jay Berwanger, passed up a chance to play for the Bears to become a foam rubber salesman. (Berwanger eventually started his own foam rubber business and became a millionaire.)

This lack of respect translated into a lack of coverage in the press. NFL scores were almost impossible to find in newspapers outside the cities with franchises. Even within those cities the coverage was spotty. As late as 1948, the Eagles' general manager at the time, Al Ennis, lamented that Philadelphia's two evening papers, the *Evening Bulletin* and the *Daily News,* sent no reporters to training camp but instead "picked up their stories on our activities from the press service releases, and by rewriting the story which appears in the *Inquirer* every morning."

As commissioner, Layden set about remaking the NFL's image. The league had been founded on September 17, 1920, when the representatives of ten Midwestern football clubs gathered in a Canton, Ohio, automobile showroom to organize the American Professional Football Association, which two years later was renamed the National Football League. At that meeting the attendees sat on the running boards and fenders of Hupmobiles, drinking beer.

Layden wanted to move the NFL to what he called a "high, dignified plane." He barred players and coaches from "lending their name to advertisements for liquor, cigaret[te]s and laxatives." He banned commercials over stadium PA systems whenever possible. Fed up with sloppy uniforms, he ordered players to wear knee-high socks, a curious preoccupation with hosiery that persists in the league to this day. (College players are permitted to wear their socks at their ankles if they choose.) Another of Layden's sartorial innovations: He ordered game officials to wear color-coded striped shirts. Referees wore black and white, umpires red and white, linesmen orange and white, and field judges green and white. One official ridiculed the dress code as a "circus on parade."

But the bombing of Pearl Harbor rearranged Layden's priorities overnight. He stopped worrying about stockings. On December 8, he was asked to assess the league's future.

"Material will be scarce because the colleges will be hit and that of course hits us," he answered. "We will do what is asked and make elastic rules as situations arise." Elastic? Layden had no idea how far the league would be stretched.

The 1941 NFL season limped to a listless conclusion. On December 14, a week after Pearl Harbor, the Bears beat the Packers in the Western Division playoff, 33-14. In the championship game at Wrigley Field a week later, the Bears defeated the Giants, 37-9. The weather was mild, yet just 13,341 fans bothered to show up, the lowest attendance for a title game in league history. And that was in football-crazy Chicago. It was a bad sign.

The next month, President Roosevelt wrote a letter to Judge Kenesaw Mountain Landis, the rigid and humorless baseball commissioner. In what came to be known as the Green Light Letter, the president urged Landis to keep baseball going for the duration of the war:

> There will be fewer people unemployed and everyone will work longer hours and harder than ever before. And that means that they ought to have a chance for recreation and for taking their minds off their work even more than before. . . . As to the players themselves, I know you agree with me that individual players who are of active military or naval age should go, without question, into the services. Even if the actual quality of the teams is lowered by the greater use of older players, this will not dampen the popularity of the sport. . . . Here is another way of looking at it—if 300 teams use 5,000 or 6,000 players, these players are a definite recreational asset to at least 20,000,000 of their fellow citizens—and that in my judgment is thoroughly worthwhile.

Roosevelt was a football fan, too. He had been captain of the freshman team at Harvard, and while he was too small to make varsity, as editor of the *Harvard Crimson*, he ceaselessly extolled the team in editorials. Yet it's no surprise that he made no mention of football in the Green Light Letter. Baseball was the only professional sport that mattered then. Lesser sports were on their own. If pro football survived the war, it would have to do so without the president's imprimatur.

Still, Elmer Layden and the team owners assumed Roosevelt's widely publicized letter to Judge Landis as their own green light, and in the spring of 1942 Layden decreed that the National Football League would continue to operate in the fall, with all ten teams participating. The usual schedule of 55 games would be played.

"But," Layden cautioned, "everything we decide today may have to be abandoned tomorrow. While we believe professional football has a definite place in the recreational program of a nation at war, nothing connected with it should or will be permitted to hinder the war effort."

On average, each NFL team had lost fewer than five players to the draft in 1941. After Pearl Harbor, though, the floodgates opened. By May 1942, 112 of the 346 players under contract to the league's teams—nearly one-third—were in the service. Even more players were sure to be gone before the fall.

Finding replacements was problematic. Many colleges were abandoning their football programs, and Uncle Sam's appetite for able-bodied young men was insatiable. More than three million were conscripted in 1942, a 200-percent increase over the previous year. As they left the workforce for an armed force, the unemployment rate plummeted (from 9.9 percent in 1941 to 4.7 percent in 1942). Defense industries were already reporting manpower shortages. If General Motors couldn't find enough workers, what hope was there for the National Football League?

By the time the 1942 season kicked off on September 13, some teams were virtually unrecognizable from the preceding year. The Eagles had lost 28 players from their 1941 roster, including their leading rusher (Jim Castiglia) and top receiver (Dick Humbert). The Giants had lost 27 players, the Dodgers 25. Not surprisingly, fan loyalty was tested. The constantly changing line-ups—not to mention more pressing concerns—caused attendance to plummet 20 percent, from an average of 20,157 per game in 1941 to 16,144 in 1942—the lowest average since 1936. When the final gun sounded on the championship game in Washington (Redskins 14, Bears 6) some owners were beginning to wonder if they shouldn't just put the league out of its misery for the duration.

■ | | | | ■

WHEN HE GRADUATED with honors from the University of Nebraska in the spring of 1938 with a degree in animal husbandry, Ted Doyle had two options: take a job with the Hormel Company, where he would have a low starting salary but could work his way up the corporate ladder to a lucrative executive position; or play professional football for $200 a game. He'd just gone into hock buying a new suit and shoes for graduation. He'd just gotten married, too. He needed money fast—and so he chose football.

"I thought that was the right decision, to get the money [right away]," Doyle explained. "I don't know if it was or not—I guess it was the wrong one. Nevertheless it was the one I made, so I lived with it. I suppose I would have been in better shape down the road if I'd've went with the Hormels."

The eldest of ten boys, Doyle was born in Maywood, Nebraska, on January 12, 1914. Growing up, he worked on his family's farm, "stacking hay and so forth." He made his high school football team but was so small he didn't play much. During his senior year, though, his weight jumped from 113 pounds to 185—all muscle, thanks to stacking hay. He went to the University of Nebraska because "it was the only school I knew."

"In those days," he said, "they didn't do much recruiting and they definitely didn't have any scholarships or anything like that. You just went to school and went out for football. Whatever happened, happened."

Doyle made the team and played tackle. In the summers he worked sorting fruit. By the time he graduated, Doyle was a beefy six-two, 224 pounds. He was a great tackle, too, a fact he attributed less to his physique than to his mind-set. Doyle said his greatest asset was his ability to psych himself up before a game. It was a slow, steady buildup, timed to peak at kickoff.

"If I could put enough pressure on myself, I could get some adrenaline flowing, and if I got that a-flowin' I could actually run over the guy opposite me."

On December 12, 1937, the New York Giants selected Doyle in the eighth round of the third NFL draft ever held. The Giants then sold his rights to the Pittsburgh Pirates (as the Steelers were then known), probably because Pirates owner Art Rooney had a penchant for players with Irish-sounding names. The following summer, Doyle and his wife, Harriet, loaded the car and drove the 970 miles from Lincoln to Pittsburgh.

The 1938 Pittsburgh Pirates were a memorable football team, though not a very good one. Since joining the NFL in 1933, the Pirates had not had a winning season (though they managed to finish 6-6 in 1936). Fed up with losing, owner Art Rooney went after the most coveted prize in the 1938 draft: Byron "Whizzer" White, the University of Colorado's flashy all-American tailback. Convinced White would boost his team's fortunes at the turnstiles as well as on the field, Rooney offered him a one-year contract for $15,800—more than any other player in the history of the league. White had planned to forgo professional football; he'd been offered a Rhodes Scholarship to study at Oxford. But Rooney's offer was too good to pass up, and he deferred the scholarship until the end of the season.

The team's coach (and backup halfback) was John Victor McNally, better known as Johnny Blood. In his prime, Blood had been an outstanding runner and pass receiver. He had logged time with some of the league's most colorful and storied franchises—the Milwaukee Badgers, the Duluth Eskimos, the Pottsville Maroons, the Green Bay Packers—earning him the nickname the

Vagabond Halfback. He was also known as the Magnificent Screwball, due to his generally erratic behavior.

Blood took his pseudonym in 1924, when he and a friend named Ralph Hanson tried out for the East 26th Street Liberties, a semipro team in Minneapolis. To preserve their college eligibility, they decided to adopt assumed names. Riding McNally's motorcycle to the tryout, they passed a theater that was showing the Rudolph Valentino movie, *Blood and Sand*. McNally shouted back to Hanson, "I'll be Blood and you be Sand."

Blood enjoyed reading Shakespeare, Chaucer, and dime novels. He was known to sign his autograph in blood by cutting his wrist. He frequented prostitutes merely for platonic companionship. "He liked an unusual conversation," remembered Clarke Hinkle, one of Blood's teammates in Green Bay.

On the train home from a game one time, he so antagonized LaVern "Lavvie" Dilweg, another Green Bay teammate, that Dilweg chased Blood all the way through the train to the rear platform. To escape, Blood climbed to the roof and ran back up the length of the moving train, leaping the gaps between cars along the way. He climbed down into the cab, surprising the engineer and the fireman.

"I've always had this thing for trains," Blood explained. "They bring something out in me."

"He was a little wild," Ted Doyle remembered. "[Blood] was a character. One time we were playing a game and he wasn't there. He was someplace else. He was playing a game in Buffalo."

The Pirates opened the 1938 season with three straight losses. On October 3, Doyle broke his arm in a game against the Giants and was sidelined for more than a month. Whizzer White ended up leading the league in rushing but the Pirates were still awful: they finished 2-9 and attendance was little improved. As expected, White left the team to study at Oxford, though Doyle claimed he quit because he felt the linemen weren't blocking for him. If that's the case, Doyle can claim some credit for White's second career, which culminated with a seat on the United States Supreme Court. (White's Rhodes Scholarship would be interrupted by the war, and he returned to the States to play for the Detroit Lions in 1940 and 1941.)

Blood returned to coach the Pirates in 1939, with the usual results. After the team lost its first three games, Blood abruptly quit on October 3—the first anniversary of the Pirates' last win. He was sick of losing.

"I would not say that my temperament was designed for coaching," Blood later conceded.

In 1940, owner Art Rooney gave the Pirates a new name, the one they carry today: the Steelers. But they remained, in Rooney's words, the "same old Pirates," finishing 2-7-2 in 1940 and 1-9-1 in 1941. (In later years frustrated fans would modify the phrase, derisively referring to the team as the "same old Steelers.") In 1942 the Steelers finally had a winning season, finishing 7-4, and Ted Doyle had his best season ever.

After the 1942 season, Doyle, who, like most players, worked a second job in the off-season, was hired at a Westinghouse factory in East Pittsburgh. He told his family and friends he was building parts for navy boats, but he was really working on the Manhattan Project. Westinghouse manufactured equipment for Y-12, the government's nuclear weapons plant in Oak Ridge, Tennessee.

"Frankly I don't think we knew what we were doing. We were making some parts. I assume that it was something that transferred uranium-235 to -238. That's what we figured out later anyhow."

It's likely that Doyle was building components for the equipment used to enrich the uranium that was put in atomic bombs.

Doyle, always ambivalent about his football career, was even more so now that he was an important part of the war effort. In June 1943, shortly before the Steelers and the Eagles merged, he wrote a letter to Bert Bell, who had become a co-owner of the Steelers two years earlier.

"Dear Bert," he wrote,

> *I would probably play football this fall if the proper arrangements could be made. At the present time I am working from*

7:30 a.m. to 4:15 p.m., and will have to continue to do so. I also would have to work six days per week most of the time. You see, we are building equipment which is wanted as fast as we can put it out. Last week we worked from 7:30 a.m. to 7:30 p.m. six days, and then worked eight hours on Sunday.

I asked for my vacation early in September, but don't know whether I will get it then or not. In fact it looks like that may be one of our busiest periods. . . .

I think it will be possible to carry on with football if we practice evenings and if we allow the boys to work as I do now. Much as I like football, we must do our part for the war effort first and furnish football recreation afterward.

Doyle's proposal would not fall on deaf ears. For more than a year, Bert Bell had advocated requiring players to work full time in defense plants during the football season. But neither man had any idea just how directly professional football—and the Steagles in particular—would contribute to the war effort.

IIIII **4** IIIII

Making Changes

On Tuesday, April 6, 1943, the NFL opened its annual meeting at the Palmer House hotel in downtown Chicago, where, it so happened, Elmer Layden kept a suite. Layden and the representatives of the league's ten clubs gathered around a large table in the hotel's ornate Crystal Room, a far cry from the Canton automobile dealership in which the league had been founded 23 years earlier. The room was filled with the sweet smell of cigar smoke, courtesy of Art Rooney's ever-present and pricey stogie.

Layden convened the meeting at 10:20 a.m., saying, "I don't believe there is any need to tell you that this is a very important meeting. I think we are all aware of the fact that the public will be scrutinizing our words and our actions very carefully throughout this meeting." He was being a bit self-aggrandizing—the public had much more important things to worry about that spring—but it was obvious that the league was imperiled. Another 150 players had been lost to the service since the end of the 1942 season. Some clubs were in ruins. The Eagles had just 16 players under contract, and they were in better shape than most other teams. Cleveland and Green Bay had just 14 players each. New York, 13. Detroit, 12. The Cardinals, ten. Pittsburgh, only six. Even the owners were marching off to war. Lex Thompson of the Eagles was an Army private, Dan Topping of the Dodgers was a Marine captain, George Halas of the Bears was a Navy lieutenant commander, and the two co-owners of the Cleveland Rams, Fred Levy and Dan Reeves were, respectively, a lieutenant colonel and a captain in the Army.

"It'll be a miracle if we operate," one coach told the *Chicago Daily Times.*

The owners had another concern, though. Professional football, hardly a lucrative business before the war, was even more risky now. Most clubs were losing money. Given the player shortage and the precipitous attendance drop the previous season, some owners simply felt it wasn't worth carrying on. By one newspaper's estimate, four of the ten clubs favored suspending operations for the duration. But the league's two most outspoken and influential owners—the Bears' George Halas and the Redskins' George Preston Marshall—adamantly opposed folding. Halas, who was training aviation mechanics at the Naval Air Technical Center in Norman, Oklahoma, was so determined to keep the league running that he managed to finagle a leave to attend the crucial meeting and lobby his colleagues. Marshall threatened to keep playing even if every other club voted to shut down: "We're going to operate if our only opposition is Georgetown University or if we have to scrimmage among ourselves." In fact, Marshall couldn't understand what the problem was.

"We're fortunate, unlike baseball, in that we only play on Sundays," he said. "Many fellows in defense work could find time to practice and play—at least in the home games. Nope, it won't be the highest caliber of football, but it'll be football." Marshall had 9,000 reasons to keep playing: that's how many season ticket orders the Redskins had already received.

Elmer Layden also opposed any cessation, insisting "we can and will play football." Of course, he didn't have much choice: the alternative was to incur the wrath of Halas and, most especially, Marshall. (Layden's resolve was further boosted by a "war clause" in his contract that stipulated he would not get paid if the league ceased operations. His annual salary was $25,000, roughly ten times the national average in 1943.)

On Tuesday afternoon, the Cleveland Rams—represented by their head coach, Charles "Chile" Walsh, and Percy Cowan, a Chicago financier who was "handling certain business affairs" for the absent owners—asked the other clubs for permission to drop out of the league for the duration of the war. With Rams co-owners Levy and Reeves in the Army, their representatives said, and with so many players lost to the service, it was no longer feasible to operate the club. (Unlike the other owners on active duty, Levy and Reeves had not assigned a full-time caretaker to look after their club.) Some owners weren't happy about it, but Cleveland's motion passed unanimously. You couldn't very well force a team to play when it didn't want to. There was a caveat though: the suspension would be for the 1943 season only, not the duration. The Rams would have to ask again if they wanted to keep sitting out the following season.

There was a silver lining to Cleveland's withdrawal: the 14 players it still had under contract would be disbursed among the league's nine remaining teams. This was accomplished by drawing the names out of a hat.

Cleveland's departure left the league with a major scheduling problem. Normally, each of the ten teams played 11 games: two against each of the other four teams in its division and three against teams from the other division. But with the league reduced to nine teams—five in the East and four in the West—that arrangement was impossible. A new schedule would have to be drawn up.

Scheduling was always a prickly matter for the NFL, particularly in the days before profit sharing. Naturally, each team was eager to schedule home games against the most popular opponents (e.g., the Redskins, Bears, and Giants). Conversely, nobody wanted the Cardinals on their home schedule. The snag this time was the Redskins-Bears game, always one of the biggest draws of the year. Here, Halas and Marshall could not agree. Each wanted the game for his home field. Layden, whose painstakingly crafted 55-game, ten-team schedule had been rendered moot by Cleveland's sudden departure, could not resolve the impasse.

The following day, the owners approved several rule changes intended to address the wartime conditions. The maximum number of players each team was allowed to carry on its roster was lowered from 33 to 25. This helped alleviate the manpower shortage (as well as reduce costs). The change also mollified the Office of Defense Transportation, which had ordered the league to reduce travel to conserve fuel and rubber for the war effort. Layden said the smaller rosters, coupled with other modifications, would cut the league's "man miles" by 37 percent from the previous season. The smaller rosters also prevented more powerful clubs from cornering the market by signing all the best available players. The owners further eliminated the minimum roster size of 22, leaving it up to Layden to determine when a team was too shorthanded.

"If a squad should drop down, for example, to 16 players," Layden said, "then I might deem it necessary to take measures to bolster the squad roster."

To get the most out of their smaller rosters, the owners approved another rule change: unlimited substitution. From its inception in the late nineteenth century, football was an endurance contest. The 11 players who started a game were expected to be on the field for all 60 minutes, playing both offense and defense, with little or no respite. The NFL permitted a player to enter a game just once each quarter, except for the fourth, when he could enter twice. Substitutions were also allowed when a player was injured—but it had better be serious. For the 1943 season, though, all restrictions were lifted. Teams were free to replace players as often as they pleased. Besides helping teams maximize their rosters, the new rule was also intended to reduce injuries, since rested players were less likely to get hurt. Most coaches, conservative by nature, opposed the change.

"I don't want a player who can't play both offense and defense," grumbled Greasy Neale, the Eagles' head coach. The owners approved unlimited substitution for the 1943 season only, citing wartime constraints, but the writing was on the wall. The change heralded the beginning of the end of the league's heroic "60-minute men."

The owners also voted to make helmets mandatory for the first time. Nobody had played bareheaded in the NFL since the Bears' Dick Plasman retired after the 1940 season, but the owners weren't taking any chances. They might have to cajole a few old-timers out of retirement and they didn't want them getting hurt. Not that the leather helmets then in use afforded much protection. Concussions were a common injury. In 1939 the John T. Riddell Company had patented a new plastic helmet that was lighter and stronger than leather (and it didn't get moldy when wet, either). But plastic was needed for the war effort, so players were stuck with the high-crowned leather headgear. Webbing inside the helmets held them in place on a player's head. Facemasks were practically nonexistent. Ted Doyle may have been the only player in the league wearing one.

"I had a cap put on my tooth and didn't want to have to replace it, so I had them put a nose guard on my helmet," Doyle explained. "'Course it wasn't a fence to hide behind like they have now, it was just a single bar that came down and another that came across the front."

The helmets were hard to decorate, though some teams tried. The Eagles painted theirs green and white, but the paint constantly chipped off, giving the helmets a shabby look that must have driven fashion-conscious Elmer Layden crazy.

One rule change the owners considered but rejected would have allowed coaches to call plays from the sidelines. Ironically, coaches were largely barred from coaching during games. The quarterback or halfback was supposed to call all the plays. The rule was a vestige of the days when coaches also played. The owners' rejection of the change was largely meaningless, though, as the rule was almost comically ignored. Every coach in the league had secret signals for calling plays. Greasy Neale used a game program. Depending on how he held it—rolled up, flat, right hand, left hand—his team knew which play to run.

The meeting concluded on Thursday, April 8, with the league's eighth annual draft. Back in 1935, Bert Bell, who still owned the Philadelphia Eagles at the time, had come up with the idea of holding an annual draft of college players, with teams choosing in the inverse order of their finish in the previous season. Prior to that, college players who had exhausted their eligibility were free to sign with any team. Inevitably the best players signed with the best teams. The draft, inaugurated in 1936, brought about the first semblance of parity to the league, and it is a credit to owners like the Bears' George Halas, the Redskins' George Preston Marshall, and the Giants' Tim Mara that they went along with the idea, putting the league's interests above their own teams'.

During the war, the league renamed the draft the "preferred negotiations list," so as to avoid any militaristic connotations. By any name, though, the 1943 draft was a fruitless exercise. Few of the draftees were expected to be available to play professional football in the fall, given their military obligations. (In 1942 only about 28 percent of all NFL draftees reported to training camp. The figure for 1943 would be closer to five percent.)

"The draft will be little more than a token affair," wrote the *Chicago Tribune*'s Edward Prell, "teams staking out claims on players, the claims to be in effect when the war is over."

To better the odds of actually landing a player or two, the league increased the number of players each team was permitted to draft from 20 to 30, prompting one official to quip, "It's just a matter of selecting 30 men who aren't going to play instead of 20."

By virtue of their perfect 0-11 record in 1942, the Detroit Lions were awarded the first pick in the draft. They chose Frank Sinkwich, an all-American halfback from the University of Georgia. But Sinkwich had already enlisted in the Marine Corps Reserve and would be reporting for active duty as soon as he graduated.

The meeting adjourned at ten o'clock that night with much unresolved. A new schedule still had to be ratified. And there were some rumblings that one or more teams might join Cleveland on the sidelines before the fall. There was even a rumor going around that the Eagles and the Steelers were planning to ask the league for permission to merge—a rumor that Eagles general manager Harry Thayer emphatically denied.

"At no time have officials of the Eagles and Steelers discussed this possibility," Thayer huffed. He should have told Art Rooney that. When asked about the rumor, the Steelers' co-owner was characteristically forthright. According to the *Chicago Tribune,* he "admitted that such a deal might be a remote possibility in the event it became apparent later in the year that neither team could recruit a squad large enough to enter the race."

To resolve the outstanding issues—and to clarify each club's status once and for all—Layden and the owners decided to hold another meeting in June. For his part, the commissioner was optimistic about the future.

"I believe we'll be able to find enough draft-exempt men to keep going," he said after the April meeting concluded. "It won't be easy, I know. Our easy source of playing material—college football ranks—is gone for the duration. We'll have to uncover new sources of supply."

One source of supply Layden and the owners did not uncover was right under their noses. It would have solved the league's manpower shortage overnight. But it would have meant exhibiting a kind of courage they did not have.

AFRICAN-AMERICANS WERE WELCOMED, though not always warmly, in the National Football League's early days. Fritz Pollard, an all-American from Brown, was one of the stars of the Akron Pros, the league's first champions in 1920. The following season Pollard was named one of the team's two co-coaches. He scored seven touchdowns to boot, tying him for the league lead.

One of Pollard's teammates was his friend Paul Robeson, who managed to play professional football on weekends, while attending Columbia University Law School and singing in New York nightclubs the rest of the week. Robeson would take the train from New York to Akron (or wherever else the Pros were playing) on Friday night, practice with the team on Saturday, play the game on Sunday, and return to New York immediately afterwards.

Between 1920 and 1933, 13 African-Americans played in the NFL, often under great stress. Each had to endure the usual epithets and indignities. In newspaper reports they were inevitably described in racial terms: "ebony panther," "dark menace," "dusky," "an Ethiopian in the woodpile."

Fritz Pollard could not use the Pros' locker room; he dressed for games at a nearby cigar factory. Nor could he eat in most Akron restaurants. On the road, he was prohibited from staying in the same hotel as his white teammates. Opposing players constantly took cheap shots at him. When he was tackled, he would roll on his back and kick his feet in the air to deter late hits.

Despite that hostility, black athletes found the NFL considerably more hospitable than professional baseball, where a "gentlemen's agreement" had kept them off the field since the late nineteenth century. Baseball's ban was strictly enforced by Judge Landis, the dogmatic commissioner, despite his public statements to the contrary. In 1943 Landis declared that "any major league club is entirely free to employ Negroes." Yet that same year, Landis scuttled Bill Veeck's attempt to purchase the Philadelphia Phillies, after rumors surfaced that Veeck was planning to stock the team with Negro League stars.

Landis frequently pointed out that there was no rule banning blacks. There was, but it was unwritten, and the owners of the 16 major league clubs adhered to it unconditionally, even when it was not in their best interests to do so. Many teams would have been vastly improved by integration. Perennial bottom feeders like the Browns and the Phillies certainly could have used a Satchel Paige or a Josh Gibson. As sports historian Alan H. Levy writes, "The fact that the leaders of the worst baseball clubs would not, could not, venture onto such a pathway to excellence, and preferred to be perennial league doormats, speaks poignantly to the depths to which the influence of Jim Crow, and the Commissioner's office, penetrated."

The early NFL was under no such influence. Teams were free to sign African-Americans. This was partly a matter of geography. Pro football was almost entirely a product of the Midwest, where racial attitudes were, in the main, less hardened and hostile than in the South. Of the 18 NFL franchises in 1922, 12 were based in just four states (Illinois, Indiana, Ohio, and Wisconsin) and one (the Oorang Indians) was a traveling team composed entirely of Native Americans.

It was also a matter of practicality.

"It was hardly clear that any pro football league would survive," writes Levy, "much less one that was all black or all white. The idea of segregation, or any other sort of segmenting, could not be considered, no matter how some owners may have wished to do so." Considering the league's tenuous finances, a color line would have been unenforceable anyway. Clubs that violated it could have been fined or boycotted, but what good would it have done the fledgling league to drive clubs out of business?

"It was not that owners of early professional football teams wanted African-American athletes to play," Levy writes, "they simply could not do much to stop anyone else from employing them."

Then George Preston Marshall came along.

Marshall was a failed actor who made his money in linen: He owned a chain of laundries in Washington. In 1932, he and two partners bought a defunct NFL franchise in Newark and moved it to Boston. They christened the team the Braves, after the city's National League baseball team (now the Atlanta Braves), with whom they shared a ballpark (Braves Field). The Braves lost $46,000 in their inaugural season. Marshall's partners wanted out and he obliged them. In 1933, Marshall renamed the team the Redskins and moved it a mile east to Fenway Park, the home of the Red Sox.

Marshall shook up the nascent NFL. His was the first team to hire a marching band and put on lavish halftime shows. He persuaded his fellow owners to split the league into two divisions and stage an annual championship game, presaging the Super Bowl by more than three decades. He also convinced them to change the rules to make the game more exciting. Restrictions on throwing the ball were lifted. The forward pass, formerly as popular as a soup line, suddenly became fashionable. Marshall was a showman and an innovator.

He was also a racist. Born in Grafton, West Virginia, in 1896 and raised in Washington, D.C., Marshall was the product of a rigidly segregated culture. In the Washington of his youth, every public institution maintained separate facilities for whites and blacks: schools, churches, restaurants, hotels, trolleys, swimming pools, ballparks. It seemed only logical to him that professional football should be likewise constituted.

At a league meeting shortly after the conclusion of the 1933 season, Marshall urged his peers to adopt a color line just like baseball's. The discussion was off the record, naturally, but Marshall's argument is easy to surmise: The country is in a depression. With so many whites out of work, how will it look if we go on hiring Negroes? It could lead to trouble.

Marshall was not beloved by his colleagues. He was arrogant, boorish, and a bit of a bully. Perhaps that's why the other owners often acquiesced to his demands. On the whole, it was easier to go along with George than to fight him. Or, perhaps, they held deep biases of their own. Whatever their motives, pro football's owners made their own "gentlemen's agreement." And with the league now financially stable, the agreement was enforceable.

Joe Lillard, a black halfback who had led the Chicago Cardinals in scoring in 1933, was not invited back to the team in 1934. Ray Kemp, who'd played for the Pittsburgh Pirates in 1933, was likewise dismissed. In fact, African-Americans would not be welcomed back to the NFL for 13 years.

Years later, the owners would deny colluding to exclude African-Americans. Steelers owner Art Rooney explained that good black players were simply too hard to find. Yet the sports pages were filled with their names: Brud Holland (Cornell), Wilmeth Sidat-Singh (Syracuse), and Ozzie Simmons (Iowa) were three of the most famous college football players in the country in the late 1930s. All were African-American. None was offered so much as a tryout with an NFL team. In December 1969, the football broadcaster and writer Myron Cope broached the subject with Bears owner George Halas in an interview:

> *There had been no ban on black ballplayers [Halas] said—*
> *"In no way, shape, or form."*
> *Why then, had the blacks vanished?*
> *"I don't know!" Halas exclaimed. "Probably it was due to the fact that no great black players were in college then. That could be the reason. But I've never given this a thought until you mentioned it. At no time has it ever been brought up. Isn't that strange?"*

In 1937, supposedly frustrated by a lack of support in Boston, George Preston Marshall moved his team to Washington. He marketed the Redskins as the Team of the South. He commissioned a fight song ("Hail to the Redskins!") that included the line "Fight for old Dixie!" (now rendered "Fight for old D.C.!"). The team played exhibition games in the Carolinas and Virginia, and its games were broadcast on radio (and, later, television) stations throughout the South. And long after every other team in the league had integrated, the Redskins remained lily white and Marshall remained committed to excluding African-Americans.

"We'll start signing Negroes when the Harlem Globetrotters start signing whites," Marshall defiantly declared in 1962. Later that year, threatened with eviction from the new, publicly owned D.C. (now RFK) Stadium, the Redskins finally started signing African-Americans.

Hatching the Steagles

I N EARLY APRIL 1943, Lex Thompson—millionaire playboy, international sportsman, owner of the Philadelphia Eagles, habitué
of Toots Shor's—was a buck private stationed at Camp Davis, a
mosquito-ridden antiaircraft-artillery training center in rural eastern North Carolina. The nearest town was miniscule Holly Ridge,
which the troops nicknamed Boom Town: "Boom, you're in and
boom, you're out!"

Thompson had enlisted in the Army the previous October,
motivated by patriotism as well as by his thirst for adventure. The
war also appealed to his competitive spirit. It was a game in which
he wanted to play. So, while his civilian colleagues were attending
the league meeting at the swanky Palmer House, Thompson was
attending officer training school and practicing his skills on the
artillery range. From this distant outpost, Thompson did his best
to keep tabs on developments in Chicago. Once or twice a day he
spoke on the telephone with Eagles general manager Harry
Thayer, who was running the team in Thompson's stead and representing him at the meeting.

In one of those phone calls, Thayer told Thompson that he
had been approached by Art Rooney with a curious proposition:
Rooney wanted to know if the Eagles would be interested in merg-

ing with the Steelers for the upcoming season. Rooney was desperate. The Steelers had just six players under contract.

"The prospects of continuing on our own look very bad," Rooney confessed to the *Pittsburgh Press.*

Rooney and his partner, Bert Bell, were determined to keep the Steelers alive in some form. The team was coming off its best season ever and they wanted to capitalize on that success. In the topsy-turvy NFL of 1942, with players coming and going like Grand Central Station at rush hour, the Steelers had managed to finish 7-4, posting the first winning season in the history of the franchise and finishing second to the Redskins in the Eastern Division. Attendance was up. The fans were excited.

The Steelers' turnaround was largely due to a rookie named Bill Dudley. Dudley was a small, slippery halfback nicknamed "Bullet Bill," not for his speed—he could barely outrun some linemen—but because he always hit his target when carrying the ball. He led the league in rushing that year and was named an all-pro.

But now Dudley was in the Army Air Forces. So was tailback Andy Tomasic. Guard Jack Sanders and quarterback Russell Cotton were in the Marine Corps. Practically the whole damn team was in uniform now: Vernon Martin, Curtis Sandig, George Gonda, Tom Brown, Milt Crain, Joe Lamas, John Woudenberg— 19 in all, just since the season ended. They were disappearing so fast that Rooney had a hard time keeping track. To make things tragically worse, starting right guard Milt Simington, an all-pro, had died of a heart attack in January at age 24. It almost seemed like the franchise was cursed.

But abandoning play, as the Cleveland Rams had done, was not an option. The 1942 season had given Steelers fans something to look forward to, and Rooney was going to give them, well, something.

The merger proposal did not immediately enthrall Eagles owner Lex Thompson. He'd sunk too much money into the Eagles to have them turned into a two-headed monster. He feared the merger would hurt the team's image and debase its name. Thompson sold a million bottles of Eye-Gene a year, so he knew a thing or two about branding. That made him an anomaly among the owners, most of whom simply named their clubs after baseball teams.

Thompson also wasn't sure about going into business with Rooney and Bert Bell. Besides, he thought he didn't need to merge with the Steelers—or anybody else. Thayer told Thompson he was "reasonably sure" the Eagles could field a team all by themselves. In addition to the 16 players the Eagles still had under contract, Thayer said they had "strings attached" to about a dozen more. That meant the Eagles would probably have enough players to fill the new, reduced roster size of 25—as long as Uncle Sam didn't get his hands on them before the season began.

But Thompson was not entirely unsympathetic to the Steelers' plight. After all, the Eagles had just lost two of their best players to the service: their star quarterback, Tommy Thompson (no relation to Lex), and their leading scorer, Len Barnum. Thompson also remembered how Rooney and Bert Bell had done him a great favor two years earlier, when they swapped franchises with him. That had spared Thompson exile in Pittsburgh, which, in his opinion, would have been only marginally better than Holly Ridge.

In some ways the merger was logical, given the wartime exigencies and the inextricably linked histories of the two teams. Merging with the Steelers might actually be good for the Eagles. Who knew? Just because they could field a team by themselves didn't mean the team would be any good. In fact, judging by their record the previous season (2-9), they were likely to be awful. Pittsburgh still had a couple of pretty good players under contract and the Eagles could use all the help they could get.

Thompson was also aware that the merger would, in his words, "contribute substantially toward ironing out the sport's difficulties." Without the merger the Steelers might have no choice but to fold, and the league was anxious to prevent that from happening to a second team.

Thompson told Thayer he'd have to think about it a while.

On June 15, 1943, at a press conference at the Racquet Club of Philadelphia, the Eagles publicly addressed the merger proposal for the first time. General manager Harry Thayer, making it clear that he was speaking for Thompson, said "on the whole" the Eagles would prefer to go it alone. However, Thayer continued, the team was willing to merge with Pittsburgh—but only if the combine was known as the Philadelphia Eagles and played the Eagles' regular number of home games in Philadelphia.

It was a lot to ask, but Steelers co-owners Bert Bell and Art Rooney were in no position to quibble. The details could be hammered out later. The next day Rooney sent Commissioner Elmer Layden a "formal application for permission to merge the Pittsburgh and Philadelphia clubs," which would be acted upon at the league's special meeting the following weekend in Chicago.

AS IF COMMISSIONER LAYDEN didn't have enough to worry about that spring, the NFL was also in danger of losing one its few remaining sources of personnel: fathers. Draft boards routinely deferred married men with children born or conceived before Pearl Harbor. (Children who entered the world before September 15, 1942—nine months and one week after Pearl Harbor—were presumed to have met the conception deadline.) As long as they maintained "bona fide family relationships" with their wives and children, "pre-Pearl" fathers, as they were known, were classified 3-A: deferred due to dependency. They were, for all practical purposes, exempt from the draft. The reasoning, as explained in paragraph 354 of the Selective Service regulations, was that the "maintenance of the family as a unit is of importance to the national well-being." If fathers were drafted, it was widely held, mothers would be forced to find work outside the home, leaving unsupervised children to fall inevitably and irretrievably into delinquency. Of all the nations that fought the war, the United States alone granted fathers this benefit. By 1943, some six million dads had been deferred. To the NFL, this was an irreplaceable talent pool. The 3-As were the veteran players who knew the game best, and they gave the league a modicum of stability. It was no surprise that the Redskins and the Bears had met in the 1942 championship game. They were the teams with the most fathers.

The NFL desperately needed dads. But the man in charge of the draft, Lewis B. Hershey, needed them more.

Hershey looked like a football player himself, barrel-chested and broad-shouldered with a thick head of closely cropped red hair. In reality he wasn't much of an athlete—he was cut from his high school basketball team in Fremont, Indiana—but, as a major general in the Army and the head of Selective Service, Hershey held great sway over professional football. His job was to give military leaders as many men as they needed to win the war. And by the beginning of 1943 it was apparent they would need a lot. Simultaneous offensives in Europe, Africa, and the Pacific were stretching the ranks to the breaking point. Yet to come were much bigger battles, including the seemingly inevitable invasions of France and Japan. The War Department wanted 11 million men in the armed forces by the end of the year. That would require the conscription of another three million men.

Steps had already been taken to meet the demand. The length of service had been extended from one year to the duration of the war plus six months. The draft age had been lowered from 21 to 18. Lowered, too, were the lofty physical standards that President Roosevelt had championed. In 1942, a draftee with fewer than six pairs of opposing teeth was classified 4-F. A year later, toothless draftees were inducted as long as they could be fitted with dentures. But it still wasn't enough.

In early April, Hershey announced that fathers would be drafted beginning July 1. Only those whose induction would cause "undue hardship" would be deferred. Family size would not be a consideration. The father of seven was as likely to be called as the father of one, though Hershey also urged draft boards to call all eligible non-fathers first.

Public opinion was squarely opposed to the Father Draft, as it came to be known. In one poll, 81 percent of all respondents said single women should be drafted before fathers. Predictably, Congress got into the act. Texas Representative Paul Kilday introduced a bill requiring that no father be drafted before a single man in any state—a bureaucratic nightmare as far as Hershey was concerned. Kilday said the draft was threatening "the preservation of the family in American life." Montana Senator Burton Wheeler introduced a similar measure.

"Taking men with several children will be breaking down morale at home," Wheeler said at a Congressional hearing. "Home morale may be more important than a big army." (To which Lt. Gen. Joseph McNarney, the Army's deputy chief of staff, replied dryly, "Better a big army than defeat by the Axis.")

Local draft boards, ever protective of their autonomy, rebelled. Some posted the names of single men with deferments—lists that came to be known as "rat files." Others said they would simply ignore Hershey's directive. The chairman of a Philadelphia draft board said, "We certainly can't throw children in the streets without supervision. If a father is forced into the Army, then the mother will have to get a job. This leaves children to shift for themselves."

Like all good soldiers, Hershey knew when to retreat but refused to surrender. He postponed the Father Draft, hoping to buy more time to convince the public, lawmakers, and draft boards of its necessity. In the meantime, he ordered the boards to reexamine and, if at all possible, reclassify previously deferred draftees. He also ordered the immediate induction of draft "slackers," men who flouted draft regulations by, for example, failing to report for a physical. There were even calls to begin drafting prison inmates. Anybody but dads.

But Hershey warned the Father Draft was inevitable—and in August he set a new date for it to begin: October 1. In a letter to local draft boards Hershey said the military's need for manpower was so acute that "one-half million fathers must be inducted before January 1, 1944." As far as NFL Commissioner Elmer Layden was concerned, the timing couldn't have been worse: October 1 was practically pro football's Opening Day.

In the days leading up to the league's June meeting, Layden was upbeat—in public, anyway. "There is a more optimistic feeling in the league than there was a year ago that we can go through the season," he told a New York sportswriter. Privately, though, Layden was deeply concerned. Training camps were due to open in less than two months. About 40 percent of the 349 players on NFL rosters in 1942 were off to war—even more than were lost after the 1941 season. And if—or, more likely, when—the Father Draft went through, that percentage would rise dramatically. To salvage the 1943 season, Layden told the owners they would have to be "ingenious" and "display the ultimate in initiative."

Chester Smith, the sports editor of the *Pittsburgh Press*, reported that "New York, Washington, Green Bay and Detroit are the only clubs in the National Football League that feel they will be able to put adequate teams on the field next fall." The Brooklyn Dodgers, according to Smith, had "lost just about everything but the water bucket." Owner Dan Topping was in the Marines. He was believed to be overseas, but his exact whereabouts were unknown. The team's two vice-presidents were also in the service. Head coach Mike Getto had quit to manage his father-in-law's hotel in Lawrence, Kansas. To replace him, Dodgers general manager Dennis Shea took it upon himself to hire Pete Cawthon, a former Texas Tech coach. Topping knew nothing of the change.

The Chicago Cardinals were in similar straits. Their roster was in tatters. Head coach Jimmy Conzelman had abandoned the team to work in the front office of baseball's St. Louis Browns. His replacement, Phil Handler, was sniffing around the Great Lakes Naval Station to see who might be available, come fall—even though the league did not yet permit active duty servicemen to play. There were rumors that the Cards, like the Rams, would have to throw in the towel. But owner Charlie Bidwill wasn't ready to give up just yet. He had something up his sleeve.

Once again, the owners met in Chicago. This time they convened in a ballroom at the Blackstone, a grand, 21-story hotel just south of the Loop on Michigan Avenue. Layden called the meeting to order at 10:30 a.m. on Saturday, June 19, 1943. It was a warm day and most of the men in the un-air-conditioned room were in their shirtsleeves. The mood was tense. At the request of Bears owner George Halas—who had once again managed to get leave from his obligations at the Navy base in Norman, Oklahoma—the meeting began with a roll call of teams and their intentions for the upcoming season:

Detroit: Operating
Philadelphia: Requesting merger with Pittsburgh
Chicago Cardinals: Requesting merger with Chicago Bears
Brooklyn: Operating
New York: Operating
Pittsburgh: Requesting merger with Philadelphia
Washington: Operating
Chicago Bears: Requesting merger with Chicago Cardinals
Green Bay: Operating

That the two Chicago teams wanted to merge was a surprise, but hardly a shock. Though they were bitter rivals on the field, their owners were old friends. Back in 1931, Charlie Bidwill had helped George Halas save the Bears from creditors by purchasing a 16-percent stake in the team for $5,000. Bidwill even served as the Bears' secretary until he bought the Cardinals in 1933, and he still held his Bears stock, a conflict of interest that would not be permitted today. Bidwill, it was widely believed, was still a Bears fan at heart, his ownership of the Cardinals notwithstanding.

Like Art Rooney, Bidwill made a fortune on the horses—but not by gambling. Bidwill owned two racetracks and a company that printed racing programs and betting slips (as well as Cardinals and Bears tickets). He bought the Cardinals on a lark for $50,000 in cash. In 1936, he and Halas signed the Madison Street agreement, which delineated each team's territory within Chicago. The Cardinals would play only on the south side of Madison, in

Comiskey Park, the Bears only on the north side, in Wrigley Field. (Before the agreement, the Cardinals had occasionally rented Wrigley, much to Halas's consternation.)

A Cardinals-Bears union would not be a marriage of equals. The Bears had finished the regular season undefeated (11-0) in 1942 and had lost fewer players to the military than most other teams. The Cardinals went 3-8 in 1942 and had already said good-bye to their top passer (Bud Schwenk) and their top receiver (Pop Ivy). Charlie Bidwill had much more to gain from the merger than George Halas. Halas likely agreed to pursue it out of loyalty to Bidwill. The fact that Bidwill was also a Bears shareholder might have had something to do with it, too.

Logistically, a Cardinals-Bears merger made more sense than a Steelers-Eagles merger. After all, Wrigley Field and Comiskey Park were separated by only a 30-minute El ride. Competitively, though, it was a different story. As woeful as the Cardinals were, they still had a couple of good players (namely back Marshall Goldberg and end Eddie Rucinski), while the Bears had won three straight Western Division crowns. The Windy City amalgam would be much more formidable than the Pennsylvania pairing.

Over the next five hours, the owners (or, in the cases of Brooklyn and Philadelphia, their representatives) debated the merger requests in increasingly testy terms. One group, led by obstreperous George Preston Marshall, adamantly opposed both mergers. This coalition—Marshall (Washington), Curly Lambeau (Green Bay), Dennis Shea (Brooklyn) and Fred Mandel (Detroit)—wanted to "crack down" on owners seeking an "easy out" of their wartime problems. They were convinced it had been a mistake to let Cleveland withdraw at the April meeting, and they opposed further contraction.

Their views were shared by the influential Arch Ward, the *Chicago Tribune* sports editor. On the eve of the meeting, Ward wrote, "Is it fair to the teams which, thru enterprise, good luck or what have you, are able to carry on to have to meet a club made up of the combined talent of Pittsburgh and Philadelphia or of the two Chicago teams? It doesn't make sense to let owners operate teams when the prospects of enjoying a profit are good and to relieve them of responsibilities when the situation is reversed."

In an attempt to block the mergers, the Marshall coalition made a motion that, if two teams merged, one of the teams would have to disperse its players among all the remaining teams in the league—just as Cleveland had done in April. That, of course, would defeat the whole purpose of merging in the first place. The motion passed 5-2, with Jack Mara, the president of the Giants (and the son of owner Tim Mara), voting with the Marshall coalition. (Steelers co-owner Art Rooney and Eagles general manager Harry Thayer voted no. Bidwill and Halas abstained.)

At 3:30 p.m., the meeting was adjourned so Thayer could call Lex Thompson down at Camp Davis to talk things over. Rooney and his partner Bert Bell used the break to lobby their colleagues. They begged the two Chicago owners to abandon their joint-operating proposal. They pleaded their case with Jack Mara, who seemed less strenuously opposed to a merger than the Marshall coalition. Elmer Layden, the commissioner, also argued on behalf of the Pennsylvanians, believing their combine would be in the best interests of the league, financially as well as competitively.

When the meeting resumed at 5:00 p.m., the Cardinals and Bears withdrew their merger request. Then Bert Bell made a motion:

> *To allow Pittsburgh and Philadelphia to merge from the end of the meeting to the close of the National Football League season, that is, the week before the playoff game, retaining their players from both teams. . . .*

Bell's motion would overturn the Marshall coalition's motion and allow the Steelers and Eagles to pool their players. (Curiously, it also assumed the combine would not win a divisional title, since the merger would expire before the championship game.)

After what one observer described as "a long and bitter debate," the motion passed by a 5-4 vote. Jack Mara had had a "softening of the heart" and changed his vote. It was a rare instance of George Preston Marshall failing to get his way.

"When the Bears and Cardinals' application was withdrawn the membership readily was agreeable to the proposals we made," Eagles general manager Harry Thayer said afterwards, rather understating the fractious deliberations. "It was felt we have legitimate reasons for wanting to combine our interests, while there was no need of the Chicago clubs doing the same."

Rooney and Bell had convinced Thayer to make two minor concessions. The combine would be known simply as the Eagles, without a city designation, and it would play most—but not all—of its home games in Philadelphia. The three men also agreed to split expenses (after player salaries) 50-50 between their two teams. (They also agreed to split profits—in the unlikely event there were any.) The combine would be based in Philadelphia, with Eagles head coach Greasy Neale and Steelers head coach Walt Kiesling serving as co–head coaches. Each team would retain the rights to the players on its roster at the time of the merger, as well as the rights to any players it signed during the merger.

Finally there was the prickly issue of uniforms. Eagles owner Lex Thompson would not allow his players to wear anything other than the team's usual colors of kelly green and white. Bell and Rooney wanted the team to wear the Steelers' black and gold jerseys, at least when it played in Pittsburgh. In the end, Thompson won out. The team would wear Eagles jerseys for every game. Bell and Rooney probably gave in because it would have been too costly to clean and maintain two sets of uniforms all season anyway.

It wasn't everything Thayer and Thompson wanted, and Bell and Rooney practically gave up the farm. But, considering the circumstances, the principals were satisfied with the merger.

"Without it," said Bert Bell, "we would have been pathetic and so would the Eagles." Back in Pittsburgh, though, there was disappointment.

"So far as anyone in Pittsburgh need be concerned," Chet Smith wrote in the *Press*, "there will be no National League football here in the fall. The temporary merger of the Steelers and Philadelphia Eagles was worked out on anything but an equitable basis."

Incredibly, at 10:45 that night, after many long hours debating contraction, the owners reconvened to discuss expansion. In a sign that better times were to come, the league had received applications for new franchises in Baltimore, Boston, and Buffalo. The owners voted unanimously to award a team in Boston to Ted Collins, the manager of singer Kate Smith (famous for her rendition of the Irving Berlin song "God Bless America"). Collins' team would not begin play until the 1944 season. The owners, however, were free to divvy up his $25,000 down payment on the $50,000 franchise fee immediately. Which they did before going to bed.

The next day, the owners tackled a bit of business that remained unfinished from the April meeting: the game schedule. One benefit of the merger was that it neatly reduced the league to two four-team divisions (the Philadelphia-Pittsburgh combine naturally having been placed in the Eastern Division). This made scheduling much more manageable than a nine-team league with two unbalanced divisions. Elmer Layden proposed that each team play two games against each of the other three teams in its division and one against each of the four teams in the other division. That would give each team ten games, one fewer than usual, but, for the first time, each team would play every other team in the league at least once. This the owners agreed to.

The hard part, as usual, was figuring out the home games. George Preston Marshall insisted on playing six of his Redskins' ten games at Griffith Stadium, which prompted Jack Mara to demand six home games for the Giants. And, since their newly constituted "Eagles" would be playing home games in two cities, Rooney, Bell, and Thayer felt entitled to an extra home game too.

It took sixteen hours of bitter and tedious negotiations over two days, but in the end, the Redskins, Giants, and Eagles got their six home games. It was decided the Eagles would play four home games in Philadelphia and two in Pittsburgh. (Each city would also get one pre-season exhibition game.) The Bears, Lions, and Dodgers would play five home games each, the Packers four, and the poor Cardinals just three—and one of those would be played in Buffalo because of a scheduling conflict at Comiskey Park. (When "tight spots develop in National League huddles," a Chicago sportswriter complained, "it always is the Cards who take a kicking around.")

With the Father Draft looming, the owners also voted to begin tapping new sources of talent. Teams were allowed to sign college undergraduates attending schools that had discontinued football. It was a rare exception to pro football's ironclad ban on signing collegians before their classes had graduated. Layden defended the change in patriotic terms: "We believe football provides a boy with training he needs for the future and if he can't get it at the college he is attending and it isn't feasible to transfer to another one where the sport is in vogue we see no reason he shouldn't be given a chance to play with one of our teams."

The owners also debated the merits of allowing active-duty military personnel to play. George Preston Marshall, who favored the idea, said, "I think that as far as this league is concerned we shouldn't pass any rule detrimental to a fellow in the service. . . . I see no reason why that fellow shouldn't play with a team in this league." Besides, he added, "All of us know damn well that we are going to have one awful job getting 20 or 25 players." (Marshall seemed to have ulterior motives: Washington was swimming in servicemen.) But other owners worried about what would happen if a grunt got hurt playing pro football. It was decided that a serviceman would be allowed to play only with the permission of his commanding officer.

After the league meeting adjourned on Monday, June 21, Bert Bell returned to his home in Philadelphia and called on an old friend who'd played for him back when he owned the Eagles. The friend hadn't played football in years, but Bell knew just what it would take to coax him out of retirement.

▌ ▏ ▏ ▏ ▏ ▌

LIKE MILLIONS OF AMERICANS in the spring of 1932, Bill Hewitt was out of work. For three seasons he'd been a stalwart on the University of Michigan's football team. But now his eligibility was used up; he couldn't play college football anymore.

"I was a semester short of graduation," Hewitt remembered, "but getting a diploma was not then my consuming passion." So he was bumming around his hometown of Bay City, Michigan, not even sure "where my next few thousand meals were coming from." Relief came in the form of a letter from Bears owner George Halas, who'd apparently heard about Hewitt from a Chicago sportswriter. Halas offered Hewitt $100 a game to play for the Bears. Hewitt countered with $110. Halas agreed, but when Hewitt showed up for training camp, he learned the contract didn't have a no-cut clause. Hewitt didn't want to take any chances, so he settled for $100 after all: "I swapped ten dollars a game for a written guarantee that I'd be kept on the payroll for the entire season."

Halas got his money's worth. Hewitt immediately became the Bears' starting left end.

The NFL had never seen anything like Bill Hewitt. On offense he was a ferocious blocker and a nimble pass catcher. On defense he was an aggressive tackler with a mean streak. He covered kickoffs and punts with wild abandon. And he did it all with his head conspicuously uncovered. Bill Hewitt was one of the last professional football players to forsake headgear. He hated helmets. He said they "handicapped" his play. He also thought they were a little sissified.

On the field you couldn't miss him. He had a full head of blonde hair and a jutting jaw. He wasn't big, just five-nine, 190 pounds, but he was quick and agile and fearless. His teammates, rather courageously, nicknamed him Stinky because when he came to Chicago he owned just one outfit (a pair of corduroy pants and a blue Michigan sweater). Fans called him the Offside Kid because, when he was playing defense, he would burst across the line of scrimmage so quickly that it was hard to believe he wasn't committing a penalty.

Hewitt was "one of the great ends of all time," George Halas said. "He had a flaming spirit."

As a rookie in 1932, Hewitt played in one of the most unusual games in NFL history. After the Bears and the Portsmouth (Ohio) Spartans finished the season tied for first place, then-Commissioner Joe Carr ordered a one-game playoff to determine the champion. The game was supposed to be played at Wrigley Field, but a blizzard forced it to be moved indoors, to Chicago Stadium. With a six-inch layer of dirt covering the arena floor, the two teams slugged it out on a field measuring just 60 yards between the goal lines and 45 between the sidelines. To accommodate the smaller dimensions, several rules were modified. Teams kicked off from the ten-yard line. After a team crossed midfield the ball was moved back 20 yards to compensate for the shortened field. The goalposts were moved from the back of the end zone to the goal line, and no field goals were allowed. And, because the field was completely surrounded by hockey dasher boards, after a player went out of bounds, the ball was placed ten yards inbounds, instead of on the sideline, as was then the custom. (This last change proved so popular that it was subsequently adopted permanently.) The Bears won this early version of an Arena League game 9-0 on a disputed touchdown, prompting a Portsmouth newspaper to denounce the game as a "sham battle on a Tom Thumb gridiron." (The Spartans did win the NFL championship three years later—but only after the team, renamed the Lions, had moved to Detroit.)

In 1933, Hewitt became a truly dominating player. Opposing teams would assign two or even three players to cover him, but to no avail.

"I never saw anything like it," his teammate Red Grange recalled. "I don't believe he made a mistake all year."

Hewitt was named an all-pro and the Bears won the championship again.

In 1934, Halas finally gave Hewitt a raise—to $130 a game. There his salary stayed for the next three seasons. His meager compensation—and the low salaries of pro football players in

general—continually frustrated Hewitt. It wasn't merely customary for players to work second jobs in the off-season; it was usually
necessary. Until the late 1950s, football cards often listed a player's second occupation. Hewitt complained that "the average professional football player is the peon of big-league sports." Not only
that: It was also impossible for players to secure meaningful, well-
paying employment away from the gridiron. "Employers don't
hand out good jobs in January, jobs with a future, to men who will
quit next August and spend four months playing at games."

By the end of the 1936 season, Hewitt had had enough. He
told Halas he was through. Halas wasn't convinced, though, so he
traded Hewitt to Philadelphia, leaving it up to Bert Bell, then the
owner of the Eagles, to convince the Offside Kid to keep playing.
Bell offered Hewitt $200 a game and a $24-a-week off-season job
as a grease monkey at a gas station. Hewitt was convinced. (In
game programs, the Eagles rather generously described Hewitt's
second occupation as "lubrication and fuel oil salesman.")

Although the Eagles were a miserable team, Hewitt's play did
not suffer. In his first season in Philadelphia he was again named
an all-pro, the first player to achieve the honor with two different
teams. In 1939, his third season in Philadelphia, Hewitt got a raise
to $250 a game. But the game was finally beginning to take a toll
on him.

"I could remember when I laughed at the veterans lined up
in the trainer's room after a game. Now I was first in line, and
when I'd had one rubdown I would go to the tail of the queue and
start all over."

After the season, Hewitt retired, seemingly for good. He settled down in Philadelphia with his wife and daughter and started
looking for a job with a future.

Then, a little more than three years later, in the summer of
1943, Bert Bell, now the co-owner of the Steelers, came calling
again.

Like Ted Doyle, Hewitt was ambivalent about pro football.
He loved the game, but he didn't mind walking away from it.

"It left me wary of people, unable to meet strangers. Years of backslapping and insincere praise made me suspicious of almost everyone."

So, Hewitt wrote, when Bell invited him to join the newly merged Philadelphia-Pittsburgh team,

> *I said "No, thank you," and he said "Aw, c'mon," and I said "Sorry," and he said "Four hundred per game." I said, "Are you going to hand me that pen or do we sit here and stall all night?"*

Bell figured Hewitt was well worth the money. Good ends were hard to come by in 1943, even if they were pushing 34 and past their prime. Besides, due to an old football injury, Hewitt was 4-F: he had a perforated eardrum. (Men with perforated eardrums were rejected for military service because they were acutely vulnerable to chemical weapons.) Not only that, he'd found work at a trucking company—an essential industry. He was positively draft-proof. The only catch was that Hewitt would have to wear a helmet for the first time in his career. It was the rule now, whether he liked it or not—and the Offside Kid most certainly did not.

6

Greasy and Walt

I N THE EARLY DAYS of professional football, head coaches were little more than figureheads, more akin to team captains. With a few notable exceptions (such as the Bears' George Halas), they were neither tacticians nor motivators. A head coach scheduled practices—if there were any—and taught his team a few simple plays. He had no game plan. He only had a game. Greasy Neale recalled what it was like playing for Jim Thorpe in 1917: "Why, we wouldn't see Thorpe when he was coaching the Canton Bulldogs until the day of the game. We didn't practice between games. Jim would give us three or four plays and then ask each man how long he thought he could play."

Early coaches had neither the time nor the inclination to devote their undivided attention to football. Like their players, most held full-time jobs during the week, and many, like Thorpe, played as well as coached. So interchangeable were head coaches that it was not unusual for a team to have two or three simultaneously. The 1927 Frankford Yellow Jackets had four: Russ Daugherity, Charley Rogers, Ed Weir, and Swede Youngstrom. By having multiple coaches, a team could be relatively certain that at least one of them would show up on Sunday (or Saturday, in Frankford's case).

By 1940, the role of the head coach had changed significantly. Player/coaches like Halas, Steve Owen of the Giants, and Curly Lambeau of the Packers had hung up their football shoes to concentrate solely on coaching. They developed new strategies. They scouted opponents. They instituted regular training regimens. And the growing popularity of the National Football League made it possible for them (and, on most teams, one or two assistants) to be compensated well enough to do the job full time. There were still occasional coaching tandems. Hunk Anderson and Luke Johnsos jointly coached the Bears for more than three seasons while Halas was in the Navy during the war. But for the most part the head coach had become the lone general leading his troops, responsible for everything from negotiating contracts to handing out paychecks. The head coach had evolved from superfluous to indispensable. He had transformed football from a simple game to a very complex one. He was now firmly in charge, and he countenanced no challenges to his authority.

When the Eagles and the Steelers merged in June of 1943, both teams' head coaches, Earle "Greasy" Neale and Walt Kiesling, were of that ilk. Each had experience reaching back to the formative days of pro football. Each also had an outsized ego and a firm belief in his infallibility when it came to matters concerning the sport. Since neither coach would accept a demotion when the teams merged, they were named co-coaches. It was an unhappy compromise, a shotgun wedding that seemed destined to end badly.

EVERYONE CALLED ALFRED EARLE NEALE "GREASY." The rather unfortunate nickname was acquired at an early age, when he called a playmate "dirty" and the playmate retorted with "greasy." In fact, Greasy Neale was quite unlike his nickname, dapper and handsome, with a pronounced widow's peak and a dimpled chin. But he never attempted to shed the sobriquet. Instead, he embraced it. When he took a coaching job at Yale in 1934, the school asked newspapers to refrain from using his nickname. But

Neale told reporters, "Yale or no Yale, if you fellows want to call me Greasy, go ahead."

Born into a poor family in Parkersburg, West Virginia, he went to work at the age of ten as a paperboy and a pinsetter at a local bowling alley. He repeated the fourth grade and dropped out of high school in his freshman year to take a job at the mills of the Parkersburg Iron & Steel Company. In his free time he played sports.

"My first love was baseball," he said, "and my consuming ambition was to become a big leaguer. The football I played as a youngster was merely a fill-in to keep busy until it was warm enough for baseball." Realizing "there wasn't much future" in the mills, in 1909 he returned to Parkersburg High, where he played—and, one year, coached—football.

In the fall of 1912, Greasy entered West Virginia Wesleyan College, his chief aims being athletic rather than academic. Playing right end, he led Wesleyan to stunning upsets of mighty West Virginia in his freshman and sophomore years, scoring touchdowns in both games. At Wesleyan he also met a lovely coed named Genevieve Horner, whom he married in 1915.

"She opened an entire new chapter in my life and gave me added incentive," he said. "She was the driving force I needed." Because he now "had the responsibilities of a husband," Neale left Wesleyan to take a job as the head football coach at tiny Muskingum College in New Concord, Ohio. He was just 23.

"Subconsciously, I suppose, I had always wanted to be a coach ever since my experience at Parkersburg High," he wrote. "The immense possibilities of football strategy always had intrigued me, plus the even more involved details of handling a squad of football players."

All the while, Neale continued to pursue his "consuming ambition" of becoming a big-league baseball player. His summers were spent toiling for minor league teams in Altoona, Saginaw, and Wheeling.

"God gave me a good pair of hands and speedy legs," he said, "but not the keen vision a professional baseball player should have." Yet, through "application and determination" he achieved his goal: In the spring of 1916 he signed a contract with the Cincinnati Reds for $1,000. But after the baseball season ended, he always returned to football.

Over the next two decades, Neale moved Zelig-like through the landscape of American sports, an early-day Deion Sanders (another two-sport star) without the attitude or the endorsement deals. In 1917 he played professional football for the legendary Canton Bulldogs under an assumed name ("Foster"), since, at the time, he was also the head football coach at his alma mater, West Virginia Wesleyan, a Southern Methodist school that frowned upon frivolous Sabbath activities like football. (The Reds would not have appreciated his moonlighting either.) In the fall of 1918, during World War I, he worked six days a week at the Wright Brothers' Dayton factory building warplanes. On Sundays he coached and played for the local pro football team, the Dayton Triangles, who finished the season undefeated. He hit .357 as the starting right fielder for the Reds in the 1919 World Series against the Chicago White Sox. Cincinnati won the series, though eight Chicago players were subsequently banned from baseball for life for conspiring to fix it. But Neale considered his achievement untainted: "I've always held to the opinion that the ill-famed Black Sox of 1919 tried to play it on the square after the first game and that our pitching was too much for them." In all, Neale played eight seasons of major league baseball, retiring with a .259 batting average.

In 1921 he became head football coach at tiny Washington and Jefferson College in Washington, Pennsylvania, guiding the Presidents to an improbable victory over Pitt and an even more improbable appearance in the 1922 Rose Bowl, where they played California to a scoreless tie. In 1930 he coached the Ironton Tanks, an independent pro football team that beat the Chicago Bears, the New York Giants, and the Portsmouth Spartans (later the Detroit Lions) in exhibition games. He also played one game for the Tanks, a few weeks shy of his 39th birthday, again using an assumed name, this time so Genevieve wouldn't find out. (She did, when he came home with a black eye.) He was the head foot-ball coach at six different colleges, compiling a cumulative record of 78-55-11. Along the way he invented the man-to-man pass de-fense and the fake reverse, and he championed "subsidization," i.e., the awarding of athletic scholarships.

In 1934, Neale was offered the head coaching job at Yale. It was a prestigious position but there was a problem: Yale had never had a coach who wasn't an alumnus. Greasy Neale, of course, was not a Yalie, and the school's alumni, who wielded a good bit of influence, objected to his guiding their football team. A compro-mise of sorts was reached: Yale hired Raymond "Ducky" Pond, a Yale graduate, as head coach. Neale was made his assistant. It seemed like a step down for Neale, but in reality Pond was mere-ly Neale's front man, a head coach in name only. Greasy ran the show and everybody knew it. For seven seasons he was the power behind the throne at Yale, a situation that was less than ideal for both men.

"I told Ducky my interests were the same as his—to see that Yale had a winning team," Neale later said. "Once this difficulty was ironed out, we got along fine." Privately, though, it must have been difficult for Neale to accept his new role. He had always been the head coach, even back at Parkersburg High.

Then, one day in 1940, Neale's secretary told him that a Yale grad named Alexis Thompson wanted to meet him for dinner.

"I'll be glad to have dinner with any alumnus of the school," Neale answered, "but who is Mr. Thompson?" When the two men met for dinner at a New Haven restaurant called Mori's, Neale learned exactly who Thompson was: an extremely wealthy young man who planned to purchase an NFL team and had been advised (by New York Giants head coach Steve Owen) to hire Neale as head coach. Neale was surprised, but he was also inclined to accept the offer. He missed being a head coach in name as well as function. Besides, Yale's athletic department was $100,000 in debt and looking for ways to cut costs. It was a good time to go.

Neale told Thompson he'd take the job, but said he wanted a three-year contract for $12,000 a year. Thompson countered with $10,000. "We settled on my figure with a minimum of bicker-ing," Neale later said. As soon as Thompson purchased the Steelers in December 1940, he named Neale head coach. When Thompson swapped franchises with Bert Bell and Art Rooney the following spring, he brought Neale along to coach the Eagles.

When he became the Eagles' head coach, Greasy Neale was nearly fifty years old. His brown hair had turned silvery gray, though he was still trim and fit enough to run pass patterns as well as his best receivers. He and Genevieve had been bouncing around football outposts most of their lives. It was time to settle down. Greasy promised Genevieve the Philadelphia job would be his last.

▮ ❘ ❘ ❘ ❘ ▮

IN 1926, OLE HAUGSRUD, a twenty-something wheeler-dealer from Duluth, Minnesota, bought an NFL franchise for one dollar. The franchise was the Duluth Kelleys (also known as the Kelley-Duluths), who were named after a local hardware store. Haugs-rud, who also agreed to assume the club's debts, immediately signed the biggest prize coming out of college that year: Ernie Nevers, a handsome all-American fullback from Stanford. Nevers had captured the nation's imagination by recovering from two broken ankles to rush for more than 100 yards against Notre Dame in the 1925 Rose Bowl. Haugsrud was able to sign Nevers because the two young men were friends. They'd played high school football together in Superior, Wisconsin, just down the road from Duluth. With Nevers signed, Haugsrud renamed his team the Eskimos—the Ernie Nevers Eskimos, to be precise—and began looking for sizeable linemen who could block for his star player. Somebody told Haugsrud about a big German kid named Kiesling who'd just graduated from St. Thomas College down in St. Paul. He was as big as a boxcar and had a mean streak.

Growing up in St. Paul, Walter Andrew Kiesling was always bigger than the other kids. When he entered Cretin High School, the football coach took one look at him and put him on the line, where he started all four years. Knute Rockne offered him a scholarship to Notre Dame, but Kiesling's mother wanted him to stay close to home, so, in 1922, Kiesling enrolled at St. Thomas. By then he was six-two, 235 pounds. His teammates called him Big Kies. One of St. Thomas's biggest rivals was Saint John's University in Collegeville, about 90 miles northwest of St. Paul. Saint John's had a flamboyant halfback named John McNally—later more famously known as Johnny Blood. Bitter opponents on the field, Kiesling and Blood became close friends off it, and their paths would cross many times in the ensuing years.

Kiesling was an outstanding college lineman—the Tommies went 29-5-1 in his four seasons there—but, like Greasy Neale, his first love was baseball. Kiesling could hit the ball a country mile, and after he graduated from St. Thomas in the spring of 1926, he signed a contract with the Minneapolis Millers of the American Association, just one step below the big leagues. There it was discovered that Kiesling couldn't hit a curve ball to save his life. The Millers' manager, Michael Joseph Kelly, gently suggested he consider another line of work.

On September 19, 1926, the Eskimos, with Kiesling on the line and Ernie Nevers and Johnny Blood in the backfield, opened the season by defeating the Kansas City Cowboys 7-0 in Duluth. The Eskimos then embarked on the most grueling road trip in the annals of professional sports. Convinced his team could get bigger gates away from Duluth, Haugsrud scheduled no more home games that season. Over the next five months the Eskimos played 28 league and exhibition contests from New York to Los Angeles, traveling 17,000 miles in the process. In the Eskimos' 29 games, Nevers played all but 26 minutes. Not that his teammates got much rest either. The team's roster usually comprised no more than 13 players, prompting Grantland Rice to dub them "the Iron Men of the North." The Eskimos were a carnivalesque enterprise. In one stretch the team played five games in eight days. Paychecks were distributed irregularly at best. One time, owner Ole Haugsrud got stiffed by the manager of the St. Louis Gunners.

"I chased him right across the football field and up the steps of the grandstand and across an open causeway," Haugsrud recalled. "I cornered the fellow in a toilet, and he gave me the seventy bucks."

With Big Kies clearing the way, Nevers scored eight touchdowns and ranked second in the league in scoring. The Eskimos finished their long, strange season with a remarkable (considering the circumstances) 6-5-3 record in league games. In 1927, though, they finished 1-8-0, largely because the league had contracted from 22 to 12 teams, eliminating the weaker clubs. The Eskimos were overmatched.

After the season, Nevers returned to Stanford to become an assistant coach. Reluctantly, Haugsrud sold the franchise for $2,000 to a buyer who moved the team, first to Orange, New Jersey, then to Newark. In 1932, the franchise, now defunct, was purchased by George Preston Marshall and moved to Boston. The team that Ole Haugsrud bought for a buck in 1926 is now known as the Washington Redskins. In 1999, the Redskins were sold to Daniel Snyder, then a 34-year-old marketing executive, for about $800 million. (Ole Haugsrud did all right, though. When he sold the Eskimos, he secured from the NFL a promise that he would get the first crack at the next franchise granted in the state of Minnesota. In 1961, he became one of the original owners of the Minnesota Vikings.)

After playing one season with the Pottsville Maroons, Walt Kiesling was reunited with Ernie Nevers. In 1929 Nevers returned to the NFL to play for the Chicago Cardinals, and urged his new team to sign Big Kies. For the next three seasons Kiesling made the blocks that opened the holes through which Nevers ran all the way into the Hall of Fame. Nevers led the league in scoring in 1929 and finished second in 1931. On Thanksgiving Day 1929, he scored 40 points in a game against the Bears, a record that still stands. In each of Nevers' three seasons in Chicago, he was named an all-pro—as was Kiesling. Nevers retired for good after the 1931 season, but Kiesling stuck around. In 1934 he moved across town to play for the Bears, who went undefeated in the regular season but lost to the Giants in the championship game. In 1936 he went to Green Bay, where he was reunited with Johnny Blood and won his only NFL championship. The following season, Blood was hired to coach the Pittsburgh Pirates and invited Kiesling to join him as a player and assistant. Kiesling finally retired from playing after the 1938 season but continued as Blood's assistant. When Blood quit three games into the 1939 season, Big Kies suddenly found himself top dog: Art Rooney promoted him to head coach.

"I plan no major changes in playing personnel at the moment," Kiesling declared upon his hiring. It was a curious mission statement; the Pirates hadn't won a game in a year. They finished the season with a record of 1-9-1. In 1940, the team, now known as the Steelers, finished 2-7-2.

Before the 1941 season, Kiesling was replaced by Bert Bell, Rooney's new partner, in an ill-conceived experiment that lasted just two games. Bell was replaced by Duquesne University head coach Aldo "Buff" Donelli, who did not give up his college job. Donelli coached the Steelers in the morning and the Dukes in the afternoon. That experiment ended after five games, when Commissioner Elmer Layden gave Donelli an ultimatum: us or them. Donelli chose them. With nowhere else to turn, Rooney called on Kiesling once more. Somewhat reluctantly, he returned. Head coaching would prove to be a role in which Walt Kiesling was never entirely comfortable. He was a lineman and was unaccustomed to the spotlight.

ALTHOUGH IT WAS SUPPOSED TO BE KNOWN simply as the Eagles—sans city—the team that resulted from the merger of the Pittsburgh and Philadelphia franchises came to be dubbed, perhaps inevitably, the Steagles. Chet Smith of the *Pittsburgh Press* appears to have been the first sportswriter to use that moniker, when, in a column published June 23, 1943, four days after the merger was approved, he said of the new hybrid, "perhaps we should call them the Steagles." In Pittsburgh the name stuck almost immediately. In Philadelphia, however, the papers continued to call the team the Philadelphia Eagles, perhaps at the insistence of Harry

Thayer, acting on Lex Thompson's behalf to protect the Eagles' name. Elsewhere, sportswriters gleefully concocted all sorts of bizarre aliases for the team with two homes: Philpitts, Philburgs, Pitt-Phils, Steaglers. But as the season progressed, most papers outside Philadelphia, including the venerable *New York Times,* adopted "Steagles," which had a nicer ring to it than the alternatives. The National Football League, however, refused to employ the portmanteau, instead referring to the team variously as the Eagles, Eagles-Steelers, and Steelers-Eagles, before settling upon "Phil-Pitt," which is how the team is listed in the league's official record book. To this day the league takes great pains to point out that "Steagles" was a nickname, not a formal appellation. The league never even bothered to register "Steagles" as a trademark (something an enterprising fan did in 2004).

On Monday, July 21, 1943, on a field near the University of Pennsylvania campus in West Philadelphia, the Steagles held their first practice. Seventeen players showed up. The Steelers and the Eagles had more players than that under contract, but due to wartime travel restrictions, only those who lived in Philadelphia during the off-season were required to attend. The rest would not report until a more formal training camp opened in August. That meant that none of the Pittsburgh contingent was present. Even Steelers head coach Walt Kiesling was absent. He couldn't get away from his summer job back home in St. Paul, processing marriage-license applications for the Ramsey County Register of Deeds.

Among the players who showed up that first day were Johnny Butler and Jack Hinkle, two unheralded halfbacks who would contribute mightily to the Steagles. Bill Hewitt was there too, returning to the gridiron for the first time in more than three years. There was little camaraderie among the players, however; no "team chemistry," as coaches describe it today. Due to the league's high turnover rate, the players barely knew each other. Only two of the 17 had played in the NFL the previous season.

For the next three weeks, the team practiced three nights a week under the tutelage of Greasy Neale. The practices were held in the evening since most players worked in defense plants during the day. The practice field, known as River Field, sat wedged between railroad tracks and the Schuylkill River. Passing locomotives belched clouds of smoke that hung over the field. The players wore white T-shirts and white shorts, with black high-top football shoes and white socks. There were no lights: practice ended when dusk surrendered to the night. There was no locker room, either. Players had to change underneath a set of bleachers. Most took the trolley or walked to practice, since nonessential driving was banned at the time, and professional football practices were, as far as the government was concerned, not essential.

The Steagles were so hungry for players that anyone who showed up was likely to be given a tryout. That's how Tom Miller ended up on the team. Miller had just been discharged from the Navy and classified 4-F after suffering a serious head injury in a midair collision during flight training at Anacostia Naval Air Station outside Washington.

"I was flying trainers and another pilot came around the wrong way," Miller remembered. "He was supposed to come around the left and instead he went around to the right. And when we came in for the landing we were a couple hundred feet off the ground and we just collided in midair there. I was banged up in my head a little bit, but he got off worse. My propeller got in his cockpit. He got his leg very badly cut."

Still recuperating, Miller went up to Philadelphia to visit Jack Hinkle, a childhood friend. Hinkle himself had recently been discharged from the military for medical reasons (he had ulcers) and was trying out for the Steagles. At Hinkle's urging, Miller went to practice one day and began catching passes. Miller, who'd played football at tiny Hampden-Sydney College in Virginia, was a decent receiver, fast, with good hands. Bert Bell was watching from the sidelines. He pulled Miller aside and asked him if he'd like to play professional football.

"I said, 'I don't know. I never thought about it,'" Miller remembered. "So he said, 'Come on in.' So he signed me to a contract—just like that. It was kind of funny. I had to be careful because I couldn't work out for a couple weeks because of my [head] injury. I could run, just so long as I didn't have any contact."

Greasy Neale devoted the early practices to teaching his charges the intricacies of the T formation. Today the T is the basis of every offensive strategy in football, but in 1943 it was still so new that most players had to learn it from scratch. Chicago Bears head coach Ralph Jones practically invented the modern T formation in the early 1930s, when he put the quarterback directly behind the center.

END   TACKLE   GUARD   CENTER   GUARD   TACKLE   END

QUARTERBACK

HALFBACK   FULLBACK   HALFBACK

After taking the snap, the quarterback had a plethora of options. He could immediately hand the ball off to the fullback or one of the halfbacks. Or he could pass it. Or he could fake a handoff and then make a pass. Or he could fake a handoff to one back, then hand it to the other. Or he could fake it to two backs and then pass. Jones also added a man in motion, an offensive player who ran across the backfield parallel to the line of scrimmage before the snap. Opposing defenses never knew what to expect. They were bewildered and, quite often, beaten. The T formation emphasized speed, agility, execution, and a bit of trickery over brute force.

"*Football became a game of brains,*" wrote Bears owner George Halas, using italics for emphasis. "Instead of knocking men down, Jones tried to entice the defense into doing something helpful for us. Best of all, the public found our brand of football exciting."

At the time, most coaches still clung to the old single-wing formation, or its cousin, the double wing. In the wing formations, the center snapped the ball a few yards back to either a halfback or the fullback, who followed a wall of blockers plowing into the opposing line.

END   TACKLE   CENTER   GUARD   GUARD   TACKLE   END

QUARTERBACK

HALFBACK   HALFBACK

FULLBACK

Three yards and a cloud of dust, as the saying went. Passing was a last resort.

The T began to gain legitimacy after the Bears used it to crush the Redskins in the 1940 championship game, 73-0 (still the most lopsided score in NFL history). Greasy Neale, soon to be hired by Lex Thompson, was in the stands at Griffith Stadium that day, and like the rest of the football world, he was shocked by the result. Neale had never run the T formation in his long coaching career. He knew little about it. He was about to start a new job in a new league, and it seemed an unlikely time to radically overhaul his coaching philosophy. But after watching Chicago make mincemeat of Washington, he decided to give the T a whirl. "If that wouldn't convince you," he said, "you'd be a very stubborn man."

A few weeks after the game, Neale was having lunch with some old friends at a Manhattan restaurant. At the table was a man who worked for Fox Movietone News, which produced the newsreels that were shown in theaters before the main feature.

"I marvel at the way you fellows seem to catch the outstanding plays of every game in the few minutes you show on the screen," Neale said naively. "How are you able to do that?"

"Oh," the man answered, "we film the entire game and select the important plays from the complete footage."

Neale nearly choked on his whiskey. "Would you by any chance have the entire footage of that Bears-Redskins game?" he asked.

"I can let you have a print for $156."

"Sold," said Neale gleefully.

For the next three months, Neale spent up to five hours a day holed up in Lex Thompson's New York apartment studying the film. By the time he emerged, he had memorized every block, run, fake, and pass in the Bears' offensive arsenal. But Neale was not interested in merely replicating the Bears' T formation. He was determined to improve upon it. He added more running plays, incorporating the best aspects of the wing formations. In the fall of 1941, the Eagles joined the Bears as the only NFL teams using the T.

Some college coaches also embraced the T formation, notably Army's Red Blaik, Notre Dame's Frank Leahy, and Stanford's Clark Shaughnessy. But most coaches, college and pro, resisted it, often bitterly. They thought its use of deception was unsportsmanlike and its use of passing unmanly. In 1943, University of Minnesota head coach Bernie Bierman dismissed the T formation as a flash in the pan. He predicted, "I don't think the T will be any more widely used than the single wing, the short punt or any of the other old standard formations." How mistaken he was: The T would eventually come to dominate football, though it would take a while. The Steelers didn't abandon the single wing for the T until 1952, becoming the last NFL team to do so.

The Steagles' summer practices ended on August 6, though Bill Hewitt, the former all-pro end who'd been coaxed out of retirement by Bert Bell, organized occasional workouts thereafter.

"As peppy as a college freshman just starting a football career," wrote the *Philadelphia Inquirer*'s Art Morrow, "Hewitt's enthusiasm has proved so infectious that it has spread throughout the squad." Even persnickety Greasy Neale pronounced himself pleased with the results of the practices.

"On the whole," Neale told Morrow, "I think we had a very satisfactory preliminary practice. . . . It is still too early to predict any championships, or anything of that sort, but I am convinced we benefited greatly by this early work."

Neale's optimism was a tad premature. The Eagles and the Steelers hadn't even merged yet, at least not on the field. The real challenge would come later that month, when training camp officially opened across town, near the campus of St. Joseph's College. That's when the Pittsburghers would be added to the mix. That's also when Walt Kiesling would arrive, and Neale would have to begin sharing the head coaching duties.

ON AUGUST 25, 1943, just four days after Lewis Hershey announced that pre-Pearl Harbor fathers would be drafted beginning October 1, NFL Commissioner Elmer Layden decreed that team rosters for the upcoming season, which had been reduced from 33 to 25 players back in April, would now be increased to 28. Layden claimed the change was due to an "improved manpower situation," but its real purpose was to allow teams to stock up on players before the beginning of the Father Draft, which would undoubtedly decimate rosters. (Some owners had wanted to increase roster sizes even more, to 35 players, but Layden feared running afoul of the Office of Defense Transportation, which had ordered the NFL to keep travel to a minimum.)

The next day, August 26, the Steagles went a step further to guard against the Father Draft.

"We're going to insist that every man work at least 40 hours a week in an essential industry, along with playing football," said Al Ennis, the Eagles' publicity director. "We don't want anyone pointing a finger at our players and charging that they aren't contributing to the war effort, even though we think football has a definite place in the American way of life." Ennis said many players were already working in defense plants anyway, and the team would help place the rest. He also said employers had shown a willingness to be flexible in allowing the players to moonlight for the Steagles. The team would run a "swing shift" training camp, with two practices per day, one in the morning and one in the evening. Players could attend whichever session suited their schedules best. Furthermore, Steelers co-owner Bert Bell said, "Pittsburgh gridders-workers who can't get away from local jobs will be allowed to appear on Sundays only." That meant Steelers tackle Ted Doyle could keep his job building uranium-enrichment components at the Westinghouse factory and still play football—just as he'd proposed in his June letter to Bell. It would make for a punishing autumn.

"In 1943 I lived in Pittsburgh all during the season," Doyle recalled. "The team was in Philadelphia. I would take a train on, say, a Friday night or a Saturday night or whatever—the day before the game—and go into Philadelphia or wherever the game was to be and then I would get a little briefing before the game, any changes in plays and those things. Then we'd play the game. I'd take the train back home Sunday night. If it happened to come back through East Pittsburgh in the morning, I'd get off the train and go to work."

Bert Bell first came up with the idea of requiring players to do war work shortly after Pearl Harbor.

"Why couldn't our professional squads be employed in defense work, cut down on the weekly practice, play on Sundays and thus combine the two and do double duty for the good of all?" he'd asked rhetorically in early January of 1942. "It isn't going to be enough to play, pay taxes, buy Defense Bonds and continue as before."

Nothing came of it in 1942, but shortly after the Steelers and Eagles merged, Bell pitched the idea to his partner Art Rooney and Eagles owner Lex Thompson, both of whom enthusiastically endorsed it. (So did Eagles head coach Greasy Neale, who had worked full time in an airplane factory while coaching and playing for the Dayton Triangles during World War I.) Their motives were not purely patriotic. Section 5(e) of the Selective Service Act authorized the deferment of "those men whose employment in industry, agriculture, or other occupations . . . is found . . . to be necessary to the maintenance of the national health, safety, or interest." By August 1943 nearly 2.4 million men had been spared induction through occupational deferments. (They were classified 2-A, 2-B, or 2-C, depending on their occupation.) While they were compelled to work at least 40 (and sometimes 48) hours a week in an "essential" industry, these men were free, in most cases, to play football on Sunday afternoons.

The task of determining whose employment was "necessary" and which industries were "essential" fell to Paul Vories McNutt, a former Indiana governor and chairman of the War Manpower Commission. President Roosevelt created the commission in April 1942 to mobilize the civilian workforce. In essence, McNutt was in charge of making sure war plants had enough workers. In August 1943 he issued two lists of occupations and activities, one labeled "non-deferrable," the other "essential." Workers on the first list were subject to immediate induction. Workers on the second were automatically eligible for deferment. The goal was to drive men from low-priority jobs to high-priority jobs.

The lists were marvelously detailed. Among the non-deferrable jobs: sign painter, taxidermist, florist, barber, bartender, gardener, soda jerk, lavatory attendant, and the manufacture of pinball machines, academic caps and gowns, and ornamental shoe buckles. (The "status of idleness" was also considered a non-deferrable activity.) The "essential" list encompassed 149 activities, from aircraft-engine mechanic to x-ray equipment serviceman.

"The time has come," McNutt said, "when every worker must justify himself in terms of his contribution to the war program."

McNutt's goal was to keep men working in essential industries—thereby keeping them out of the Army. This put him in diametric opposition to Lewis Hershey, the head of Selective Service, and inevitably led to conflict between the two men. To make matters worse, McNutt was Hershey's boss, since Roosevelt had given the WMC authority over Selective Service. (One of Hershey's subordinates joked that Selective Service's insignia should be "a Hershey bar with McNutts in it.") Both McNutt and Hershey were Hoosiers, born and raised in Indiana, but their personalities were as different as Indianapolis and Amsterdam. Hershey was a blunt, no-nonsense military man. McNutt was a smooth-talking, silver-haired politician. Hershey believed McNutt's list of "essential" activities was too broad. After all, how critical were tanners to the war effort? He wrote McNutt, "I will not transmit any order from you for classification," and notified draft boards that the WMC chairman's lists were merely advisory and not binding, ironically citing the very autonomy that had undermined Hershey's efforts to draft fathers. A perturbed McNutt complained to Roosevelt, who reasserted the WMC's supremacy.

Occupations and industries that did not appear on either of McNutt's lists existed in a kind of bureaucratic no-man's-land. Men engaged in those activities—including bank and grocery store clerks, automobile repairmen, and tailors—were subject to induction when their draft numbers came up in the normal course of events. Among this group, too, were professional athletes. As far as Paul McNutt was concerned, they were neither nonessential nor critical.

"The usefulness of the sport is a separate question from the 'essentiality' of individuals who play it," McNutt explained cryptically. "Thus it may well be that it is desirable that Blankville have a ball team. But Blankville may lose certain members of that team to higher priority industries—even members that might be 'essential' to winning the pennant. The pennant is not 'essential.'" In other words, the only way for a professional athlete to secure an occupational deferment was to work a second job in an essential industry.

The Steagles were the only pro sports team to require its players to take war jobs. On the whole, the players did not object to the extra work. Most of them needed the money anyway. In the NFL, a salary of $200 a game was typical. At the Budd factory in North Philadelphia, experienced workers were commanding as much as $73 a week. Annualized, the factory job was more lucrative.

And the war plants were eager to hire the players. In 1943, demand for workers was so intense that unemployment fell to under two percent—still a record low. One third of the shipyards on the West Coast were behind schedule. Desperate plant managers began "scamping" workers—stealing them from other plants. In Buffalo, one factory sent telegrams to another factory's workers, offering them higher paying jobs immediately. One personnel manager complained that "the way to get one good man is to hire four because three will quit." Wartime employers were caught in a bind: as the number of soldiers increased, so did the number of workers required to feed, clothe, arm, and transport them, while the number of available workers simultaneously shrank. The United States produced a staggering amount of materiel during the war: 8,200 warships, 86,000 tanks, 300,000 planes, 15 million guns, 20 million helmets, 41 billion rounds of ammunition. It took an estimated 20 million workers to make it all—a force nearly twice the size of the military's. The war stimulated many changes in the American workplace, changes that were both momentous and contentious.

On June 25, 1941, President Roosevelt signed Executive Order 8802, which called for "the full and equitable participation of all workers in defense industries, without discrimination because of race, creed, color or national origin." Black leaders hailed the order as "the most significant move on the part of the Government since the Emancipation Proclamation." During the war, the number of African-Americans employed in the manufacturing sector rose by 600,000 to two million, and the percentage employed in war plants jumped from 2.5 percent to almost ten percent. The changes were not unanimously acclaimed. When the federal Committee on Fair Employment Practice directed Southern railroads to hire more black engineers and conductors, the popular syndicated columnist Raymond Clapper complained that only "mischief, disunity and further irritation of race relations" would result. The committee, Clapper wrote, was ignoring "the deep complex of human emotions bound up in the matter." In early June of 1943, some 25,000 white workers at an engine plant in Detroit walked off the job to protest the promotion of three black workers.

Equally contentious was the reaction to the influx of women in the workplace. About six million women worked in defense plants during the war. Many took jobs long reserved for men. They were welders, electricians, toolmakers, plumbers, mechanics, and, yes, riveters. They contributed mightily to the war effort and discovered a new world outside the home. As a female worker at the Puget Sound Navy Yard put it, "somehow the kitchen lacks the glamour of a bustling shipyard."

More than one-third of the female war workers were married and had children younger than 14, a statistic that was widely regarded as alarming. The fear, as with the Father Draft, was that children would be neglected. It was a fear that was not completely unfounded. Exposés in *Fortune* and the *Saturday Evening Post* depicted children locked alone in freezing houses and sleeping in automobiles while their mothers worked. In response, the government began funding day-care programs for the first time. The Swan Island Center at the Kasier shipyard in Portland, Oregon, was a model day-care center. It operated around the clock to accommodate mothers on every shift. The cost, including meals, was 75 cents per child per day ($1.25 for two children). By the end of the war, more than 3,000 publicly funded day-care centers were caring for more than 130,000 children across the country. The centers were also credited with dramatically increasing worker productivity.

The mere sight of women in coveralls was enough to trigger conniption fits in some. It appalled the popular advice columnist Dorothy Dix (real name Elizabeth Meriwether Gilmer; definitely not to be confused with the nineteenth-century social activist Dorothea Dix).

"The reason that women pass up the frills and furbelows of their sex for the hard-boiled shirts and tubular britches of men," Dix wrote in 1943, "is because they are so naturally lacking in femininity that they try to turn themselves into imitation men as a compensation for not being the real thing." In a *Philadelphia Evening Bulletin* story headlined "Will Slacks Produce a Crop of Old Maids? 'No,' Girls Say, 'We'll Get Our Men After War,'" an 18-year-old shipyard worker named Eleanor Penczak defended her "masculine" attire: "We're here to work—not to look glamorous. And anybody who thinks our main job in life should be to go around looking feminine just doesn't appreciate the needs of the day."

Women working in war plants were sometimes subjected to virulent sexual harassment. Catcalls were common.

"You'd think those fellows down there had never seen a girl," said a sympathetic male at the Boeing plant in Seattle. "Every time a skirt would whip by up there, you could hear the whistles above the riveting, and I'll bet the girls could feel the focus of every eye in the place."

Labor shortages allowed women to make inroads even in the resoundingly virile world of football. In the fall of 1943, Bell Township High School in rural western Pennsylvania, apparently unable to find a qualified and willing male, hired a 22-year-old gym teacher named Pauline Rugh to coach the football team. Rugh was a recent graduate of Penn State, and she returned to her alma mater for a quick tutorial.

"It is physically impossible to teach you all about football in three days," Penn State coach Bob Higgins lectured her, "but we'll get you started and then depend on you to ask questions as new problems arise." In newspaper stories Rugh was invariably described as "comely." Typical was what Red Smith, later a Pulitzer Prize-winning *New York Times* columnist, wrote in the *Philadelphia Record*: "As far as local records show, Miss Rugh is the first she-coach of a recognized team of males in the history of the sport. What's more, she is reliably described as a very tasty dish, a blonde with a couple of eyes like this, O O, and a throbbing contralto voice."

Rugh seemed uncomfortable with all the attention. She did her best to avoid the reporters and "picture men" who camped on her doorway. Yet her attempts to shun publicity only stirred more interest in her story. "This," noted the *Pittsburgh Post-Gazette*'s Havey Boyle, "probably, is a technique that works in other feminine adventures, too, marriage being one of the more notable."

Bell Township High School's wartime experiment, however noble, failed. The team lost all eight games it played and was outscored 219-13 in the process.

The Eagles and the Steelers hoped their own wartime experiment would end more happily.

Unfit for Military Service

A t 8:00 A.M. ON SUNDAY, SEPTEMBER 5, 1943, Al Wistert, fresh off the college all-star game and his draft physical, reported to the Steagles training camp, which had already been under way for ten days. He could hardly believe his eyes. To reduce travel, Commissioner Elmer Layden had ordered all NFL teams to hold their camps close to home. The Steagles chose for their training site a hard, rocky field at 54th Street and City Line Avenue, between a Standard Oil gas station and a dumping ground for construction debris. Bits of broken glass and tin cans were scattered everywhere. It was a far cry from the immaculate, manicured grounds Wistert had enjoyed at the University of Michigan. The locker room, a short walk away in a field house at St. Joseph's College, was cramped and musty. Three dim lightbulbs hung from the ceiling. The showers consisted of three nozzles sticking out of the wall, with a wooden grate for a drain.

"I was thinking that the NFL was the next step up," Wistert recalled. "I could hardly see my way around the locker room, and the lockers were so small that I couldn't get my shoes in. I had to stand them on end to get them in the locker. And I'm supposed to be stepping up in class? Holy smokes!"

Wistert changed into his pads and charged onto the field. The team was supposed to hold an intra-squad scrimmage that morning. But Greasy Neale and Walt Kiesling were nowhere to be found. The team's two coaches, who were both living at the Hotel Philadelphian, had not received their wakeup calls, so the players just lolled about in the late-summer heat. Wistert approached Bill Hewitt, who was sitting on a rock smoking a cigarette.

"You couldn't miss him," Wistert said. "He looked like a gorilla." Hewitt had played football at Michigan with Wistert's older brother Whitey, and Wistert was counting on Hewitt to show him around and introduce him to his new teammates. But when Wistert offered his hand to Hewitt, the Offside Kid just got up and walked away without saying a word. In fact, all the players ignored Wistert, because they were envious of his supposed $4,500 contract.

"It was kind of a nightmare for me," recalled Wistert. It took him several days to figure out what was going on—and many more to convince his teammates that he was actually making less than they assumed.

Around 11:00 a.m. Neale and Kiesling finally showed up, to be greeted by much ribbing from their players, who jokingly threatened to fine them. It was a rare moment of levity in a training camp that, in just ten days, had grown extremely tense. Wistert could tell immediately that the two coaches couldn't stand each other.

"Kiesling and Neale got along like a cat and a dog," Wistert said. "At times they would argue on the field in front of all the players. It was just crazy."

Greasy Neale and Walt Kiesling barely knew each other when their respective teams merged in June. In their long football careers, they had met on the gridiron just three times, as opposing coaches when the Eagles played the Steelers in 1941 and 1942. (The results: one Eagles win, one Steelers win, and one tie.)

They got off on the wrong foot when Kiesling arrived in Philadelphia on August 18 and discovered that Neale had unilaterally installed the T formation while Kiesling was still in St. Paul. Big Kies was an old fashioned single-winger. He despised the T, which he found unnecessarily complicated and a bit effete.

In appearance, disposition, and coaching style, Neale and Kiesling were complete opposites.

On game days Neale always wore a jacket and tie, with a trench coat and a fedora. He was curious, quick-witted, and un-afraid of change (as evidenced by his late conversion to the T formation). He was also gloriously profane.

"He was creative about it," said Al Wistert. "He never said 'son of a bitch' or 'goddamn.'" Among Neale's favorites: "You couldn't knock a sick whore off a shit pot!" "You stand around like a bear cub playin' with his prick!" "They killed Christ and let you live!"

Neale was hard on his players. He'd fine them for the most innocuous infractions. But he was always fair and never mean and whatever his faults his players would come to adore him.

"I loved Greasy," halfback Jack Hinkle said. "He was like a father to me. The only players who didn't get along with Greasy were the first-year men. Greasy loved the veterans. He'd say, 'Give me a team of veterans and I'll win the title.'"

Neale believed in making a football team "a family affair" and enjoyed golfing and playing bridge with his "boys" while his wife Genevieve socialized with their wives.

"It is to be doubted," wrote the *New York Times* sports columnist Arthur Daley, "that any coach ever inspired deeper loyalty and affection from his players than did Greasy."

"He's in my prayers every night," said Vic Sears, a soft-spoken tackle who played nine seasons for Neale in Philadelphia.

Disheveled and stern, Walt Kiesling was less revered. After his playing days, his weight ballooned to more than 300 pounds. His clothes always seemed a size too small, and in photographs his tie is invariably crooked. He was dull and unimaginative. He liked to begin every game with the same play, running his fullback into the middle of the line. When Steelers owner Art Rooney finally insisted he begin a game with a pass, Kiesling sabotaged the play by ordering one of his linemen to jump offside.

"If this pass play works," he told the team, "that Rooney will be down here every week giving us plays." He constantly berated his players, loudly and publicly.

"Seldom did Kiesling praise the athletes he coached," wrote the longtime Steelers broadcaster Joe Tucker. "He had been a standout by performance and expected and demanded that everyone who wore the Pittsburgh uniform play to his potential."

On one especially hot day at the Steagles training camp, Kiesling ordered all the water buckets removed from the field.

"You can't get into condition by swilling water down your throats," the corpulent coach roared, apparently ignorant of the benefits of hydration.

In Pittsburgh, his players disliked him so much they once threatened to go on strike. Art Rooney liked him, though, and that was all that mattered.

"He was a tremendous coach," Rooney said, "and not only that, a great guy." Indeed, Rooney seemed to have a better opinion of Kiesling's head coaching skills than even Kiesling himself.

"The thing about Walt was that he preferred to be an assistant," said Ole Haugsrud, who signed Kiesling to his first pro contract in Duluth. "He was available whenever the Steelers needed somebody, yet he would much rather be an assistant than the boss."

Neale and Kiesling were fundamentally different people.

"Greasy had a sense of humor, and he was a confident, upbeat guy," recalled Frank "Bucko" Kilroy, a rookie tackle on the Steagles in 1943. "I wouldn't say Kiesling didn't have a sense of humor, but he was more serious."

The two coaches clashed incessantly. Neale, having toiled in Ducky Pond's shadow at Yale for seven long seasons, was not prepared to share the spotlight with Kiesling. Inflexible and dogmatic, Kiesling was incapable of compromising with Neale.

"They hated each other," recalled Vic Sears matter-of-factly. But they did have one thing in common: Both men suffered from an overabundance of self-esteem.

"When Greasy Neale is the head coach there is nobody else gonna be the head coach," Al Wistert said. "He was a very domineering person."

"Kies was a great coach," Rooney said of Kiesling, "but everything with Kies was that nobody knew football *better* than Kies."

As training camp wore on, the animosity between the two coaches only deepened. Wistert said, "I can remember one day when Greasy Neale got all upset and he threw his cardboard armful of plays that he had down on the grass field and stomped off the field! He was quitting! It was pretty bad, I'll tell ya."

To ease tensions, Steelers co-owner Bert Bell suggested the two head coaches divide their duties rather than collaborating: Neale would coach the offense, Kiesling the defense. It was a division of labor rarely attempted in pro football; until then, coaching duties were usually divided between the line and the backfield, not offense and defense. It was a good arrangement, said Ray Graves, a lantern-jawed center who played for the Steagles.

"I think Kiesling was more of a defensive coach and felt like that was the most important part of the game and I think Greasy Neale was a little more wide open and wanted a little more offense. I think he stressed offense more."

On the whole, the players didn't get along much better than the coaches at the beginning of training camp. Only about ten of the 30-odd players who eventually reported to camp were under contract to Pittsburgh. In the minority and far from home, the Steelers naturally formed a clique and tended not to socialize with the Eagles.

"There was a little antagonism," recalled Eagles tackle Vic Sears. "There were tensions. It wasn't a good situation for anybody."

The merger also produced all sorts of unexpected job competition. Eberle "Elbie" Schultz had been a starting tackle for the Steelers the previous season. After the merger he was supplanted by the Eagles' Sears, who said Schultz was quite disgruntled: "He hated my guts. He absolutely hated me." (Schultz eventually won a starting job, but as a guard, not a tackle.)

Mostly, though, it was the Eagles who felt aggrieved. Steelers co-owners Art Rooney and Bert Bell and Eagles general manager Harry Thayer had informally agreed to a quota system, guaranteeing the outnumbered Steelers a minimum number of starting positions. This unavoidably fostered resentment. When Ray Graves, the Eagles' starting center in 1942, reported for training camp, he suddenly found himself demoted to second string behind Al Wukits, a Steelers rookie.

"There were some personal feelings there" was how Graves put it, diplomatically, many years later. (Graves eventually won back his starting position.) Al Wistert, an all-American at Michigan, was not pleased to learn he would be playing behind Steelers tackle Ted Doyle—and that Doyle would not even be practicing with the team during the week. (Doyle did manage to get enough time off from the Westinghouse plant to attend training camp for a week.)

"I didn't like that very much," Wistert said. "I had never been second string. So I was not very happy." Nor was Wistert happy when Greasy Neale moved him from left tackle to right tackle.

Nowhere was the job competition more intense than among the quarterbacks. Then as now, the quarterback was the key to the T formation. This was even more true then, when the quarterback, not the coach, called (or, at least, was supposed to call) all the plays. The Eagles had lost a splendid one when Tommy Thompson went into the Army after the 1942 season. (The Steelers had lost their best passer, "Bullet" Bill Dudley, to the Army Air Forces.) In the early practices, Greasy Neale had auditioned several candidates for the position, including Steve Sader, a Philadelphia sandlot player with no college experience, and Donald MacGregor, an ex-con from Des Moines who'd led his prison team to the Iowa Semipro Championship. Even the burly end Bill Hewitt, who knew the T formation from his days with the Bears, took a few snaps. But none of the candidates sufficiently impressed Neale, so he invited a dozen quarterbacks to training camp. One was a diminutive southpaw named Alexander Sherman.

If not for the war, Allie Sherman might never have played a down in the National Football League. Born and raised in Brooklyn, the son of Russian Jews, he was an exceptionally bright student who graduated from high school at 16. He enrolled at Brooklyn College, where, although he weighed just 120 pounds, he tried out for the football team. Head coach Lou Oshins was so desperate for personnel that he installed the underage, undersized egghead into the starting lineup—as a blocking back in the single wing. It was not a successful venture. The Kingsmen usually got pummeled.

The summer before Sherman's junior year, Oshins decided to switch to the T formation, and anointed Sherman his quarterback. Oshins bought a copy of *The Modern T Formation,* a how-to book by George Halas, Ralph Jones, and Clark Shaughnessy. Each week, he ripped a chapter out of the spiral-bound book and sent it to Sherman, who was waiting tables in the Catskills. Sherman studied each chapter religiously. He learned the T well, and the Kingsmen's fortunes improved.

By the time he graduated (*cum laude*) from Brooklyn College in 1943, Allie Sherman was five-ten, 160 pounds—and barely 20 years old. He looked more like a law student than a football player. But he knew the T formation inside out—which is exactly what Greasy Neale was looking for. The Eagles sent Sherman a letter inviting him to training camp.

Another quarterback competing for the starting job was Henry Leroy "Roy" Zimmerman, a tall, lanky Mormon whose background differed markedly from Allie Sherman's. Around 1930, when Zimmerman was 12 years old, his family's farm in Tonganoxie, Kansas, was obliterated by a dust storm. With their scanty belongings strapped to a Model A, the Zimmermans joined the great western migration depicted in John Steinbeck's celebrated novel, *The Grapes of Wrath,* eventually settling in southern California.

As a high school halfback, Zimmerman caught the eye of San Jose State College head coach Dudley DeGroot, who offered him a scholarship. On the gridiron Zimmerman could do it all: run, pass, punt, kick, and play defense. In 1939, his senior year at San Jose State, he led the Spartans to a perfect 13-0 record. The following spring Zimmerman signed a contract with the Washington Redskins.

Unfortunately, Zimmerman's experience in Washington was not entirely positive. As Sammy Baugh's backup he learned a lot but didn't get much playing time. In his first three seasons he completed just six passes (and threw five interceptions). He had trouble getting along with his teammates. According to Merrell Whittlesey, who covered the team for the *Washington Post,* "Zimmerman made few friends in his three years with the Redskins." He also had a nasty run-in with Redskins owner George Preston Marshall.

Zimmerman's dispute with Marshall concerned money. As the reigning NFL champions in the summer of 1943, the Redskins were scheduled to play a team of college all-stars in the annual game sponsored by the *Chicago Tribune.* (This was the same game in which Al Wistert played for the collegians.) Zimmerman felt he deserved extra compensation for the game, since it wasn't on the regular league schedule. Marshall felt otherwise. Eagles general manager Harry Thayer, who was in Chicago for the game, caught wind of the dispute and immediately broached trade talks with Marshall. Zimmerman barely played in the game on August 25, as the college team humiliated the Redskins, 27-7. The very next day, Marshall traded Zimmerman to Philadelphia for two second-stringers, center Ken Hayden and end Jack Smith. The trade, it was reported, was Marshall's "form of punishment" for Zimmerman's recalcitrance. It was one of the most lopsided trades in league history, made possible by Marshall's arrogance and Thayer's shrewdness.

Greasy Neale was elated. Although Zimmerman had never played the T formation, he was big (six-two, 200 pounds) and he had an exceptionally strong arm. In fact, Zimmerman had been a major league pitching prospect until a knee injury ended his baseball career. He was also a superb punter and kicker. Furthermore, he was extremely unlikely to be drafted by the military. Not only was he a father, he also helped run his family's farm in California and was a part-time police officer, both grounds for deferment.

Zimmerman couldn't have been happier either. He was relieved to be out of Baugh's shadow and from under George Preston Marshall's thumb. With the Steagles, he would finally get a chance to prove himself in the National Football League. There were opportunities for revenge, too: The Steagles would play the Redskins twice. Zimmerman had already circled the dates on his calendar.

But first he would have to win the starting job.

IF TRUTH IS THE FIRST CASUALTY of war, then the rigorous screening of inductees is the second. As a war drags on and the need for soldiers heightens, the physical standards for their induction decline proportionately. This was the case during World War II, during which, for example, the minimum uncorrected eyesight requirement was lowered from 20/100 in each eye to 20/200. Of the first one million men drafted, some 400,000—40 percent— were rejected as unfit for service, mainly due to bad teeth, poor hearing or eyesight, or illiteracy. By 1943, though, men lacking some fingers and toes were likely to be inducted, as were illiterate draftees and men with VD. Even amputees got a good hard look before being classified 4-F.

In the fall of 1943, as the Father Draft neared, opponents of it applied enormous pressure on the War Department and Selective Service to reduce the minimum physical requirements even further, so as to prevent the drafting of fathers.

But the military, perhaps to its credit, considered some standards immutable. The minimum height (60 inches) and weight (105 pounds) requirements went unchanged throughout the war. The maximums—78 inches and "overweight which is greatly out of proportion to the height"—went unchanged too, winning deferments for a handful of oversized football players, notably Green Bay's Buford "Baby" Ray, a six-six, 250-pound tackle. Likewise, some defects were deemed unacceptable no matter how dire the need for soldiers. A host of maladies large and small— ulcers, perforated eardrums, high blood pressure, diabetes, chronic sleepwalking—earned otherwise able-bodied men an automatic 4-F classification, rendering them unfit for military service but not for professional football.

Such was the case with Al Wistert. On September 20, 1943, 15 days after he reported to training camp, the former Michigan tackle got a telephone call from his draft board back in Chicago. Wistert wouldn't be going into the service after all. He was 4-F. The x-rays taken of his left wrist during his draft physical had revealed evidence of osteomyelitis, an infection of the bone that sets in when a bone is broken or operated on. Wistert had broken his wrist playing football at Michigan, and had had it operated on twice thereafter. When he learned that he was being rejected for military service because of osteomyelitis, Wistert had mixed feelings. On the one hand, he was "kinda worried." Osteomyelitis was especially dangerous before the widespread use of antibiotics (penicillin was still an experimental drug in 1943). The infection, if it spread, could result in amputation or even death. On the other hand, Wistert said, "I wanted to play pro football. And the sooner I could get to playing pro football the better I liked it. So I don't know that I was real disappointed when they turned me down."

Wistert was just one of many 4-Fs who would prove invaluable to the National Football League during the war, and to the Steagles in particular. Fifteen of the 24 players who appeared in five or more Steagles games were military rejects—a whopping 62 percent.

Eagles tackle Vic Sears had ulcers, and since ulcers can bleed, sometimes profusely, the military refused men who had them. Sears wanted to fight: He'd been in the ROTC program at Oregon State.

"All my buddies who were with me in college went to the South Pacific for four years," Sears recalled. "Never got a leave. But I didn't go. I always had trouble with stomach ulcers. One year I damn near bled to death the night before a game."

Eagles center Ray Graves was born deaf in his left ear. He volunteered for the Army Air Forces anyway and managed to hide his disability for six months, until he was assigned to a base near Atlanta, where he underwent a rigorous physical.

"When they found out," Graves said, "they said they didn't want any deaf pilots. So I was 4-F right there and they discharged me."

Steelers end Tony Bova was nearly blind in one eye and not much better off in the other. He wore contact lenses, which at the time were made of glass or hard plastic. Contacts were so uncommon, in fact, that Bova was never asked whether he was wearing them when he took the eye exam for his Navy physical. He passed the exam but, like Graves, his defect was eventually discovered, and Bova was discharged. He wore the contacts when he played football.

"He was a legitimate receiver," remembered Dan Rooney, Art's son, who was 11 in 1943 and occasionally traveled with the team. "I guess he could hear the ball coming."

And the list went on for the Steagles. End Larry Cabrelli had a bad knee. Fullback Charlie Gauer had a bad knee and ulcers. End Bill Hewitt and quarterback Allie Sherman had perforated eardrums. Halfback Jack Hinkle had ulcers. Fullback Ben Kish and end Tom Miller had disqualifying head injuries. Center Al Wukits had a hernia. Guard Eddie Michaels was so deaf he had to take his helmet off in the huddle to hear the play being called.

"Let's face it, there was a war going on," Vic Sears said. "If you were healthy you were in it." The preponderance of 4-Fs in the NFL was not entirely coincidental. Football players were probably more likely than the average draftee to have disqualifying conditions, due to the violent nature of their profession. Head injuries, perforated eardrums, crippled joints, and broken bones were occupational hazards that could also keep a man out of the Army.

There was a special bond among the Steagles' 4-Fs, who believed, in some small way, they were contributing to the war effort. If they couldn't fight the war, at least they could take people's minds off it.

"I think everybody realized that somewhere on the home front we oughta have some entertainment," said Ray Graves. "We all realized that we owed something to entertain in our capacity. It was a challenge that we all accepted in a real rough time."

The Steagles weren't all 4-Fs. Halfback Dean Steward was classified 1-A and was just waiting for his local draft board to call him. (It did, but not until the end of the football season.) Guard Rocco Canale was in the Army. Canale, a five-eleven, 240-pound lineman from Boston College whose brawny physique earned him the nickname "The Walking Billboard," was stationed at Mitchell Field near New York City. His commanding officer was sympathetic to his desire to play pro football and agreed to let Canale play for the Steagles on weekends.

A similar arrangement allowed Frank "Bucko" Kilroy to play for the Steagles. Kilroy, a 240-pound redhead, was a punishing lineman with a reputation for playing rough. In one scouting report he was described simply as "MEAN." *Life* magazine once identified him as the dirtiest player in the league. (Kilroy sued the magazine for libel and won an $11,600 judgment.) Kilroy was in the Merchant Marine, so he was automatically deferred from the draft.

"I was doing mostly convoy duty in the North Atlantic and the Mediterranean, first on cargo ships and then on transports," Kilroy said. "You name it, I was on it. Scary." But, like Rocco Canale, Kilroy had understanding superiors. "Believe it or not, they'd ship me back to New York for the football season. I used to come into Philadelphia on Friday night and practice two days with the team and then play on Sunday. But the moment the football season was over I was back on the North Atlantic on convoy duties."

During the war, numerous servicemen and mariners managed to get away from their duties long enough play a little pro football. In 1944, Hank Soar was stationed in Massachusetts and Pennsylvania, but still played for the Giants. Tim Mara, the owner of the team, "didn't like it because I wasn't there working out all week long," Soar recalled. "I said, 'I don't like it either but what the hell can I do about it? I'm in the Army!'"

Another player who was on active duty was the Green Bay Packers' Tony Canadeo. In 1944, he was in the Army, stationed at Fort Bliss in Texas. When his wife had a baby that fall, Canadeo was given a furlough to return home. When Packers head coach Curly Lambeau found out he was back in town, he convinced him to suit up again, and Canadeo played three games for Green Bay before returning to Fort Bliss.

Of course, most servicemen couldn't play pro football on the side. Once they were inducted, their careers were put on hold—sometimes permanently. A few days before the Steagles played the Bears in an exhibition game in Philadelphia on September 16, fullback Joe Hoague informed Walt Kiesling and Greasy Neale that he had passed his Navy physical. Hoague, who had played for the Steelers in 1942, was ordered to report to Fort Schuyler in New York on September 28. As a going-away present, Kiesling and Neale put Hoague in the starting lineup against the Bears, his last pro football game until 1946. During training camp, the Steagles also lost Frank Hrabetin to the Navy. At six-four, Hrabetin was just two inches shy of the maximum allowable height for induction. Hrabetin had played tackle for the Eagles in 1942. Like Hoague, he wouldn't return to pro ball until after the war. Hoague and Hrabetin were fortunate. By the time many players returned from the war, they were too old or too infirm to return to the game.

LATE ON THE NIGHT OF FRIDAY, SEPTEMBER 10, 1943, the Steagles gathered at 30th Street Station in Philadelphia and boarded the Pennsylvania Railroad's Pittsburgh Night Express. Most of the players rode coach, as sleeping car accommodations were reserved for high-priority passengers. The train chugged westward through the night, across the Amish farmland of Lancaster County, down into the Susquehanna Valley, and over the Alleghenies along Altoona's famous Horseshoe Curve, a serpentine stretch of track that connected the Midwest to the Eastern seaboard and was considered so vital to the war effort that it was under military control for the duration. The trip took more than seven hours. It was a long way to go for a home game. When the train finally pulled into Pittsburgh's Penn Station early Saturday morning, its brakes hissing, the players, tired and stiff after the long ride, wearily divided into two groups. The Philadelphians squeezed into cabs and headed to the Schenley Hotel. The Pittsburghers scattered for their homes. That night the two groups reunited at Forbes Field for the debut of the Phil-Pitt Steagles. They would play the vaunted Green Bay Packers. It was just a preseason exhibition game, so it wouldn't count in the standings, but it would go a long way toward determining whether this makeshift squad was any good.

Wartime Pittsburgh was a dark place. The steel, iron, and aluminum mills were running around the clock. Their furnaces were fired by bituminous coal, and their smokestacks filled the air with a thick smog that all but erased the sun. A pall hung over the city, quite literally. Sometimes it got so bad that the streetlights stayed on all day. A fine black dust blanketed the city, whispering through keyholes and transoms. It was, quite simply, pollution, but the locals had another name for it: black sugar. To them it was manna, a reassuring sign of economic recovery and a reminder that the mills were humming again after a long depression. They gladly and gratefully swept it from their porches in the morning.

In the darkness and deprivation, the city took a special delight in football. Then, as now, Pittsburgh was a football town. The city was the home of the country's first professional team (the Allegheny Athletic Association in 1892), three powerful collegiate programs (Pitt, Duquesne, and Carnegie Tech), dozens of legendary high school teams, and, of course, the Steelers.

Pittsburghers weren't sure what to make of the Steagles, though. They felt like they'd gotten the short end of the stick in the merger. Of the 33 players on the Steagles roster for the Green Bay game, just five had played for Pittsburgh in 1942. Steelers fans were also miffed that only three "home" games would be played in Pittsburgh—and one of those was the exhibition against Green Bay. It didn't help matters that the team wore the Eagles' colors of green and white instead of the Steelers' black and gold.

To reassure Pittsburgh fans that the Steagles were, indeed, their team, Al Ennis, the Eagles' publicity director, published "A Message To The Loyal Pittsburgh Fans From The Philadelphia Eagles" in the program for the Packers game.

"The object of the merger," he wrote, "was to provide the loyal fans of both cities with a team worthy of their support. . . . We don't say we will win the championship, but you can depend upon this—we'll be in there fighting for it every minute of every game." The program also included a skit poking fun at the team's unofficial name:

J.Q. Fan: "Jeeves, bring me my top hat, cow bell and cane. I'm off to Forbes Field to follow the Steagles!"

Jeeves: "The what, mawster? Are you sure you are feeling well, sir?"

J.Q.: "Certainly I'm all right, I feel great!"

Jeeves: "Well sir, I was only wondering why you were going out to chase some silly old dawgs on a nice night like this, and in Forbes Field, of all places, if you don't mind me saying so."

J.Q.: "I do mind you saying so. And I didn't say beagles, Jeeves, you blockhead. I said 'Steagles'—spelled S-T-E-A-G-L-E-S."

If Steelers fans found it hard to embrace a team comprising mostly Philadelphia Eagles, many Eagles found it just as hard to represent Pittsburgh on the field.

"The Eagles, we all felt like it was our team," remembered Ray Graves. "It was a wartime creation that we had to live with. The Eagles did feel like the Eagles should have been first [in the name]. It should have been Eagles-Steagles."

Tackle Al Wistert concurred: "I never had any feeling that we were a Pittsburgh team. . . . Frankly, we didn't think about Pittsburgh being one of our hometown locations." Ted Doyle, a Steeler, respectfully disagreed. He said it definitely felt like the Steagles represented Pittsburgh. Vic Sears, an Eagle, subscribed to neither point of view.

"We were Steagles," Sears said. "We weren't Eagles. We weren't Steelers. We were Steagles."

In any event, Pittsburgh was at least willing to give the Steagles a chance. An impressive crowd of 18,369 turned out to see the quasi-home team take on the Packers at Forbes Field.

Opened in 1909, the ballpark was named for John Forbes, the British general who captured Fort Duquesne from the French in 1758. Built on a pie-shaped parcel in the Oakland neighborhood two miles east of downtown, the ballpark's grandstands wrapped around the baseball infield in a narrow V shape, like a giant pair of tweezers, which made it a good venue for football, since the fans were relatively close to the action along both sidelines. One end zone was in the trough of the V, where home plate was for the park's primary tenants, the Pirates. The other was in right-centerfield, at the open end of the V. The turf was as hard as a sidewalk (or a pavement, as Philadelphians call it), supposedly to benefit the groundball-hitting Pirates. It was also the dirtiest field in the NFL, covered as it was by a thin layer of black sugar. After playing there "it took you two days to get the soot out from under your fingernails," remembered Steagles tackle Bucko Kilroy.

Green Bay was a formidable opponent. The Packers had finished 8-2-1 in 1942, finishing second to the undefeated Bears in the Western Division. Veteran receiver Don Hutson, who doubled as the team's kicker, held so many records for receptions and scoring that his nickname was "Mr. Most." The Packers' best passer, Cecil Isbell, had retired, but head coach Curly Lambeau found two able replacements in Tony Canadeo (known as "The Gray Ghost of Gonzaga" for his prematurely gray hair and his alma mater) and Irv Comp, a rookie from tiny Benedictine College in Atchison, Kansas.

Lambeau himself was returning for his 25th season at the helm of the Packers. He'd organized the team in 1919, when he was just 21, securing the sponsorship of the Indian Packing Company. Two years later Green Bay joined the nascent National Football League, winning five championships between 1929 and 1939.

Although he'd been practicing with the Steagles barely two weeks, Roy Zimmerman was tabbed by Greasy Neale to start the game at quarterback. Neale mainly wanted to see how well the veteran passer was learning the T formation. Allie Sherman, the 20-year-old rookie from Brooklyn College, still hoped to win the job by the time the regular season began.

The Packers won the coin toss and elected to receive. At 8:30 p.m., Zimmerman kicked off for the Steagles. But instead of booting the ball far downfield, he tried an onside kick. The Packers were caught napping. The Steagles recovered the ball on the Green Bay 38. Three plays later, halfback Jack Hinkle took a handoff from Zimmerman and carried the ball into the end zone from seven yards out as the crowd roared in appreciation. Maybe this was a team worth rooting for after all. Less than a minute into the game it was 7-0 Steagles. But the Packers, who had never lost to either the Steelers or the Eagles, quickly retaliated, tying the score on a 55-yard touchdown pass. After a Zimmerman field goal, Green Bay scored another touchdown, and at halftime the score was Packers 14, Steagles 10.

It was an unseasonably chilly evening, and many fans, still accustomed to Pittsburgh's stifling summer heat, had come to the game in short sleeves. As the game wore on, and the mercury dipped into the 50s, some resourceful spectators kept warm by burning newspapers at their feet, an egregious violation of municipal codes and common sense. By the intermission small fires dotted the grandstands, casting the ballpark in an orange glow.

In the third quarter the Packers scored another touchdown, on a 55-yard pass from Canadeo to Hutson. By now the Steagles' "train legs" were showing. They looked tired and slow. Green Bay, on the other hand, was well rested. To minimize travel, the team had arrived in Pittsburgh the previous Monday, on its way home from an exhibition game in Baltimore. While the Steagles spent the week toiling in shipyards and factories, the Packers took up residence at the only hostelry that could accommodate them for so many days: the Northside YMCA. ("Hotel reservations were hard to get," Canadeo recalled of the war years, "but we just put a lot of people in a couple of rooms.") The Packers had been practicing all week at a playground on Monument Hill, romping through drills "like college boys," according to the *Pittsburgh Post-Gazette*. Rarely in NFL history has the visiting team arrived four days before the home team.

In the final quarter, Green Bay added a touchdown on a returned fumble, making the final score 28-10. The disappointed fans stomped out their fires and filed for the exits. The next day the Steagles rode the train back east to Philadelphia, completing the 600-mile round trip for a home game. Monday morning they were back at work.

Despite the loss, Greasy Neale and Walt Kiesling saw some promising signs in the Green Bay game. The Steagles had more first downs than the Packers (17-11) and more total yards (484-399). On offense the linemen were stellar, opening gaping holes for the ball carriers in their wake. Jack Hinkle alone rushed for more than 200 yards. The Steagles "did everything but win," Art Morrow wrote in the *Inquirer* the next day.

But not all the reviews were so positive. Roy Zimmerman passed for just 29 yards, and the Steagles fumbled the ball three times, a malady that would plague them all season. Most disappointing of all, however, was the play of former all-pro end Bill Hewitt, the highest-paid Steagle. At 34, Hewitt was a shadow of his former self. He missed several tackles, and the explosive quickness that had earned him the nickname The Offside Kid was gone.

"Bill was out of condition and I felt so sorry for him," recalled tackle Vic Sears. "It was terrible. It was not Bill's fault. It was people comin' in and thinkin' he can skip five, ten years and still play. You can't. It was sad."

Hewitt had actually been retired less than four years; it only seemed like he'd been away much longer than that. In the interim he'd held physically undemanding jobs at an advertising agency and a trucking company. Steagles tackle Al Wistert remembered how Hewitt always reeked of liniment.

"He spread something like Absorbine Jr. all over his body because it was aching so bad. And in order to get ready for practice or a game he'd cover himself with liniment."

Hewitt was also having a hard time playing with a helmet on. Returning to the sidelines, he would often throw it off, in frustration and contempt. Said Steagles end Tom Miller, "He'd take that helmet off and he'd throw it into the sidelines and Greasy would pick it up and tell him, 'Put this on! You gotta wear it!' He hated that helmet."

On the whole, though, Greasy Neale pronounced himself pleased with the Steagles' showing against the Packers.

"The mistakes we made were all honest ones," he said after the game. "I really cannot blame the players for them. I think they learned a lot from this one."

The Steagles would get another crack at the Packers in the regular season, and the stakes would be much higher.

Neale and Kiesling didn't have much time to prepare for the Steagles' second and final preseason game, which was the following Thursday night in Philadelphia against the fearsome Chicago Bears. To win, the Steagles would have to play much better than they had against Green Bay. Still, Neale was confident: "Any team that can outgain the Packers by nearly 100 yards must be regarded as a threat. I would not go so far as to predict a victory over the Bears, but I certainly feel that the Eagles"—Neale couldn't bring himself to call his team anything else—"have a chance."

PHILADELPHIA, LIKE PITTSBURGH, was a wartime boomtown, and the city's factories were specially retooled for the times. Instead of steam engines, the Baldwin Locomotive Works turned out light tanks. Instead of railroad cars, the Budd Company made airplane parts and ammunition. Four shipyards along the Delaware River churned out vessels for the Navy and the Merchant Marine. More than 500 companies in and around Philadelphia held defense contracts totaling more than $1 billion. By 1944, one of every four workers in the city was directly employed in war production.

Probably even a greater proportion had, at one time or another, visited Shibe Park.

Opened in 1909 (the same year as Forbes Field) and named for one of the owners of the Philadelphia Athletics, the ballpark was the city's primary civic venue, a kind of secular cathedral. Built in the Beaux Arts style, with a magnificent domed tower rising five stories over the main entrance at 21st and Lehigh, it hosted political rallies and religious revivals as well as sporting events. Shibe Park was a gathering place for bluebloods and the new blood alike.

Despite hot, sticky weather and a persistent rain, more than 30,000 fans packed the ballpark on the night of Thursday, September 16, to watch the Steagles make their Philadelphia debut in an exhibition game against the Bears. The unusually high turnout was the result of the visiting team's renown, as well as a relentless promotional campaign on the part of the *Philadelphia Inquirer*, which sponsored the game as a fund-raiser for its charitable arm. As pro football games went, it was a glittery affair. *Inquirer* publisher Walter Annenberg was there, of course, as were Philadelphia Mayor Bernard Samuel and most of the City Council. Washington Redskins owner George Preston Marshall also attended, as did New York Giants owner Tim Mara. Eagles owner Lex Thompson was present too. Thompson had just completed officer training school and was now a second lieutenant in the Army. According to the papers, he was able to get a "brief leave" to watch the game.

Chicago opened the scoring with a 68-yard touchdown pass in the first quarter, but the Steagles answered in the second frame. Halfback Johnny Butler, a rookie from the University of Tennessee, returned an interception deep in Steagles territory to the Phil-Pitt 32. From there, Butler and fellow halfback Jack Hinkle took turns carrying the ball downfield. On fourth-and-goal from the Bears three-yard line, Butler plowed into the end zone behind left tackle Vic Sears. A few minutes later the half ended. Much to the surprise and delight of the home crowd, the score was 7-7.

During the interval there was a war bond drive. President Roosevelt had launched the third major bond drive of the war just eight days earlier, during one of his famous fireside chats. The war was largely financed through the sale of such bonds, which came in denominations ranging from $10 to $1,000. They were sold at 75 percent of their face value and could be redeemed for their full value, plus 2.9 percent interest, in ten years. Eight out of every 13 Americans—more than 60 percent of the population, including children—chipped in and bought $185 billion in bonds during the war. (By removing that money from the economy, the sale of war bonds also helped stem inflation.)

Bond drives were a staple of life on the home front. Movie stars and sports heroes were dispatched to the smallest villages and hamlets to drum up sales. One of the most memorable drives took place in September 1942, when more than 300 movie stars, including Bette Davis, Rita Hayworth, and Dorothy Lamour, fanned out across the country, attending rallies in hundreds of towns and selling more than $800 million in bonds.

One of the most unusual bond drives took place at the Polo Grounds in New York on June 26, 1944, when the Yankees, Dodgers, and Giants played a three-way baseball game. The Dodgers and Yankees played the first, fourth, and seventh innings, the Dodgers and Giants played the second, fifth, and eighth, and the Yankees and Giants played the third, sixth, and ninth. The price of admission was a war bond. The exhibition raised more than $56 million. The final score was Dodgers 5, Yankees 1, Giants 0.

Pro football did its part, too. The NFL sponsored rallies generating more than $4 million in sales in 1942, and the halftime rally at the Steagles-Bears game on September 16, 1943, raised an additional $364,150.

After the bond drive wrapped up, the teams returned to the soggy field. Early in the third quarter the Steagles missed a chance to take the lead when Zimmerman shanked a 30-yard field goal attempt. Then the Bears pounced. On the ensuing drive, quarterback Sid Luckman lobbed a 17-yard touchdown pass to Harry

Clark to give Chicago a 14-7 lead. Luckman threw another touchdown pass in the fourth quarter. The final score was Bears 20, Steagles 7.

When the game ended, the Steagles collapsed, exhausted, on the field. They'd played two games in two cities in five days, against two of the league's best teams, working in war plants all the while. This was the downside of the war-work requirement. Some of the players were working eight hours a day, six days a week, in addition to playing professional football. It was a grueling, exhausting schedule. Steelers co-owner Bert Bell recognized it.

"If all the clubs were playing under the same conditions," Bell said, "we'd have a better chance. But we are the only club with 100 percent of our personnel in war work. As a result, some of our inexperienced players may look greener and make more mistakes than they would if they had plenty of time to practice. . . . The players are tired, too, and the coaches can't bear down on them as they would otherwise."

Once again the Steagles' linemen and running backs played well but the passing game was awful. Roy Zimmerman completed just one pass, though it wasn't entirely his fault: Steagles receivers dropped several passes, at least two of which might have resulted in touchdowns. By all accounts the Steagles were a mediocre football team. Despite getting off to a good start in both preseason games, they ended up losing them by a combined score of 48-17. Even the most optimistic fans in Philadelphia and Pittsburgh had low expectations for the upcoming season.

8

Birds of Steel

WHEN THE STEAGLES' TRAINING CAMP ENDED in late September, so scarce were competent players that Kiesling and Neale decided to keep only 25 men on the roster, even though the limit had been raised to 28. What was the point in having three extra players if they weren't any good? Just seven of the 25 players were under contract to the Steelers. Just two (tackle Al Wistert and center Al Wukits) had been selected in the NFL draft the previous April. (A third, guard Rocco Canale, would join the team after the season started.) Steelers co-owner Bert Bell begged the military to assign Pittsburgh's No. 1 pick, University of Minnesota halfback Bill Daley, to a Navy training program at Penn or Villanova, but to no avail. Daley ended up at the University of Michigan, where he played football for Fritz Crisler and was named an all-American. (The NCAA routinely allowed servicemen stationed on campuses to play college football.)

With the twice-daily training sessions over, the Steagles practiced Tuesday through Saturday nights for the rest of the season, usually for three hours beginning at six o'clock. The practices were held in Philadelphia at either Shibe Park or Parkside Field, a small ballpark near Fairmount Park that was the home of the Philadelphia Stars Negro League baseball team. The players arrived by trolley, bus, or subway, weary from their war jobs. Many worked at the shipyards that lined the Delaware River.

"I worked in a shipyard over in Camden," recalled Al Wistert. "I was a company inspector—I didn't know what I was inspecting, but I was supposed to be checking to make sure that a ship when it was ready to be launched had all of the equipment in it that it was supposed to have."

Several other players worked at Bendix Aviation, which manufactured airplane parts, while others worked at smaller factories. During the war, the standard workweek was as long as 48 hours: eight hours a day, Monday through Saturday. The players spent at least another 15 hours a week on football.

"You worked all day, and you practiced all night, and by the end of the day you were tired as hell," remembered Jack Hinkle, who worked at Bendix.

The Steagles would open the regular season at Shibe Park on October 2, against the Dodgers. On the eve of the game, Greasy Neale was cautiously optimistic about the forthcoming campaign. He told sportswriter Grantland Rice, "With the pick of both teams, meaning the Eagles and Steelers, we'll have a chance." Neutral prognosticators had mixed expectations. *Philadelphia Record* columnist Red Smith predicted "wartime sports' strangest hybrids" would be "a pretty good ball club." But the United Press was less positive, picking the Steagles to finish third in the four-team Eastern Division, behind the Redskins and the Giants, and ahead of only the dreadful Dodgers.

The Steagles did have a great line and good ball carriers. But their passing game was anemic and they had butterfingered receivers, who dropped passes and fumbled the ball with alarming regularity. If past seasons were any indicator, the team would stink. Since joining the league in 1933, the Eagles had never had a winning season and the Steelers had had just one, in 1942, and that squad had been dismantled by the war. As Red Smith put the question, "Take two teams which in most years past have rated a sub-zero figure on the form charts, add them together, and does the sum equal a passing grade?" In the jumbled world of wartime sports, the answer was anybody's guess.

THE RESCHEDULED FATHER DRAFT was supposed to begin on October 1. But just as they had in July, local draft boards refused to cooperate, despite Selective Service director Lewis Hershey's pleas. Hershey had written beseechingly to every member of every draft board:

> *Your work as a local board member has been most outstanding in our war effort, and I know that you will maintain that record by continuing to defer the necessary men and fill the calls of the armed forces. That being so, we have but one alternative: To complete our calls by taking fathers as they may be needed after all other available men have been exhausted. . . . We are challenged as never before. Let us be guided by the greatest good in determining our course. The decisions will be difficult and many times unpleasant, but we can bear the burden, knowing that these decisions will bring the end we are all seeking—the early and complete surrender of our enemies.*

But many boards still refused to call fathers, even if it meant failing to meet their monthly induction quotas.

"We found that we would have to call four fathers to fill our quota," said a board official in Philadelphia. "We decided just to be short four men and call none at all."

The *Philadelphia Record* said, "Several board chairmen expressed indignation at Selective Service headquarters' plans to proceed with drafting fathers. They said that instead they will take as many from war plants as they can before inducting a single father. 'And we will disregard the War Manpower Commission's manning table plans to do it,' they added."

Military planners were aghast. During the three months ending September 30, the Army had requested 585,000 men but only 447,000 were inducted, a 24-percent shortfall. Generals in the field were complaining about the shortage. The war, the planners said, could not be won without fathers. The Army's deputy chief of staff, Lt. Gen. Joseph McNarney, warned gravely of the consequences of "ignoring the considered judgment of our military leaders, arrived at after careful and prolonged study."

Once again, Congress got involved. Texas Representative Paul Kilday and Montana Senator Burton Wheeler reintroduced their bills to delay the induction of fathers. Kilday's called for a permanent delay, Wheeler's a temporary one.

Public opposition to the Father Draft was still strong. If anything, opponents had more ammunition than they'd had back in July. Italy had surrendered since then. Wasn't the end of the war, in Europe at least, imminent? And couldn't the Axis Powers be bombed into submission anyway? It seemed to opponents of the Father Draft that the military simply wanted too many men. To them the drafting of fathers also represented the superfluous and dangerous crossing of a threshold—into "total war."

Hershey, who was well liked by many in Congress (and was a nimble politician himself), worked behind the scenes to help draft legislation that would simultaneously kick-start the Father Draft and pacify its opponents. In December, both houses passed a bill requiring local draft boards to call pre-Pearl fathers, but only after all eligible nonfathers in their jurisdiction had been called. It was called the "Take Fathers Last" bill, but in actuality it merely codified what had been Hershey's position all along: fathers would be drafted last, but fathers would be drafted.

The bill also included a provision separating Selective Service from the War Manpower Commission, thereby removing Lewis Hershey from the supervision of Paul McNutt. Other than ending what Hershey called his "bondage time," the bill didn't change a thing.

"What kind of legislation is that?" a bemused President Roosevelt asked. "The answer, of course," wrote historian George Q. Flynn, "was political legislation." Although he considered the bill rather silly, Roosevelt signed it. The Father Draft would finally begin on December 10, 1943. By then, of course, the NFL season would nearly be over. The long and largely pointless debate had saved pro football for 1943.

To the Steagles, however, the issue was irrelevant. They weren't just playing football. They were also doing essential war work.

WHEN THE BROOKLYN DODGERS finally got around to hiring Pete Cawthon to be their head football coach in June 1943, there actually were no Brooklyn Dodgers: the team had no players under contract. Off to a late start, with the cream of the sparse crop of available talent already harvested by other teams, Cawthon resorted to desperate measures. Like many wartime employers, he took out half-page advertisements in major newspapers, seeking employees—the last and perhaps only "help wanted" ads ever placed by an NFL team looking for players.

Lew Jones nearly spit out his coffee when he saw one of the ads in a Dallas paper one morning in July. Jones had played for Cawthon at Texas Tech and was still fiercely loyal to his old coach. Jones, who was 31 and hadn't played football for nearly ten years, telephoned Cawthon immediately.

"I'm out of shape," he said. "And I'm thirty pounds over-weight. But if you want me, I'll take the weight off and come to Brooklyn to help out."

Cawthon let out a whoop of joy. "Do I *want* you! Man, those are the sweetest words I've heard in years. If I have you, I'll have one good guard I can depend on. Get that blubber off and get up here the first minute you can."

Jones quickly recruited several other former Red Raiders to join him in Brooklyn: G.L. "Country" Webb, Bill Davis, Floy "Pete" Owens. The Dodgers training camp turned into a veritable Texas Tech reunion.

It's surprising that Cawthon managed to cobble together a team at all. Less surprising is the fact that it wasn't a very good one. The Texas Tech bunch was old and flabby and, apart from a handful of veterans (Pug Manders, Bruiser Kinard, Dean

McAdams), the rest of the team consisted of untested and untalented rookies.

"We simply do not have enough experienced players," Cawthon moaned. It didn't help matters that on the first day of camp McAdams tripped over his helmet and tore a muscle in his left shoulder.

When the Dodgers came to Philadelphia to play the Steagles, the two teams already had a feud going. Back in July, Brooklyn general manager Dennis Shea had called the Steagles a "town team" for requiring its players to work war jobs.

"We're not going to operate with any part-time players who work at other jobs during the week," Shea sniped. "It labels us as Humpty Dumpty outfits. We're still going to charge big league prices so we ought to have big league teams." For good measure, Shea added that "there was no good reason for the Philadelphia-Pittsburgh combine" in the first place.

Shea's words were the 1943 equivalent of billboard material. They grated on the Steagles, who were busting their butts five or six days a week in defense factories and five nights a week on the practice field. They certainly didn't consider themselves "part-time players," and they were determined to show the Dodgers just what a "town team" could do.

The weather was perfect, but on the night of Saturday, October 2, barely 11,000 fans came to Shibe Park in Philadelphia to watch the Steagles take flight for the first time in a regular season contest. The game had not been as heavily promoted as the *Inquirer*-sponsored exhibition game against the Bears, but the main reason for the low turnout was competition. Earlier that afternoon, 30,000 fans had packed Franklin Field to watch Penn rout Yale, 41-7. (Penn led the nation in college football attendance in 1943.) Then there were the baseball A's, who had played a doubleheader against the Indians earlier in the day at Shibe Park, losing their 103rd and 104th games of the season. With all that going on, it's not surprising that so few Philadelphians were willing to shell out $3.50 for a reserved seat to watch a team that was only half theirs. The Steagles' opponent was a factor, too: The Dodgers, who had been shut out by Detroit 27-0 a week earlier, were not exactly a big draw.

Roy Zimmerman was still the Steagles starting quarterback. He had not thrown the ball particularly well during training camp—in the two exhibition games he completed just five passes for 35 yards—but Greasy Neale thought Zimmerman had taken to the T formation "like a cat takes to milk." Zimmerman executed the complicated running plays like a magician, faking handoffs with a legerdemain that befuddled opposing defenses. Besides, with the way the front line was blocking and the backs were running—the Steagles had racked up more than 500 rushing yards in the two exhibition games—it was clear that passing was not to be the team's primary offensive weapon.

Understandably, Allie Sherman was disappointed by Neale's decision. But Sherman, who aspired to be a head coach one day, took advantage of his time on the sidelines by becoming Neale's de facto assistant. Sherman shadowed Neale constantly, studying his every move. Neale encouraged his young protégé. He recognized that Sherman was "a serious student of the game" and that he "had real possibilities as a coach."

At 8:45 p.m., Zimmerman kicked off and the Birds of Steel took wing.

About four minutes into the game, the Steagles had the ball on their own 20-yard line. Rookie halfback Johnny Butler took a handoff from Zimmerman, sliced through a yawning hole in the line, and ran 69 yards to the Brooklyn 11.

Butler had been drafted by the Steelers in 1941 but spurned the team to take a job with Western Union in Charleston, South Carolina. He was convinced to join the Steagles by Eagles center Ray Graves, who had been Butler's roommate at the University of Tennessee. Butler had explosive speed; he could shoot through holes in the blink of an eye. He had so impressed Neale in training camp that he earned a starting position at left halfback. Only problem was, he was due to report for his Army physical in six days.

Butler's run set up a 22-yard field goal by Zimmerman. Later in the first quarter Zimmerman recovered a Dodgers fumble on the Brooklyn 17. Butler carried the ball into the end zone from the ten, dragging a Brooklyn tackler with him the last two yards. Zimmerman kicked the extra point to give the Steagles a 10-0 lead. Early in the second quarter, Zimmerman completed a nice 40-yard pass to myopic end Tony Bova. Three plays later, pre-Pearl father Ernie Steele bulled his way into the end zone from the Brooklyn ten, culminating a lovely 78-yard drive. The score was 17-0 and the sparse crowd was roaring itself hoarse.

The rest of the game was scoreless, but the Steagles dominated until the final gun. Especially magnificent was the performance of the three Eagles and two Steelers who made up the front line: left tackle Vic Sears, left guard Elbie Schultz, center Ray Graves, right guard Eddie Michaels, and right tackle Ted Doyle. (Equally impressive were their respective substitutes: Bucko Kilroy, Gordon Paschka, Al Wukits, Ed Conti, and Al Wistert.) The Steagles' linemen simply manhandled their Brooklyn counterparts. On offense they opened holes that the running backs sailed through for more than 200 total rushing yards. On defense they were even more spectacular. They completely shut down the Dodgers' running game, continually tackling Brooklyn ball carriers before they even reached the line of scrimmage. In fact, it was one of the most impressive defensive performances in NFL history. The Dodgers were held to -33 (yes, minus 33) yards rushing—still the third lowest total ever recorded. The Steagles also intercepted three Brooklyn passes and allowed the Dodgers to get inside the Phil-Pitt 40-yard line only twice. Not bad for a Humpty Dumpty outfit.

It wasn't a flawless performance. Zimmerman, who'd injured his groin running into an unyielding turnstile at Parkside Field the night before, played in great pain and completed just three of 12 passes, and the Steagles fumbled four times. But the team's overall performance was astounding, even considering the competition. Louis Effrat of the *New York Times* said the Steagles were "superb" against the Dodgers, operating with "smoothness, speed and general efficiency." New York Giants head coach Steve Owen, whose team the Steagles would play next, watched the game from the press box at Shibe Park. He left Philadelphia "deeply impressed."

The Steagles were less impressive a week later against the Giants. They had two punts blocked and three passes intercepted. They fumbled ten times, setting an NFL record that still stands.

And they still won.

SHIBE PARK, THE HOME OF BASEBALL'S PHILLIES AND A'S, was a tough place to watch football. Unlike Forbes Field, it was poorly suited to the gridiron's geometrics. With goalposts erected along the first base line and in front of the left field fence, the grandstands were close to the end zones and far from the sidelines. Kickoffs sometimes sailed into the upper deck. After the baseball season, temporary bleachers were erected along the sideline in the outfield. The bleachers brought spectators much closer to the action, but they were rickety, uncovered, and uncomfortable.

"Shibe Park discouraged football fans," writes Bruce Kuklick in his history of the ballpark, *To Every Thing a Season*. "Indeed, many Eagles patrons went to Shibe Park as much for the masculine thrill of braving the winter outside as for witnessing the team."

Due to the scheduling vagaries resulting from NFL teams sharing ballparks with baseball teams, the New York Giants' game against the Steagles at Shibe Park on October 9 was their first of the season. (The Detroit Lions, by contrast, had already played three games.) The late start was just fine with Giants head coach Steve Owen. The big Oklahoman had an ace up his sleeve and he wanted to keep it there as long as possible. The ace was named Bill Paschal.

Like Allie Sherman, William Avner Paschal, Jr., likely would not have played pro football if not for the war. Paschal was a football and track star at Tech High in Atlanta. In his senior year he hurt his knee when he fell out of the top bunk of a bunk bed. He still earned a scholarship to Georgia Tech, but played only three minutes before reinjuring the knee. After an operation to remove cartilage, Paschal dropped out of college and went to work as a switchman for the Central of Georgia Railway.

In the summer of 1943, he bumped into his old college coach, Bill Alexander, who wired Grantland Rice in New York, asking him to pass Paschal's name along to Giants coach Steve Owen.

"With what I've got left," Owen told Rice, "I'll take a chance. . . . I can pretty near use anybody now."

When Paschal showed up at the Giants training camp at Bear Mountain, New York, Owen could hardly believe his eyes.

"The kid is one of the best running backs I've seen in years," Stout Steve gushed about his six-foot, 190-pound diamond in the rough. "He is not only a fast, quick starter, but he runs hard and drives on through." And the best part was that, because of his knee, Paschal was 4-F.

After their convincing win over Brooklyn, Greasy Neale and Walt Kiesling worried that the Steagles might be overconfident going into the Giants game. It seemed an unwarranted concern. Since joining the league ten years earlier, Philadelphia and Pittsburgh were a combined 7-31-1 against New York. The Eagles hadn't beaten the Giants in five years. Greasy Neale was 0-4 against them since coming to Philadelphia in 1941, a record that profoundly embarrassed him, since he and Steve Owen were close friends. In 1921, Neale tried to persuade Owen to play for him at Washington and Jefferson. Owen declined, but the two young men—Neale was 30, Owen 23—struck up a friendship that endured over the decades. When Lex Thompson bought an NFL franchise in 1940, it was Steve Owen who urged him to hire Greasy Neale.

On Friday, October 8, the Steagles got some good news: Speedy halfback Johnny Butler had failed his Army physical. He was 4-F due to poor eyesight and bad knees. (Like Bill Paschal, Butler had had the cartilage in one knee removed.) The next night Butler was in the starting lineup against the Giants.

109

More than 15,000 fans passed through Shibe Park's creaky turnstiles to see the game, a nearly 40 percent increase over the previous week's attendance. The Steagles' brain trust—Bert Bell, Art Rooney, and Harry Thayer—must have been very pleased. Sure, part of the increase was due to the end of the baseball season. But undoubtedly the team's electrifying performance against Brooklyn had piqued fan interest. It also didn't hurt that Lex Thompson was there with his latest girlfriend, a popular B-movie actress named Anne Shirley.

Among Eagles fans, Thompson's gossip-column lifestyle was as much discussed as the team's performance on the field. The millionaire owner was constantly surrounded by an ever-changing retinue of famous and near-famous lovers, drinking buddies, and hangers-on. His appearance at a game never hurt the gate.

The Steagles won the coin toss and elected to receive. Johnny Butler took the opening kickoff in the end zone. He ran out a few yards, then lateraled the ball to Jack Hinkle, who looked upfield to see a wall of blue jerseys converging on him. Hinkle was hell bent on having a good game. He wanted to show Giants coach Steve Owen a thing or two.

At Syracuse University, Hinkle had been an unheralded blocking back who rarely carried the ball. He signed with the Giants in 1940, but was cut after three games.

"I got into an argument with Steve Owen and they released me," Hinkle recalled. When asked what the argument was about, all Hinkle would say was, "Something asinine."

In 1941, Hinkle played for a team called the New York Americans in one of the many incarnations of an American Football League. The season ended just in time for him to sign with the Eagles for the final game of the 1941 season—at Washington on Pearl Harbor Day. Though drafted into the Army, he was discharged after a year because of his stomach ulcers. The Eagles took him back in 1943, and in training camp Greasy Neale turned him into a running back instead of a blocking back, which delighted Hinkle. He wasn't very fast—"They clocked me by the calendar," he liked to joke—but he was tenacious.

"When he gets in a game, he's a slambang player," Neale said. "A bull, that's what he is." He also had a good pedigree: One of his distant cousins was Clarke Hinkle, a legendary Green Bay fullback.

It was also during the Steagles training camp that Hinkle met an 18-year-old brunette from Overbrook named Joane Haggerty. They would marry the following February. In the stands, Joane would cheer him on so vociferously—"LET'S GO, HONEY!"— that his teammates eventually gave Hinkle the nickname "Honey."

Yes, 1943 was shaping up to be a very good year for Jack Hinkle. And now he was going to make it even better. As he stood searching for a crack in the onrushing blue wall, Hinkle thought about how good it would feel to show Steve Owen just what he was missing. Then Hinkle dropped the ball. He barely managed to recover his fumble, collapsing on the ball on the six-yard line an instant before the blue wall came crashing down. Hinkle got up, brushed himself off, and sheepishly joined the huddle, where Roy Zimmerman gave him a shot at redemption by calling "41 Outside"—Hinkle's favorite play.

Three backs lined up behind Zimmerman. Johnny Butler was on the left. Ben Kish, a six-foot, 200-pound fullback who had recently been discharged from the military after suffering a head injury, lined up directly behind Zimmerman. Hinkle was on the right. Zimmerman took the snap, wheeled to his left, and faked a handoff to Butler. Then he pivoted 180 degrees to his right and stuck the ball in Hinkle's belly. Hinkle slipped through a crack between Eddie Michaels, the deaf right guard, and Ted Doyle, the right tackle who'd taken the train in from Pittsburgh the night before. By the time the Giants collared him, Hinkle had advanced the ball 37 yards to the 43-yard line. The crowd was going wild.

Up in the press box, though, Ross Kaufman, the official statistician, got the numbers all mixed up. On his scorecard, he mistakenly attributed the 37-yard run to No. 27 (Butler) instead of No. 43 (Hinkle). Officially, Jack Hinkle never ran those 37 yards.

"I didn't realize the mistake until the next practice," Hinkle recalled. "The coach posted the stats and had me for a long gain of 16 yards! I knew that was wrong but I didn't make a fuss. At the time, it hardly seemed worth correcting."

On the next two plays the Steagles were called for penalties, and on the third Zimmerman threw a pass that the Giants' Len Younce intercepted and returned for a touchdown. Butler fumbled the ensuing kickoff out of the end zone for a touchback, so the Steagles kept possession, but on third down Hinkle attempted a surprise punt, which didn't surprise the Giants, who blocked it and recovered the ball on the one. Bill Paschal strolled into the end zone on the next play. Less than four minutes into the game the score was 14-0 in favor of the Giants. Jack Hinkle wasn't making much of an impression on Steve Owen (or anyone else), and the crowd wasn't going wild anymore. Before the quarter ended, the Steagles had fumbled three more times and had a second punt blocked.

At the beginning of the second quarter, the Steagles finally put together a drive without a fumble, interception, or blocked punt. From his own 42-yard line, Zimmerman completed a 44-yard pass to Bobby Thurbon, a rookie halfback from the University of Pittsburgh. Then Thurbon and fullback Ben Kish took turns carrying the ball to the four. From there, Ernie Steele followed a Vic Sears block and stepped into the end zone untouched. Zimmerman added the extra point to make the score 14-7.

Early in the fourth quarter, the Giants nearly made it 21-7. They had a first down on the Phil-Pitt five-yard line, but four times the Steagles smothered Bill Paschal short of the goal line. Then, with less than six minutes remaining in the game, the Steagles tied the score on an 11-yard, fourth-down pass from Zimmerman to Thurbon. On their next possession the Steagles scored again, this time on a 31-yard pass from Zimmerman to rookie end Tom Miller. With less than two minutes left and the Steagles leading 21-14, the Giants threatened to even the score, until Jack Hinkle finally gave Steve Owen something to chew on: Hinkle intercepted a New York pass on his own five-yard line and returned it 91 yards to the New York four. It would be the longest run of his career, and it clinched the game.

With time winding down, Neale sent Allie Sherman in for Zimmerman at quarterback, with strict instructions to run out the clock. But when Sherman reached the huddle, tackle Ted Doyle had something else in mind.

"I had found that I could run over the guy opposite me on the line of scrimmage," Doyle remembered. "So when he [Sherman] came into the huddle, I said to him, 'Just duck in behind me and we'll go.' And so when the ball was snapped he took it and ducked in behind me and we went over for a touchdown."

It was a subversive display of camaraderie between a Steeler and an Eagle, one a grizzled veteran, the other a 20-year-old rookie. It was hard for Neale to be too angry, though. He'd finally beaten Steve Owen. The final score was 28-14.

It was a wild game. The *New York Herald Tribune* called it "one of the most exciting games the professionals have turned up in a long time." Rarely has a football team looked as bumbling as the Steagles and still won by two touchdowns. As in the Brooklyn game, all credit was due the linemen: Sears, Schultz, Graves, Michaels, Doyle, and their substitutes. Their average weight was around 215 pounds, small even for the time, and positively lilliputian by modern standards. (The average lineman in the NFL today weighs around 300 pounds.) But the Steagles linemen were moving in perfect synchronicity, each executing his assignment with crisp precision. On offense they blocked flawlessly, performing Greasy Neale's complicated and highly choreographed T formation to, well, a T. On defense they simply stopped opposing running backs dead in their tracks. They held Bill Paschal to only about 30 yards rushing, and the entire Giants team to just 42 yards. In their first two games the Steagles had allowed just nine rushing yards in 56 rushing attempts—a ridiculously miniscule average of less than six inches per attempt! In fact, the whole team, line and backs, was playing great defense, much to the credit of Walt Kiesling. The Steagles had shut out Brooklyn and held New York to two cheap touchdowns (one was scored on an interception return and the other was the direct result of a blocked punt). For all the attention Neale's T formation generated, it was Kiesling's old-fashioned, hard-nosed defense that was largely responsible for the Steagles' fast start. Tackle Bucko Kilroy, for one, believed Kiesling's contributions were underappreciated. Kilroy called Kiesling "an innovator" and "the guy who started the basics" of modern NFL defenses.

The win over the Giants, however, was undeniably ugly. The Steagles' ten fumbles (half of which the Giants recovered) broke the previous record of eight, first set by the Redskins against the Steelers in 1937 and subsequently tied by five other teams. The Steagles' record of ten fumbles has since been equaled three times but is still unsurpassed. In all, the Steagles fumbled 14 times in their first two games. One possible explanation: the ball. Both games were played at night, and at the time the NFL used a football that was dyed white (with a black circle painted around each end) for night games, to make it easier for fans and players to see. (Before television, the lighting in ballparks was frequently murky.) Some players complained that the white ball was harder to hold onto than the usual brown ball.

"I didn't like it," Cleveland Browns quarterback Otto Graham once said of the white ball. "The paint they used was slick. . . . It was very slippery." But the slippery-ball theory fails to explain why the Steagles' opponents in the first two games fumbled just five times. (The white ball went the way of the wing formation in 1956, when television networks demanded better lighting in ballparks.) Steagles tackle Bucko Kilroy blamed the T formation for all the fumbles.

"You have to remember," he said, "a lot of guys were just learning the T, where you exchange the ball on every play. In the single wing, the halfback takes the snap and runs with it. We exchanged the ball on every play. It took time to straighten that out."

Perhaps the numerous fumbles were indicative of the overall quality of play in the NFL in 1943. There was undoubtedly a diminution in talent, as lesser lights were recruited to replace departing stars. Sid Luckman, the Chicago Bears' star quarterback, said the game slid back "about ten years or so" in 1943, and

Walt Kiesling rated the league as "between 30 and 40 percent weaker than in 1942." Statistics, to some extent, support that view. Between 1941 and 1943 the average number of points per game rose by a touchdown, from 32.9 to 38.9, as seasoned (and deferred) passers like Luckman and the Redskins' Sammy Baugh took advantage of inexperienced defenses.

"The caliber of play wasn't top notch," admitted Bucko Kilroy years later. "But the games were competitive and . . . we loved what we were doing."

League officials did not pretend the game was what it used to be. Before the 1943 season began, Giants owner Tim Mara said, "The 4-F boys playing the game this year will make it stand for 'Fine, fast, furious football!'"

Whatever its cause, the fumbling had to stop. The Steagles' next opponent was the Chicago Bears—and they weren't going to beat the Bears by two touchdowns if they fumbled ten times. Greasy Neale would work on that all week at practice, forcing his backs to "run a gauntlet" of teammates in an exercise designed to teach them, painfully, the price that must be paid to hold onto a football. For the time being, though, both Neale and Walt Kiesling were happy with how things stood: The Steagles were 2-0 and in first place in the Eastern Division.

After the Giants game, Lex Thompson took the team to Bookbinder's restaurant to celebrate. He treated them to lobster, which was not rationed and was fast becoming a fashionable alternative to steak, much to the delight of Maine lobstermen.

Allie Sherman did not join his teammates, however. Feeling a little homesick, he was going back to Brooklyn for the first time since he'd come to Philadelphia for training camp. Right after the game, fresh from scoring his first NFL touchdown, he walked the six blocks from Shibe Park to the North Philadelphia train station on Broad Street. While he was waiting on the platform he saw a large group of large men approaching. It was the Giants. Sherman slipped into the background and listened while Steve Owen chewed out his players for losing to such a rinky-dink outfit as the Steagles.

When he boarded the train, Sherman was careful to avoid the Giants' car.

BY NOW, RELATIONS AMONG THE STEAGLES were improving. Their common plight—working long hours in defense jobs all day in addition to playing professional football, a rugged and violent game—helped foster better relations. Mostly, though, the players were just getting to know each other better.

"I think we all got a little better acquainted and appreciated each other," said Ray Graves.

It also helped that nearly the entire team lived together. As part of his effort to make football "a family affair," Greasy Neale required the players, even the Pittsburghers, to live at the Hotel Philadelphian, an imposing, 600-room edifice on the southwest corner of 39th and Chestnut in West Philadelphia. (The handful of players who owned homes in Philadelphia were exempted from this policy, as was Ted Doyle, who didn't want to leave his job at the Westinghouse factory and was allowed to commute to games from Pittsburgh.) The hotel was where Neale kept a suite, and where Walt Kiesling lived during the 1943 season. Vic Sears remembered that Neale did not give the players much choice in the matter.

"Greasy said, 'I want you here. We have our meetings here. You gotta be here.'"

Not that the players had many other options. Housing in Philadelphia was scarce. The booming war industries attracted tens of thousands of workers to the city, but wartime restrictions on raw materials like lumber made it impossible to build new homes. The newcomers were herded into hastily subdivided row houses or makeshift trailer parks, and often charged exorbitant rents, despite a ban on gouging. Life at the Hotel Philadelphian was practically idyllic by comparison. The rates were subsidized by the team. The players paid about a dollar a day, a considerable break from the hotel's daily rate of three dollars.

Greasy Neale's motives weren't purely altruistic, of course. The residency requirement facilitated nightly "skull sessions" in the hotel ballroom after practice, at which the players were forced to watch game film for an hour or more while Neale fumbled clumsily with the projector. Ever since he'd learned the T formation by studying the raw newsreel footage of the 1940 championship game, Neale was a firm believer in the benefits of game film. He'd make his players watch the same play over and over, carefully pointing out what everybody had done wrong and only rarely acknowledging what anybody had done right.

The Eagles hired a lone cameraman to film their home games from the Shibe Park press box. The film had to be developed, of course, and it usually wasn't ready until Tuesday or Wednesday. The films of opposing teams were obtained through an underground network of football coaches who traded films like Grateful Dead fans would later trade bootleg recordings of the group's concerts. The league discouraged the practice but it grew so pervasive that it was codified after the war: Teams were required to submit films of their previous three games to their next opponent.

After eight hours in the factory, three hours on the practice field, and another hour or more of skull sessions, there wasn't much time left for the players to carouse. Mostly they just hung out in the hotel's Penguin Lounge or at Smokey Joe's, a popular tavern near the Penn campus. They also played cards, usually bridge, often in Neale's suite. They frequently ate together at a nearby Horn & Hardart Automat, a practice that Neale encouraged vigorously because the food was cheap.

The close quarters practically compelled friendship, recalled Eagles center Ray Graves.

"We made some real close friends with them [the Steelers]," Graves said. "I tell ya—ya had to, riding up and down the elevator with 'em—ya had to get pretty well acquainted."

Graves said the living arrangements had the added benefit of keeping the players on a short leash.

"The team and the wives and the children lived there. My daughter helped run the elevator! It was a family and it kept the husbands in line. . . . Johnny Butler went out one night and came back late, and I'll tell ya, one of the wives saw him comin' in and got on him. I'll tell ya, they kept the husbands pretty straight. I think it was a good thing. We were a family."

On Friday nights, Neale would host a cocktail party for the team in the Penguin Lounge.

Though he never had any of his own, Neale was quite fond of children. He enjoyed bouncing the players' babies on his knee, babbling to them in baby talk. The older children regarded him as an uncle, and he showered them with treats.

"He was something," said Ray Graves. "He had a lot of different personalities. He liked the kids . . . and they loved him. And he could be the toughest, meanest guy you ever played under, too."

The primary reason for the improving relations among the players—even more than the collegial atmosphere of the Hotel Philadelphian—was the Steagles' record: 2-0. The team was undefeated and in first place. When they played the Bears on October 17, the two teams would meet as equals in the standings. The Steagles were in first place in the Eastern Division, the Bears were tied for first in the West.

"When you're winnin'," said Ray Graves, "everything's a little better."

But even winning was not enough to thaw the frosty relationship between the teams' two co-head coaches. Walt Kiesling was feeling marginalized. Greasy Neale seemed incapable of ceding any authority to Kiesling, which naturally upset the big man. "Greasy ran the show," said Vic Sears. "He just took over."

Kiesling felt slighted. He also felt Neale was slighting the Steelers on the team. At one practice Kiesling got so upset with Neale for calling one of the Steelers a "statue of shit" that he pulled them off the field.

"I think Greasy tried to be as fair [to the Steeler players] as he could," Sears said. "I don't think anybody could have been happy about the situation. It wasn't a good situation for anybody." Halfback Jack Hinkle agreed: "The conflict was understandable. Kiesling was just sticking up for his own kids."

Halfback Ernie Steele remembered a time late in the season when Neale was ill in bed and Kiesling went to visit him. Steele said Kiesling sat in a chair and began reading a newspaper in silence.

"Greasy said, 'I'm layin' here dyin' and you're reading the goddamn newspaper!?' Kiesling said, 'If you're gonna die, you're gonna die. I can't do anything about it.' They were something, those two."

9

Chicago

ON THURSDAY, APRIL 8, 1943, the federal Office of Price Administration decreed that, effective the following Tuesday, the length of matchsticks would be decreased by roughly ten percent to conserve wood. The OPA also ordered match manufacturers to begin packing matches "half with the heads one way and half in the opposite direction," thereby reducing the amount of paper required for packaging.

Four months later, six statuesque young women picketed the OPA offices in San Francisco to draw attention to the plight of "tall gals who cannot get long stockings." "The new OPA ceiling on stockings is about 29 inches and they end slightly above the knees," said one protester. "So we have to go barelegged and it ain't dignified."

From the length of matchsticks to the length of stockings, the Office of Price Administration controlled virtually every facet of daily life in the United States during the war. The most obvious manifestation of this control was rationing. The massive amount of material needed to supply the armed forces led to shortages of everything from steel to soap.

At various times, the list of rationed goods included rubber, automobiles, typewriters, sugar, bicycles, gasoline, farm machinery, boots, oil, farm fences, coffee, oil and coal stoves, shoes, processed foods (including juices and canned, frozen, and dried fruits and vegetables), firewood, liquor, canned milk, cigarettes, butter, meats, fats, and cheese.

Rationing was administered by the OPA through 5,500 local boards, similar to the draft boards. Each household was periodically issued a ration book, which contained rows of different colored stamps, each of which was assigned a point value and a letter. The OPA also assigned each rationed item a point value based on its scarcity—the scarcer the item, the higher the point value. A consumer wishing to buy, say, pork chops, might be required to surrender 15 red "B" points in addition to the purchase price.

But no amount of rationing could prevent periodic shortages of certain goods. Newspapers were filled with stories of "famines": butter famines, whiskey famines, beef famines, gasoline famines. A shortage of sheet steel led to a license plate famine in Pennsylvania. So, instead of issuing new plates during the war, the state distributed small metal tags that were attached to the old plates, a system that would be adopted permanently (with stickers replacing the metal tags) in the late 1950s. There was even a penny famine, owing to the military's demand for copper. The government responded by minting pennies out of steel in 1943, a development that drove consumers and shopkeepers crazy, since the shiny coins closely resembled dimes.

The booming wartime economy obliterated the remnants of the Great Depression. Inflation was the new concern. With many goods in short supply, prices would naturally rise. With workers in great demand, wages, too, would increase. Inflation would not only raise the cost of fighting the war; FDR feared it would also have a corrosive effect on morale. To keep a lid on it, the OPA froze the prices of many goods and services. The wages of many workers were likewise frozen.

No detail was too mundane to escape the scrutiny of the OPA. It imposed price controls on "the cutting and maintenance of lawns," thus freezing the wages of kids who mowed yards for pocket change. In restaurants, the OPA ruled, diners were permitted a cocktail, soup, or dessert—but not all three. On New Year's

Eve 1943, nightclubs were instructed to charge no more for drinks and meals than they had one year earlier. Minor violations of the rationing regulations usually resulted in a 30-day suspension of ration privileges—not an insignificant penalty, given that many basic necessities were not legally obtainable without ration stamps. More serious violations, such as trafficking in black market goods or counterfeit ration stamps, were punishable by up to ten years' imprisonment and a $10,000 fine. It wasn't only patriotism that contributed to the program's high compliance rate.

The burden of coping with the inconveniences, sacrifices, and privations of wartime America fell most heavily upon women. With their husbands at war or at work, women assumed total management of the household. Propaganda campaigns specifically targeted women, urging them to "Use it up, wear it out, make it do or do without." In *Don't You Know There's a War On?*, his seminal book about life on the home front, Richard Lingeman writes of the wartime woman: "She was a soldier and her kitchen a combination frontline bunker and rear-echelon miniature war plant."

While Steagles tackle Ted Doyle labored in the Westinghouse factory and on the football field, his wife was left to manage the household while raising two children, a three-year-old boy and a two-year-old girl.

"I was busy," Harriet Doyle remembered. Like countless millions of other patriotic American homemakers, she saved kitchen fats and turned them in to her butcher, so they could be converted into glycerin to make gunpowder. She assiduously recycled tin cans, observed "meatless Fridays," and cultivated a small "Victory Garden" to supplement the family's diet. Finding shoes for her children was one of the greatest difficulties Doyle encountered.

"Their feet were growin' all the time! And with two of 'em, why, it was interesting. But when we ran out of ration coupons, our neighbors would help us out."

Technically that was a violation of OPA regulations: ration stamps were to be used only by the household to which they'd been assigned. In fact, they were to be removed from the booklet only in the presence of the shopkeeper to whom they were being redeemed. The reality, said Harriet Doyle, was very different.

"We exchanged ration coupons with the neighbors all the time. There was an elderly couple next door that didn't have any children, so they gave us extra coupons. And a bachelor who lived across the street shared coupons, too."

Like every other American institution, the National Football League was forced to adapt to wartime conditions.

"Equipment was very scarce," recalled Dan Rooney, the son of the Steelers' founder. "We kept it in the basement of our house so we didn't lose it. Cleats were really hard to get because they were a rubber product." Footballs were hard to get too, because their bladders were made of rubber. What little equipment that was available was often appropriated by the military for recreational use. What's more, travel restrictions made it difficult for "non-priority" travelers like football players to get seats on trains. When Ted Doyle commuted to games, he shared a berth with Bill Cullen, one of the Steelers' radio announcers (and later a popular TV game show host), an arrangement that probably garnered Doyle more airtime than the average lineman. Ballpark concessions were difficult to procure as well. A bottle shortage rendered soft drinks ("soda" in Philadelphia, "pop" in Pittsburgh) a precious commodity. Paper for game programs was also in short supply. And it was almost impossible to get the uniforms cleaned, since laundry services were inundated with military business. After his first day at training camp, tackle Al Wistert handed his sweat-soaked jersey and pants to the Eagles' trainer, Fred Schubach.

"We can't get laundry service," Schubach barked. "Wear that stuff a while!" Wistert took his uniform back home to his wife Ellie, who cleaned it in the tub.

In some ways the wartime conditions actually benefited the National Football League. Games were played on Sundays, many workers' only day off. The ballparks were close to trolley lines or other public transportation, so fans could get there without expending precious gas rations. And, by the fall of 1943, nearly 300 colleges had dropped their football programs for want of players, thereby eliminating the pro game's primary competition.

Although football had not yet acquired much of the martial vernacular that has since come to characterize it—"blitz" and "bomb" meant very different things in 1943—the game's obvious parallels with war also may have contributed to its popularity on the home front. The objectives of penetrating enemy territory while defending your own, the recurring and often violent physical confrontations: football was a benign substitute for the real thing. Nor did the NFL discourage the perception. On the cover of game programs, images of soldiers and football players were frequently juxtaposed. While one threw a hand grenade, for example, the other threw a touchdown pass.

The league presented football not merely as diversionary, but as necessary.

"Democracy makes us a pacific people," said Chicago Cardinals head coach Jimmy Conzelman in a 1942 radio broadcast. "The young man must be toughened not only physically but mentally. He must become accustomed to violence. Football is the No. 1 medium for attuning a man to body contact and violent physical shock. It teaches that after all there isn't anything so terrifying about a punch in the puss."

Football also gave Americans a respite from fear, especially in the gray autumn of 1943, when the United States had already been at war for two long years and no end was in sight. The threat of invasion had subsided: In October, the government even lifted a ban on the publication and broadcasting of weather reports. Americans were confident, but victory in Europe and especially Asia was still far from certain.

"We were all concerned about the war," remembered Harriet Doyle. "Our hopes were high but we were very concerned. It was something that we prayed and hoped for, that everything would turn out all right. Ted had a brother in and so did I. [Ted's brother was killed in action.] It definitely concerned us all. I was very happy that my husband didn't have to go in. It's very selfish, but with two children—I would've had my hands full."

There were few entertaining escapes that autumn. Baseball was over, and Hollywood, awash in unctuous patriotism, offered an endless stream of banal war movies, the most popular of which, *This Is the Army,* starred Ronald Reagan. Popular music was similarly preoccupied (e.g., "Praise the Lord and Pass the Ammunition" by Kay Kyser). Football provided a release. After dropping off precipitously in 1942, attendance rebounded dramatically the following season, with war- and work-weary fans turning out in droves. The NFL would average 24,228 fans per game in 1943, a 33-percent increase over the previous season and the best in league history at that time.

"Fans had found football a good way to forget the war for a few hours," is how Bears owner George Halas explained it.

In Philadelphia and Pittsburgh—cities where first-place teams were as common as palm trees—the Steagles' early success excited sports fans. Suddenly, unexpectedly, they had a winner, albeit one with an unusual name and pedigree.

"The Steagles have been a distinct surprise," gushed Chet Smith in the *Pittsburgh Press* after the Giants game. Even the scribes of the Midwest, professional football's epicenter, were impressed. In the *Chicago Tribune,* Edward Prell wrote that the "whispering is growing louder that here is a team which may represent the east in the championship playoffs." When a reporter told Vic Sears that the Steagles had a good line "considering the times," the ulcerous tackle bristled.

"Look," he said, "this is a good line, war or no war."

Bert Bell was asked if the Eagles had ever started the season with two wins.

"Hell," he laughed, "I don't even remember them ever winning two games in a row before!"

In fact the Eagles never had started a season with consecutive victories, and the Steelers had just twice, in 1936 and 1937.

Bell could not contain his enthusiasm for the Steagles.

"Their spirit is wonderful," he said. "We have no great, outstanding players, but we do have what's better. That's a squad of players that think they can win a ball game. And by golly, that's what counts." As for their next opponent, the mighty Chicago Bears, Bell said, "I'm not saying we'll beat them." But, he hastened to add, "They can be beat. . . . It will be a ball game."

On the evening of Friday, October 15, the Steagles departed Philadelphia on a train bound for Chicago. The trip would take more than 15 hours, their longest road trip of the season by far. (The second longest were the trips to Pittsburgh for home games.) En route the train picked up the Pittsburgh contingent, including Ted Doyle and the Steelers' radio announcers, Joe Tucker and Bill Cullen. It was reported that "quite a number" of Steelers fans boarded the train as well, even though the Office of Defense Transportation had instructed pro football teams to "restrict sales of tickets to residents of the area in which the game is played" in order to make space on trains available for soldiers and other people "traveling on war business." Like so many wartime rules, this one was greeted with a wink and a nod. The Steelers fans could buy their tickets at the Wrigley Field box office, where no one would bother to ask them where they were from.

Pullman cars were available for the players to sleep in, but it was still a long, uncomfortable ride. Greasy Neale didn't mind, though. The Eagles head coach enjoyed long train trips. He believed they fostered the kind of family atmosphere he strived for among his players. On the train the players read, played cards, and hung out in the dining car. Even when air travel became common after the war, Neale preferred the rails, believing that "flying has a deleterious emotional effect on certain players which it is well to avoid." He felt that "train travel on the whole, is much more restful, and brings the team to its destination in better physical condition, and in a more emotionally stable frame of mind" than air travel.

"I think Greasy might've owned stock in the railroad," joked center Ray Graves.

The train pulled into Chicago around nine o'clock Saturday

The Steagles starting lineup, photographed September 15, 1943. The front line (left to right): Larry Cabrelli, Frank "Bucko" Kilroy, Eddie Michaels, Ray Graves, Elbie Schultz, Vic Sears, and Bill Hewitt. The backfield (left to right): Jack Hinkle, Roy Zimmerman, Ben Kish, and Ernie Steele. (Hewitt and Hinkle would later switch to different uniform numbers.) *Photo courtesy Temple University Libraries, Urban Archives, Philadelphia, PA*

The Steagles play leapfrog during a break in training camp near St. Joseph's College in Philadelphia, September 10, 1943. At the upper right is backup quarterback Allie Sherman. *Photo courtesy Temple University Libraries, Urban Archives, Philadelphia, PA*

The Steagles practice a running play during training camp as co-head coach Greasy Neale watches intently, September 10, 1943. Neale spent much of training camp teaching the team the intricacies of the T formation. *Photo courtesy Temple University Libraries, Urban Archives, Philadelphia, PA*

When the Steelers and Eagles merged, the Eagles' owner, Lex Thompson, was in the Army. Here Thompson is shown practicing on the antiaircraft-artillery range at Camp Davis in North Carolina. *Photo courtesy Temple University Libraries, Urban Archives, Philadelphia, PA*

Harriet and Ted Doyle, around the time of their marriage in 1938, the same year Ted Doyle signed with the Steelers (then known as the Pirates). *Photo courtesy Jo Hanshaw*

Servicemen share a program in the stands at the Steagles-Bears exhibition game at Shibe Park, Philadelphia, September 16, 1943. Throughout the war, many members of the armed forces spoke out in favor of the continuation of professional sports. *Photo courtesy Temple University Libraries, Urban Archives, Philadelphia, PA*

The Steagles vs. the Chicago Bears, Shibe Park, Philadelphia, September 16, 1943. Except for the Green Bay Packers, every team in the NFL played its home games in a major league baseball park at the time. *Photo courtesy Temple University Libraries, Urban Archives, Philadelphia, PA*

The Steagles' Roy Zimmerman tackles New York Giants end Will Walls during the Steagles' 28-14 victory over the Giants at Shibe Park, Philadelphia, October 9, 1943. Rushing to assist Zimmerman is his teammate, Ben Kish (44). Note the white football, which the NFL used in night games at the time. *Photo courtesy Temple University Libraries, Urban Archives, Philadelphia, PA*

Al Wistert in 1940, his sophomore season at the University of Michigan. He was drafted by the Eagles in 1943. *Photo courtesy Temple University Libraries, Urban Archives, Philadelphia, PA*

Bill Hewitt in the 1930s, when he played for the Chicago Bears. In 1943, Hewitt was coaxed out of retirement to play for the Steagles. A new rule required him to wear a helmet for the first time in his career. *Photo courtesy Pro Football Hall of Fame/WireImage .com*

Earle "Greasy" Neale shortly before he became the head coach of the Philadelphia Eagles in 1941. Neale shared head coaching duties with Pittsburgh's Walt Kiesling when the two teams merged in 1943. *Photo courtesy Pro Football Hall of Fame/WireImage .com*

Demonstrating their defensive prowess, the Steagles encircle Green Bay Packer Tony Canadeo at Shibe Park, Philadelphia, December 5, 1943. Among the Steagles are Tom Miller (89), Ed Conti (67), Tony Bova (85), and Ray Graves (52). *Photo courtesy Temple University Libraries, Urban Archives, Philadelphia, PA*

Steagles halfback Jack Hinkle (43) runs for a touchdown against the Green Bay Packers at Shibe Park, Philadelphia, December 5, 1943. Blocking for Hinkle are Ben Kish (44) and Tony Bova (85). *Photo courtesy Temple University Libraries, Urban Archives, Philadelphia, PA*

morning, and the team went straight to Wrigley Field for a brief workout to shake off their train legs and inspect the turf. Afterwards they checked into the Edgewater Beach Hotel on the far north side, where they ate lunch in the café. Greasy Neale was a punctilious coach, and his rules for road trips were rigid. He seems to have had a particular fixation on food.

"All meals are to be eaten in the hotel coffee shop," players were instructed in a handout, "and checks must be signed by players. If two or more players have their meal together, each of the players must sign the check." Among the other rules: smoking was permitted "at all times" except during meals, in meetings, in the locker room, or on the field; no gambling was permitted except for penny ante poker, rummy ("with small stakes"), pinochle ("at five cents per hundred"), and bridge ("at 1/20th cent a point"); and no drinking of beer or whiskey was permitted "at any time except when the entire squad is granted permission by the Head Coach."

Curfew the night before a game was 10:00 p.m., but in Chicago all the players were already in bed well before then. They knew they needed all the rest they could get. Their task the next day was gargantuan. The Bears were redoubtable; they hadn't lost a regular season game since before Pearl Harbor. Their roster was loaded with older, experienced players, including five future members of the Pro Football Hall of Fame (Danny Fortmann, Sid Luckman, George Musso, Bronko Nagurski, and Clyde Turner). Apart from the departure of owner George Halas for the Navy, the Bears were largely unscathed by the war. It seemed a bit suspicious, actually.

BACK IN MID SEPTEMBER, just before the start of the season, the Bears had issued a press release announcing that five more players were returning to the team for the upcoming campaign. The release also noted the jobs the players would be leaving to join the team:

■ Harry Clark, a pipe fitter at a defense plant in Morgantown, West Virginia.

- Al Hoptowit, a farm worker in the Yakima Valley of Washington state.

- Dante Magnani, a pipe fitter at the Mare Island Navy Yard in California.

- Hampton Pool, a mechanic at a shipyard in Sunnydale, California.

- Clyde "Bulldog" Turner, a civilian Army employee in Abilene, Texas.

As was customary, the release was published nearly verbatim in the Chicago papers. Almost immediately, the phone at the Chicago office of the War Manpower Commission began ringing. Callers were angry. Why were these men being allowed to leave important war jobs to play pro football? William Spencer, the top WMC official in Chicago, decided to find out. Declaring it "a matter of public morale," Spencer said his investigation would determine whether there was any "irregularity" in the transfer of the players from essential industries to a nonessential one.

"If rules have been violated," Spencer promised, "I will attempt to straighten them out."

As part of a "job stabilization program" begun in late 1942, the WMC required a worker to obtain a "certificate of availability" from his employer before leaving a war job. This was supposed to prevent a worker from leaving his employer in a lurch when he quit. Employers were not allowed to hire a worker who did not have a certificate of availability. The goal of the program was to keep workers from leaving essential jobs without good cause—to simply go to a higher paying job, for example. In fact, it bound workers to their employers: You needed your boss's permission to quit a war job. At issue was whether the five Bears in question had obtained their certificates of availability. Also at issue was the question of which employer was "regular" and which was "vacation." If the football club was considered the players' regular employer, then their war work was merely "supplemental," and not under the jurisdiction of the WMC. However, if the Bears were their vacation employer, that was another matter altogether.

Ralph Brizzolara, who was running the Bears while George Halas was in the Navy, insisted the team had done nothing wrong.

"If there has been any violation," he said, "it was entirely inadvertent."

To NFL Commissioner Elmer Layden, the whole situation was keenly embarrassing.

"The league clubs have always cooperated in the war effort," the image-conscious commissioner said. "If there are any irregularities we want to know about them too and they will be corrected. The war comes first."

The possible repercussions were enormous.

"If the players failed to obtain certificates of availability," Spencer said, "it would be doubtful if they would be permitted to continue playing football. They might have to return to essential industry."

There was also the possibility that the players would be reclassified 1-A and inducted immediately. And it wasn't just the Bears who would be affected. A negative ruling would affect the entire league, and all of professional sports for that matter, since most teams employed players who worked in war plants during the off-season. If those players were not permitted to leave their war jobs, pro sports would be out of business. It was estimated that three-fourths of all major league baseball players were doing war work after the baseball season ended.

"It goes without saying, of course," wrote *New York Herald Tribune* sportswriter Arthur E. Patterson, "that if these men were frozen to their war jobs, there just wouldn't be any baseball in 1944."

One pro sports team, however, had no such concerns. Since the Steagles required all players to hold war jobs, the issue to them was moot.

"We turned our practices upside down to make sure that the men would not let their war work suffer," Harry Thayer said, rather smugly, in reference to the investigation of the Bears. "I venture to say that by the time we open our regular season . . . every man on the squad will be in fact a full-time war worker and a part-time football player."

Ralph Brizzolara met with William Spencer at the WMC office on September 23, just three days before the Bears opened the season in Green Bay. Elmer Layden met with Spencer the next day. Pending the outcome of the investigation, Spencer ruled that the five Bears in question would be allowed to play football. The team, meanwhile, launched a public relations counteroffensive. On October 8, it made a show of announcing that it would soon be losing four players to the military. Bill Geyer, Bill Osmanski, Johnny Siegal, and Bill Steinkemper would all be joining the Navy within three weeks.

GEORGE HALAS NOT ONLY OWNED the Chicago Bears, he coached them, too. Except for three seasons in the early 1930s, when Ralph Jones took the reins, he was the team's only head coach from its founding in 1920 until the Navy recalled him halfway through the 1942 season. In his absence, Halas delegated the coaching duties to Luke Johnsos and Hunk Anderson, two former Bears who had also served as assistant coaches under Halas before his departure. Johnsos was in charge of the offense and Anderson oversaw the defense. It was an arrangement similar to Walt Kiesling and Greasy Neale's, with one added benefit: Johnsos and Anderson actually got along.

"The division could have caused trouble, but didn't," Johnsos recalled. "Neither of us told the other what to do."

Even without Halas at the helm, the Bears were nearly unstoppable. Since he'd left they'd lost just once, a 14-6 heartbreaker to the Redskins in the 1942 championship game. After opening the 1943 campaign with a 21-21 tie in Green Bay, the Bears defeated the Lions and the Cardinals by a combined score of 47-21. One of the Bears' stars was Bronko Nagurski, who'd retired at the end of the 1937 season, but was lured back in 1943. In his prime, Nagurski was a powerful fullback, so strong that more than one tackler was knocked unconscious trying to bring him down. He was nearly 35 now, older even than Bill Hewitt, and not as fast as he used to be, so the Bears moved him to tackle, where he acquitted himself nicely.

"Bronk was still as strong as a bull," writes his biographer, Jim Dent. "It took two strong men to move him, much less block him out of the play." Nagurski returned to the Bears out of loyalty to Halas, as well as for the money: $500 a game, more than he'd ever made before.

The 1943 Bears continued Halas's tradition of playing smash-mouth football: "a crushing ground game and a weekly accumulation of sizeable penalties," as the *Tribune*'s Edward Prell put it. But they could also throw the ball. Quarterback Sid Luckman was leading the league in passing, and seven of the Bears' ten touchdowns so far in 1943 had been scored through the air. Luckman was a Columbia grad with a golden arm. He couldn't throw the ball very far or very hard, but he could throw it with stunning accuracy.

"He couldn't throw too good," said Luckman's longtime teammate Clyde "Bulldog" Turner, "but he'd complete 'em."

The Bears' increasing use of the pass led some to claim the club had "turned sissy" by "subordinating their running game to an aerial attack," a charge that Luckman emphatically denied.

The Steagles-Bears game was rife with subplots. It would be a battle of the only two teams in the league running the T formation. Greasy Neale had learned the T by studying film of the Bears; now he hoped to give them a taste of their own medicine. The game also pitted the league's two best defenses against each other. The Steagles were No. 1 in run defense and overall defense, while the Bears were tops in pass defense. The game would also be a homecoming of sorts for Bill Hewitt, who had started his career with the Bears before being traded to the Eagles. Hewitt had not distinguished himself with his play in the Steagles' first two games and he was determined to make an impression against his old friends. The bookmakers favored Chicago, but the Steagles were confident and the Bears were wary.

"They've got a tough ball club," Bears assistant coach Paddy

Driscoll said a few days before the game, "and we know we've got to get together and go to the limit on Sunday."

SATURDAY, OCTOBER 16, 1943, was a red-letter day in Chicago. At 10:48 that morning, Mayor Edward J. Kelly snipped a red, white, and blue ribbon to formally open the city's first subway, a 4.9-mile stretch of tracks running underneath State Street. Chicago had wanted to build a subway since the turn of the century but couldn't afford to until FDR turned on the federal money spigot during the Depression. With a $23 million grant, the city constructed the most modern subway in the world, with a state-of-the-art ventilation system, escalators, and fluorescent lighting. A single, 3,500-foot platform, one of the longest in the world, connected every station between Lake and Congress streets. The stations themselves were designed in the Art Moderne style, each with a color scheme revealed in accents like light fixtures. And a ride cost just ten cents.

The ribbon-cutting ceremony took place in the Madison Street station. On the street above, thousands of Chicagoans braved a chilly north wind to witness a spectacular hour-long parade. The subway was a remarkable feat of engineering, given the city's soft, sandy substrate. It was also hailed as a way to take pressure off the city's overcrowded elevated trains, which carried up to a million passengers every day.

October 16 was a red-letter day in Chicago for another reason: it was on that day that William Spencer, the regional director of the War Manpower Commission, ruled that the five players who had left war jobs to join the Bears had *not* violated WMC regulations. Spencer ruled that the players were "under contract to the football club and subject to recall at the start of the season." He also ruled that their "principal occupation" was football, so "any jobs accepted by the players during off-season periods constitute supplemental employment, not subject to WMC regulation." In other words, it didn't matter whether they had certificates of availability. Spencer also pointed out that none of the players' employers had complained to the WMC about their leaving at the start of the football season, "indicating they understood the services of the players were only on a temporary basis." The five were free to keep playing ball, as were all other professional athletes who worked in war plants during the off-season. Bears fans were delighted. The team itself—indeed all of professional sports—was simply relieved.

The Bears did get a bit of bad news that Saturday, however: their star tackle Bronko Nagurski had to hurry home to International Falls, Minnesota. His mother was ill, two of his farmhands had quit, and his father's grocery store was short of staff. To the Steagles, of course, this was very good news.

The next afternoon, nearly 22,000 curious fans ventured to Wrigley Field for a peek at the two-headed monster called the Steagles. Today it seems an unlikely venue for football, but Wrigley Field was the Bears' home for fifty seasons. When the team, then known as the Staleys (after the starch company that originally sponsored the team), moved from Decatur, Illinois, to Chicago in 1921, George Halas met with William L. Veeck, Sr., the president of the Chicago Cubs, to discuss renting Wrigley Field from the baseball team. Veeck wanted what was to become the standard rent for NFL teams in major league ballparks: 15 percent of the gate receipts and all concessions. Halas agreed, happy he didn't have to pay a fixed rent. With temporary bleachers erected in the outfield, the ballpark accommodated about 46,000 fans for football. After the 1970 season, the league passed a rule requiring all teams to play in venues with a minimum seating capacity of 50,000, forcing the Bears to move downtown to Soldier Field. Football and Wrigley Field were a good fit—but a tight one. A gridiron barely fit within the "Friendly Confines." In the outfield, one corner of the end zone came within inches of the brick outfield wall, which wasn't covered with ivy until 1937. Bronko Nagurski once crashed into the wall headfirst after scoring a touchdown. Back on the sidelines, Nagurski is said to have told Halas, "That last guy gave me quite a lick!" A corner of the opposite end zone actually went into the first base dugout. The Bears eventually padded the outfield wall and laid foam rubber in the dugout to protect players.

The previous day's winds had died down, and the weather that Sunday was clear and cool, a delicious day for football. At two o'clock the Bears' Bob Snyder kicked off to the Steagles. Roy Zimmerman returned the kick to the Phil-Pitt 38. On first down, halfback Ernie Steele carried the ball two yards to the 40. On second down, Zimmerman tossed a long pass to Steele, who caught the ball on the Chicago 24 and ran it the rest of the way into the end zone. Zimmerman added the extra point, and just 80 seconds into the game the score was 7-0 Steagles. Wrigley Field was stunned into silence, but back at the Hotel Philadelphian loud shrieks of joy could be heard coming from one of the suites. As they did whenever the Steagles played away from Philadelphia, the players' wives had gathered to listen to the game on the radio.

After Steele's touchdown, Zimmerman kicked off to the Bears' Dante Magnani. Magnani had played for the Cleveland Rams in 1942. He was among the players distributed to the remaining clubs when the Rams folded for the season. The Bears literally picked his name out of a hat. Magnani took the kickoff on his own four-yard line. Somewhere around the 20 he burst through a wave of green-shirted Steagles and sprinted down the sideline. At the Phil-Pitt 12 he barely outran Ernie Steele's desperate lunge. After that, Magnani could have run into the dugout, through the locker room, and all the way down Addison Street to the lake, and still no Steagle would have caught him.

Magnani's 96-yard kickoff return opened the floodgates. The Bears scored six more touchdowns before the Steagles tacked on two meaningless fourth-quarter scores. The final was Chicago 48, Phil-Pitt 21. It was the most points the Bears had ever racked up against either the Steelers or the Eagles. (The fact that it was also the most points either Pennsylvania squad had ever scored against Chicago was no consolation.) The Bears scored three touchdowns on passes, two on runs, one on a kickoff return, and one on a punt return. They rushed for 205 yards. The Steagles rushed for just 60. The Phil-Pitt line, so ballyhooed entering the game, "fell apart like a one-hoss shay," according to the *Philadelphia Record*. Al Wistert, who started the game at right tackle, took some of the blame. It was the rookie's first NFL game back in his hometown. "I got over-anxious," he recalled.

> *My main responsibility was to close the inside gap, between me and the guard next to me. Well, after a couple plays, I figured I would try to fake inside then slide outside, to stop the runner going that way, see. Well, Luckman figured out what was going on and they ran inside me a couple times. The linebacker expected me to close that gap, so they got good gains. I was going against Greasy's orders and he gave me hell after the game. He said, "Where were you today? You were supposed to stop the inside run!" And I said, "Well, I tried to slide outside. I guess I gambled and lost." And he said, "You didn't lose; the team lost!"*

It wasn't all Wistert's fault, of course. There was plenty of blame to go around. None of the linemen performed well; it was almost as if they'd forgotten how to block and tackle. The running backs spun their wheels all day. Roy Zimmerman completed just six of 24 passes. (Sid Luckman, meanwhile, completed 13 of 25.) The defeat was total. In the *Pittsburgh Press*, Cecil Muldoon called it a "humiliation." To Jack Sell of the *Post-Gazette*, the game was "a long story of disaster."

"They beat the pants off us," was how Ernie Steele put it. Ted Doyle agreed.

"We got the hell beat out of us," said Doyle. "You try to forget that type of game."

The loss distressed Greasy Neale profoundly. In the locker room after the game, he lambasted the squad.

"You can't win ball games in this league by playing high school football!" he screamed. It was a long train ride home. At least the Steagles wouldn't have to play the Bears again—unless they met in the championship game, a possibility that suddenly seemed much more remote.

In Milwaukee, the Redskins had won their second straight game, throttling the Packers 33-7. And in New York, the Giants had clobbered the Dodgers 20-0, with rookie Bill Paschal scoring two touchdowns. The Steagles weren't in first place anymore. The standings now read:

	W	L	T	Pct.
Redskins	2	0	0	1.000
Steagles	2	1	0	.667
Giants	1	1	0	.500
Dodgers	0	4	0	.000

At practice the following Tuesday, quarterback Roy Zimmerman tried to rally the dispirited Steagles.

"Boys," he told them, "we lost a ball game Sunday—but we've won two. We made mistakes against the Bears, plenty of them. Let's get out there now and find out why we made them, and what we can do about it."

The mistakes needed to be corrected quickly: In five days the Steagles would play the Giants, and the Giants had revenge on their minds.

ON THE MORNING OF SUNDAY, OCTOBER 24, the Steagles took a train to New York to play the Giants. Due to a shortage of hotel rooms for "nonessential" travelers (and to save money), the team would return to Philadelphia immediately after the game. The Giants were eager to avenge their opening game loss to the Steagles, though Giants head coach Steve Owen wasn't about to give them anything to post on their locker room wall.

"The Steagles have a real good team," he said a few days

before the game, adding that he merely hoped the Giants would "give a better account" of themselves than they had a fortnight earlier. Among the bookies the Steagles were adjudged "slight favorites."

It was a cold, blustery day, but 42,681 fans filled the Polo Grounds anyway, setting attendance records for a Giants home opener and for any Steelers or Eagles game anywhere ever. Since the stadium was considered an attractive enemy target, certain wartime precautions were in place. Each of the 56,000 seats was labeled with instructions for fans to follow in the event of an aerial attack. Some were labeled "Follow Green Arrow," some "Follow Red Arrow," and some "Sit Tight." Fans, the game program noted, were "expected to comply with these instructions" during a bombardment.

In the first quarter the Giants scored touchdowns on a blocked punt return and a long pass. Early in the second quarter, Roy Zimmerman, who had badly bruised his hip making a block early in the game, limped off the field and never returned to the game. The Steagles were thoroughly demoralized. On the sidelines, Greasy Neale and Walt Kiesling seethed. Neale prowled the sidelines constantly, his trench coat flapping behind him. From the opening kickoff until the final gun he harangued his players and the officiating crew in equal measure, chain-smoking all the while, littering the field with the butts. When Neale suffered a heart attack during a game late in the 1942 season, the only surprise was that it was mild.

Walt Kielsing, dowdy in a baseball cap and sweatshirt, was no less demonstrative. His team could do little right in his eyes, even when it was winning, but especially when it was losing, and after every play he screamed at the offending parties in a manner that disheartened rather than motivated. Together on the sidelines, the two ranting coaches made for an odd sight, each always roaming and spitting invective, seemingly unaware of the other. They rarely interacted during a game, and when they did the tone was accusatory.

"They would blame each other when something went wrong," said tackle Bucko Kilroy. Occasionally an unlucky player would find himself the object of the two coaches' wraths simultaneously, leaving him no choice but to ignore both.

Nothing went the Steagles' way that afternoon at the Polo Grounds. On those rare occasions when they did make a good play, it would inevitably be nullified by a penalty. It almost seemed like the cards were stacked against them.

"I had a buddy, Len Younce, that played for New York," said Vic Sears. "And every time we made a touchdown or a big play they [the officials] would give us a penalty. And he told me after the game, 'You couldn't win.' And that's the way it was. You couldn't win. And the coach [Steve Owen] played golf with Greasy and told him the same thing: 'You couldn't win.'"

It would be hard to blame the officials for this debacle, though. In the second quarter the Giants scored two more touchdowns, and in the third they scored two more—six in all. Bill Paschal ran for two, Emery Nix and Tuffy Leemans each passed for one, and two blocked punts were returned for scores. (Leemans, who had postponed his retirement after Pearl Harbor, would finally hang up his spikes after the 1943 season.)

Allie Sherman, who played 55 minutes, performed admirably in relief of Roy Zimmerman. He passed for more than 100 yards and steered the Steagles to two touchdowns late in the fourth quarter, but by then the game had long been decided. The Giants won, 42-14.

Once again the Steagles line was terrible. In the first two games it had been a brick wall. Now, wrote Cecil Muldoon, it was "a dish of jelly." Muldoon's sarcastic lead in the *Pittsburgh Press* the next day neatly summed up the Steagles' plummeting fortunes:

NEW YORK, October 25—Lost, strayed or stolen—one offense and one defense. Finder please return to Greasy Neale, Phil-Pitt coach, Philadelphia, Pa. Also liberal reward for anybody sending in book on fundamentals of football.

The Steagles' collapse mystified the team, as well as the sportswriters who covered it.

"No one," wrote Chet Smith in the *Press*, "has been able to offer a satisfactory answer as to what made the Steagles come apart after they had taken the Brooklyn Dodgers and the Giants in the first two games. . . . There is no adequate manner to explain a net difference of 42 points in the first and second contests with the Giants."

In the *Philadelphia Record*, Red Smith called the Steagles a "Jekyll-Hyde combination." Jack Sell's theory made as much sense as any. Writing in the *Pittsburgh Post-Gazette*, he noted how the team's first two games were played at night and its second two during the day: "The Pittsburgh-Philadelphia Steagles are a peculiar bunch of pro gridders who seem allergic to daylight and sunshine."

After the game, the coaches threatened unspecified "changes" unless "some of the players [showed] an improvement." An unnamed "spokesman"—probably Greasy Neale—told the papers, "We would be better off to have fewer players and have men who really wanted to win—not just go through the motions." The Steagles' collapse threatened the team's fragile unity. Al Wistert for one had had enough of Neale's profane rants:

> *At the University of Michigan, the coaching staff was a gang of high class people. I never heard any cursing out there on the field. And of course I was raised mainly by my mother and my sisters and I didn't hear any cursing around home. Greasy Neale, every other word he used was a swear word! And that shocked me and it threw me for a loop, so for that first year, I just despised the man, really, and I couldn't get along with him. He wanted to know what was wrong with me. I was supposed to be an all-American football player. "Now what's going on here?" he said. "You're not performing that way." And I said, "I just can't play football for you. You don't know how to handle men. And I can never play football for you." Well, we never spoke the rest of the season.*

To fans the team was beginning to resemble a cross between the same old Steelers and the same old Eagles: The worst of both worlds. With the Redskins winning again, 13-7 over the Cardinals, the Steagles were now in third place, a long fall from the lofty perch they'd occupied just two weeks earlier.

	W	L	T	Pct.
Redskins	3	0	0	1.000
Giants	2	1	0	.667
Steagles	2	2	0	.500
Dodgers	0	5	0	.000

A fresh start was possible, though. The following week the Steagles would return to Pittsburgh to play their first regular season game at Forbes Field. And, fortunately for them, their opponent was the Chicago Cardinals.

ııııı **10** ıııı

Strikes

ALTHOUGH THEY WERE OUTNUMBERED by the Eagles on the team, several Steelers made key contributions to the Steagles, notably end Tony Bova, halfback Johnny Butler, and tackle Ted Doyle. Yet many Pittsburghers felt their team's contributions to the combine were being ignored by Philadelphia. The City of Brotherly Love seemed to be conveniently forgetting the fact that it shared its football team with the Steel City. *Pittsburgh Press* sports editor Chet Smith noted that Eagles owner Lex Thompson had even ordered the team's radio announcer, By Saam, to refrain from uttering the words "Pittsburgh" or "Steagles" on the air when the team played the Bears in Chicago.

"There was not the slightest suggestion on the air that the eleven on the field was a combination of two squads," Smith wrote, "but in one way, the fact that the ears and minds of the good Quakers were not besmirched was entirely satisfactory, for they had to accept full responsibility for the awful shellacking that was administered."

The merger certainly brought the complex relationship between the two cities into sharp focus.

"In Philadelphia," Smith complained, "the merger has received virtually no recognition. There they are known as the Eagles and that is that." It was true. The *Philadelphia Inquirer*'s Art

Morrow dismissed the setup as a "business merger only," and, while the *Inquirer* and the city's evening paper, the *Bulletin,* tended to call the team "Eagles-Steelers" on first reference in stories, the papers reverted to "Eagles" in subsequent references. James W. Cururin, a Steel City soldier stationed in Maryland, wrote the *Post-Gazette* to decry the short shrift given the Steelers.

"I would like to know why Philadelphia papers I get here don't give Pittsburgh any credit for a pro football team," he wrote. "All I read about is the 'Philadelphia Eagles.' Why not give Pittsburgh some credit?"

Although they share the same state and are connected by the Pennsylvania Turnpike, America's first superhighway, Pittsburgh and Philadelphia are divided, physically and psychologically, by the Allegheny Mountains, a sandstone curtain that bisects the state longitudinally. Today the Alleghenies can be easily traversed on the turnpike, but as recently as the nineteenth century the mountains were an insuperable obstacle to the westward expansion of the United States. As a result, Philadelphia and Pittsburgh have quite distinct histories and personalities. In the mid 1700s, while the Founding Fathers were plotting a revolution in Philadelphia, Fort Duquesne (as Pittsburgh was then known) was little more than a swamp, "much infested with venomous Serpents and Muskeetose." Philadelphia was a sophisticated colonial capital, rapidly emerging as the second most influential English-speaking city in the world. Fort Duquesne was a French-controlled outpost in the wilderness, 20 days away on horseback.

In 1758 John Forbes captured the fort for the British and renamed it in honor of Prime Minister William Pitt. The British took advantage of the area's most abundant natural resource, a resource they knew well from home: coal. Soon coal-fired glass- and ironworks were producing supplies for the pioneers making their way west. By 1817 Pittsburgh boasted more than 250 factories, but it wasn't until the 1870s, when the iron horse finally conquered the Alleghenies, that the city really began to grow, its factories at last connected to the Eastern seaboard. Between 1850 and 1900 Pittsburgh's population rose nearly sevenfold, from

46,601 to 321,616. By the time the United States entered World War II, Pittsburgh was the nation's tenth largest city, with a population approaching 700,000. Philadelphia was the third largest, with nearly two million inhabitants.

Both cities were major industrial centers during the war, but of two very different kinds. While Pittsburgh manufactured the raw materials (aluminum, glass, iron, steel), Philadelphia made the finished products (ships, light tanks, airplane parts, ammunition). Pittsburgh was aligned with the great manufacturing centers of the Midwest, Cleveland and Detroit, and its culture was deeply influenced by the waves of immigrants from Central and Eastern Europe whose labors made possible its remarkable prosperity. Philadelphia was decidedly more Eastern, and still shaped by the patrician values of its WASP elite.

Their coal was different, too. Eastern Pennsylvania's homes and factories were fueled by anthracite, a hard coal that burns much cleaner than the softer bituminous variety prevalent west of the Alleghenies. As a result, Pittsburgh was dirtier than Philadelphia, and self-conscious about it. Philadelphians, meanwhile, struggled with their own perceived shortcomings. Wedged between New York and Washington, the two most important cities in the country, Philadelphia could not help but feel inferior. The city's glories were long past. Even the skyline was stunted: A gentlemen's agreement forbade the construction of buildings taller than the 500-foot tower of city hall. In 1940, the renowned Philadelphia architect and urban planner Edmund Bacon called his hometown "the worst, most backward, stupid city that I ever heard of."

Considering their disparate histories and personalities, it's not surprising that the merger of their football teams presented certain difficulties. Philadelphia ignored Pittsburgh's contributions, and Pittsburgh didn't like it. Yet, to a remarkable degree, the Steagles also united the two cities, and in a way that geography and politics never could. In some tiny ways, the Steagles overcame the differences between their two hometowns. The "Phil.-Pitt." that appeared in the agate type of the NFL standings

143

in sports pages represented a breakthrough of sorts. The two cities shared in the unexpected joy of the team's two wins, and commiserated in the misery of the two losses.

"It is a compliment to the club that both Philadelphia and Pittsburgh claim the eleven as its own," wrote Havey Boyle in the *Pittsburgh Post-Gazette.* "They are in [a] better position than Charley Case, the one-time vaudevillian, who said that two cities had a row about his birth place. Chicago insisted he was born in New York and New York insisted he was a Chicagoan."

BEFORE A CHICAGO CARDINALS WORKOUT one day in early October 1943, Clint Wager, a six-foot-six-inch end, was practicing his punting. When a teammate called out to him unexpectedly, Wager was startled. He missed the ball completely and his knee smashed into his forehead. He went into the clubhouse, where the Cardinals' head coach, Phil Handler, "noticed the forehead was dented" and urged him to go to the hospital. X-rays revealed a hairline fracture. By missing the ball and cracking his own skull, Clint Wager neatly (if painfully) epitomized the laughably inept Cardinals franchise.

Founded in Chicago in 1899 as the Morgan Athletic Club, the team became known as the Cardinals in 1901 when its owner, Chris O'Brien, bought a pile of used uniforms from the University of Illinois. The jerseys had faded from a deep maroon to a dull red, which O'Brien cheerfully pronounced "cardinal red." Later known as the Racine Cardinals (because they played at a ballpark on Racine Avenue), the team was a charter member of the National Football League and, now based in Phoenix, Arizona, is one of only two founding members still in the league. The other is the Bears, a team as different from the Cardinals as night from day. While George Halas built the Bears into a powerhouse, the Cardinals became laughingstocks, an afterthought in their own city, not merely perennial losers but cannon fodder for the rest of the league.

In 1929, O'Brien sold the Cardinals to a Chicago dentist named David Jones, who briefly made the team reputable by signing the legendary halfback Ernie Nevers. But that respectability proved fleeting. In 1933, Jones sold the Cardinals to Charlie Bidwill, who restored them to their usual place at the bottom of the Western Division. By 1943 the Cardinals had had just one winning season since Bidwill bought them, going 6-4-2 in 1935—and still managing to finish last. The war siphoned off what little talent the team had, and after the 1942 season the head coach, Jimmy Conzelman, abandoned the franchise for a front-office job with baseball's lowly St. Louis Browns, an indication of just how far the Cardinals had sunk.

After their attempted merger with the Bears was thwarted in June, the Cardinals finally got around to hiring Conzelman's replacement, Phil Handler, who was in pretty much the same boat as Pete Cawthon in Brooklyn—except Handler, who had been Conzelman's assistant for 11 seasons, didn't have the same reservoir of talent from which to draw as Cawthon did (through his Texas Tech connections). Then, in an early season exhibition game, the Cardinals' best player, Marshall Goldberg, broke his ankle. Handler was reportedly reduced to recruiting personnel from the nearby Great Lakes Naval Station, who played under assumed names. The Cardinals lost their first five games by an average score of 21-6. Their sixth game would be in Pittsburgh against the Steagles.

To Greasy Neale, losing to the Bears and Giants, while unacceptable, was at least understandable. They were good teams. But losing to the Cardinals—that would be genuinely embarrassing. That was Neale and Walt Kiesling's constant refrain as they prepared their charges for the game. A reckoning was at hand. Either the Steagles would rise to 3-2 and stay in the Eastern Division race or fall to 2-3 and, for all intents and purposes, be eliminated from it. The two coaches emphasized the gravity of the situation by carrying out their threat to make changes. When the lineup was posted on Saturday, Tony Bova replaced Bill Hewitt at left end and Tom Miller replaced Larry Cabrelli at right end. The coaches explained that they were sacrificing "experience to gain the speed necessary to rush the passer. " It was a remarkable comedown for

Hewitt. Once a perennial all-pro, so quick his nickname was the Offside Kid, he'd been usurped by a half-blind Steeler.

The Steagles left Philadelphia on Saturday morning. Again, the visiting team beat them to Pittsburgh by nearly a week. The Cardinals had come to the city on their way home from a loss in Washington the previous Sunday and worked out at Forbes Field all week. Indeed, the Cardinals spent more time practicing at Forbes Field that week than the Steagles did all season.

On October 31, 1943—Halloween—more than 16,000 fans streamed into Forbes Field to watch their Steelers play football in the green-and-white costume of the Philadelphia Eagles. The crowd was bigger than at either of the Steagles' two regular season games in Philadelphia, an indication of the keen interest in the team in Pittsburgh.

"Our Steagles are coming home!" wrote Chet Smith in the *Pittsburgh Press* on the eve of the game.

The game began ominously for the home team. On the Steagles' first play from scrimmage, Zimmerman, still hobbled by a bruised hip, was sacked and fumbled the ball. The Cardinals recovered on the Phil-Pitt 17. Two plays later, though, Steagles defensive back Ben Kish intercepted a Chicago pass on the 14 and raced 86 yards straight down the right sideline for a touchdown. The Steagles caught the Cardinals unawares on the ensuing kickoff, with Jack Hinkle recovering a perfectly executed onside kick on the Chicago 42. Three plays later Zimmerman fired a 32-yard touchdown pass to Tony Bova. Just like that it was 14-0.

This time the Steagles kicked deep. The Cardinals' Don Cahill tried to catch the ball on his own ten, but it deflected off his hands and rolled into the end zone. Cahill casually went back to down the ball for a touchback but, just as he touched it, Jack Hinkle swooped in and snatched it. Cahill didn't know the rule, but Hinkle did: Having already touched the ball before it entered the end zone, Cahill could not merely down it. He had to return it. It was a live ball. The Steagles were awarded a touchdown. The Cardinals protested bitterly to linesman Charley Berry, but the call stood.

Four minutes into the first quarter the score was 21-0 and the game was effectively over. The Cardinals never put up a fight and the Steagles won easily. The final score was 34-13. The linemen had returned to top form, holding the Cardinals to just 31 rushing yards while the Steagles racked up 167. Tony Bova, Bill Hewitt's replacement, scored two touchdowns. It was not a flawless performance by any means—the Steagles fumbled four times—but it was satisfactory. And with the Giants losing to the Packers, the Steagles had recaptured sole possession of second place. Washington remained undefeated atop the division by dispatching Brooklyn, 48-10. Sammy Baugh set a new NFL record by passing for six touchdowns in that game. When they heard about that, the Steagles must have groaned: They were playing the Redskins the following week in Philadelphia.

But as the fans streamed out of Forbes Field that Sunday, their minds were not long occupied by thoughts of their triumphant Steagles: The nation's coal miners were threatening to go on strike in less than seven hours, at midnight. If they did, Pittsburgh's factories would grind to a halt. War production everywhere would be imperiled. Homes would go unheated. It would make for a very long, cold November.

COAL PROVIDED HALF THE NATION'S ENERGY during the war. It fired the mighty foundries that smelted ore at 3,000°F to make iron and steel. It fueled the factories that shaped those metals into everything from battleships to bullets, and it was burned in humble basement furnaces in millions of homes. The country couldn't run without coal, and the war certainly couldn't be won without it, which is why John L. Lewis, the president of the United Mine Workers union, joined other labor leaders in making a "No-Strike Pledge" immediately after Pearl Harbor.

"Our nation is at war and coal production must not cease," he explained to wildcat strikers in July 1942. "Our every effort must be directed toward this end." Less than a year later, though, Lewis was singing a different tune.

In the spring of 1941, the UMW had won a 16 percent wage

increase for miners. But in April 1942 the government announced that, as part of its anti-inflation program, industrial workers were allowed to make no more than 15 percent above their pay on New Year's Day 1941. Miners were therefore ineligible for further increases. Yet prices, despite all the government's efforts, continued to rise, especially at company stores in the coalfields, where the OPA was simply ignored.

"Two months ago we paid 45 cents per peck of potatoes, now we must pay 75 cents for same thing," Steve Kerlik, a Russian-born miner in western Pennsylvania, complained in the spring of 1943. "If you work and can't buy food, then one day you strike."

Many miners were also heavily in debt to the company stores as a result of the Depression. By the time their accounts were settled on payday, some were left with no more than two dollars in hand.

At the same time, the miners were making many sacrifices. Lewis biographers Melvyn Dubofsky and Warren Van Tine write, "The longer hours and increased mechanization imposed by the wartime demand for coal made mining—already one of the most dangerous jobs in America—even more dangerous. The statistics of miners dead and injured offered Lewis an ultimate justification for wartime strikes. He understood . . . that for miners the battle for production on the home front produced its own body count."

In January 1943, half of eastern Pennsylvania's anthracite miners went on strike, demanding a raise of two dollars a day to nine dollars. Lewis did not authorize the walkout, and he ordered the miners back to work. But it taught him a valuable lesson.

"Lewis," Dubofsky and Van Tine write, "recognizing that the membership had decided the direction it would march, artfully maneuvered his way to the head of the parade."

The no-strike pledge was history. Besides a two-dollar raise, Lewis demanded double time for working Sundays, compensation for the tools that miners were required to buy, and, most controversially, "portal-to-portal" pay for the time it took miners to descend the shafts into the mines at the beginning of the day and return aboveground at the end. (For some miners, the trip took upwards of an hour each way.) Mine operators were not happy, nor was the government, which said the demands, if met, would light the fuse on inflation.

Miners went on strike once in May and twice in June, and in each instance temporary agreements were reached to get them to return to work. The latest agreement would expire at 12:01 a.m. on Monday, November 1.

Although many Americans sympathized with the miners—in one survey, 58 percent said they recognized "some justice" in their demands—the strikes made Lewis one of the most hated men in America.

"Speaking for the American soldier," said an editorial in *Stars and Stripes,* "John L. Lewis, damn your coal-black soul!"

On Monday, November 1, with no new contract in place, 500,000 miners stayed home from work. There were no picket lines or pep rallies, no whistles or chants. There was no need for any of that. The miners were united. None needed convincing to stay home. Given the wartime labor shortage, the strikers were, quite literally, irreplaceable. Roosevelt briefly considered jailing them until his Interior Secretary, Harold Ickes, reminded the president that "a jailed miner produces no more coal than a striking miner." Roosevelt couldn't send troops in either, because, as the union's rallying cry went, "You can't mine coal with bayonets."

Panic buying in the days leading up to the strike had depleted coal reserves, and by Monday afternoon, the first day of the strike, there was already talk of imposing a national blackout to conserve the combustible rocks. In Pittsburgh, the *Press* reported, "there is not a single lump of coal available for retail sale." In the city's fashionable Squirrel Hill neighborhood, desperate homeowners descended on a construction site where a seam of coal had been unearthed. In Philadelphia, a coal rationing plan went into effect, and no household with a supply of ten days or more already on hand was permitted to buy any more.

More ominously, the strike threatened to cripple war production nationwide. The Carnegie-Illinois Steel Corporation announced that the strike would force it to begin reducing iron and steel production Wednesday or Thursday. Mills that had been operating at 100 percent of capacity prepared to reduce to zero. Shortly before 5:00 p.m. on Monday, President Roosevelt seized control of the nation's 3,000 mines and put Interior Secretary Ickes in charge of them. Roosevelt also ordered the strikers back to work the following day, an order the miners refused to obey. They would only answer to another president: John L. Lewis. Meanwhile, Lewis and Ickes began negotiating a settlement.

On Wednesday, U.S. Steel announced that it was shutting down nine blast furnaces in Pittsburgh and Youngstown. Shortly after six o'clock that night, Lewis and Ickes announced that a settlement had been reached.

The miners won a raise of $1.50 a day to $8.50. (Anthracite miners received a slightly smaller increase.) They also won a 45-minute allowance for portal-to-portal travel. The papers immediately hailed the settlement as a smashing victory for Lewis and the miners, but the fine print told a different story. The agreement increased the miners' workday by one hour and reduced their lunch break from 30 minutes to 15, prompting one commentator to quip, "Lewis bargained for eight months and the miners lost their lunch." Before the strike the miners had worked seven hours a day for seven dollars. After the strike they worked eight-and-a-half hours—for eight-and-a-half dollars.

The details did not concern most Americans, though. All that mattered was that coal would be mined again.

However questionable their victory, the miners' militancy emboldened other workers, and, for the rest of the war, strikes would plague vital industries.

The strife would not affect professional football, however. Each player signed a contract with a "reserve clause" that bound him to his employer in perpetuity. There was no free agency. If the player and the club could not agree on a salary, then the salary would be "such as the Club may fix." The players had no benefits: no health insurance, no life insurance, no pension. There was no minimum salary, and players were usually not paid for exhibition games (the source of Roy Zimmerman's dispute with Redskins owner George Preston Marshall). The owners would not formally recognize a players' union until 1968.

AT TRAINING CAMP IN 1937, Redskins head coach Ray Flaherty was showing a hotshot rookie named Sammy Baugh how to throw a pass.

"Sammy, you're in the pros now," Flaherty said to the strapping cowboy from Sweetwater, Texas, "and they want the football where they can catch it. Hit 'em in the eye."

Baugh looked at his coach and asked, "Which eye?"

He wasn't joking.

An all-American football player at Texas Christian University in 1935 and 1936, Samuel Adrian Baugh was planning to pursue a baseball career until George Preston Marshall enticed him to Washington with a contract believed to be worth $8,000. Marshall got a bargain. By the time "Slingin' Sammy" retired after the 1952 season, he was the NFL's career leader in passing attempts (2,995), completions (1,693), completion percentage (56.5), touchdown passes (188), and passing yardage (21,886). Those records have since been eclipsed, but Baugh's influence has not. Almost single-handedly Baugh dragged professional football into the modern era. When he came into the league, passing was an act of desperation. When he left, it was *de rigueur*.

Baugh is remembered as one of the greatest quarterbacks in NFL history, but he wasn't even a quarterback for his first seven seasons in the league. The Redskins didn't adopt the T formation until 1944. Before then Baugh was a tailback, usually in the wing formation, which afforded the passer little protection.

Baugh's extraordinary talents were not limited to passing. He was also one of the greatest punters in NFL history. His lifetime average of 45.1 yards per punt still ranks second all-time. He was an outstanding defensive back as well, intercepting 31 passes before he stopped playing both ways after the 1945 season. And he did it all with good humor and grace and not a trace of pride.

In 1943, Sammy Baugh was at the height of his considerable powers—and the opposition was bereft of talent. (Since he owned a cattle ranch in Texas, Baugh was deferred from the draft.) He would end the season leading the league in passing, punting, and interceptions—football's version of the "triple crown," and a feat never to be duplicated in today's game of specialized players. In 1943, Sammy Baugh was practically unstoppable.

But Greasy Neale and Walt Kiesling thought they could stop him.

Persistent rain limited the Steagles to just two full practice sessions in the week before the Redskins game. At those practices and in the nightly "skull sessions" at the Hotel Philadelphian, Neale and Kiesling drilled into their team the importance of harassing, hampering, and harrying Sammy Baugh. The coaches believed "the best way to stop an aerial attack is to rush the passer so that he must get his tosses off hurriedly." The Steagles would rush Baugh relentlessly to put him off his game.

Redskins head coach Arthur "Dutch" Bergman had his own strategy for winning, and it seemed to be working. Bergman inherited the team when his predecessor, Ray Flaherty, joined the Navy after the 1942 season. Bergman, who had played for Knute Rockne at Notre Dame, immediately replaced Flaherty's single-wing formation with something called the Notre Dame box. (Suffice it to say that it involved a lot of players moving around in the backfield before the snap, but Sammy Baugh still passed a lot.) Considering that the Redskins had just won the championship with the single wing, it was a risky move. But the Redskins responded positively to the new formation and reeled off four straight wins to begin the season. Including the previous year, they had won 13 games in a row.

Philadelphia had not seen the Steagles since their unexpected victory over the Giants at Shibe Park four weeks earlier. Absence, apparently, had made the heart grow fonder: Advance ticket sales for the game were said to be the highest in the history of the Eagles franchise.

Nobody was anticipating the game more keenly than Steagles quarterback Roy Zimmerman. He'd been looking forward to it since the day he was traded from the Redskins to the Eagles.

While the *Washington Times-Herald* claimed Zimmerman "was never completely popular with his teammates" in Washington, he seemed to have no trouble making friends on his new team.

"Zim was a nice person," said halfback Ernie Steele. His teammates also appreciated Zimmerman's leadership.

"He came up and did a pretty good job," said center Ray Graves. "I think he was a good quarterback and took charge pretty good." In Washington, though, Zimmerman was not missed.

"If he were still with Washington," the *Times-Herald* sniffed, "he'd still be sitting out most of the Redskin games." Shortly before the game, a rumor circulated that the Redskins intended to "do a job" on their old teammate. The Steagles intended to do likewise on Sammy Baugh.

Bookmakers made the Redskins ten-point favorites. The point spread was a relatively new concept in 1943. Previously, most bookies set odds. For example, the odds of the Redskins winning would have been 5-to-7, while the odds of the Eagles winning would have been 5-to-1. The point spread was popular with gamblers because it allowed them to bet on underdogs without having to worry about the underdogs actually winning—all they had to do was lose by fewer points than the spread. Bookies liked it too. Under the odds system they could be wiped out if, say, a 100-to-1 long shot actually won. The point spread minimized risk. By adjusting the spread according to the wagering, a shrewd bookie could balance his bets on either side of it and collect his commission—the "vigorish" or "vig." The point spread led to an explosive growth in gambling on pro football and, not coincidentally, in the game's popularity.

The Redskins arrived at Shibe Park about two hours before the 2:30 p.m. kickoff on Sunday, November 7. It was a warm day and by game time the ballpark was filled with, in Art Morrow's words, "a howling, excited multitude of 32,693." The crowd included 3,000 servicemen attending as guests of the Steagles, as well as hundreds of Redskins fans who'd made the trip north. It was the largest audience ever assembled for a National Football League game in Philadelphia.

The multitude was howling and excited nine minutes into the second quarter, when Larry Cabrelli intercepted a Sammy Baugh pass and returned it 24 yards to give the Steagles a 7-0 lead.

The Redskins answered less than four minutes later, when Baugh lobbed a 15-yard pass over the crossbar and into the arms of his favorite receiver, Wilbur Moore, who was dashing across the back of the end zone.

At halftime the score was 7-7.

During the intermission, volunteers from the Navy League passed through the stands collecting donations for the purchase of cigarettes for the troops overseas. According to the organization, servicemen considered smokes "next in importance to food and ammunition."

"Give generously," the Navy League implored. "The least we can do is to keep cartons of cigarettes flowing to them in a constant stream." The tobacco companies did their part by donating millions of cigarettes directly to the armed forces.

Less than a minute into the fourth quarter, with the game still tied at 7-7 and the ball on the Steagles 23, Roy Zimmerman dropped back to punt. The Redskins were well aware that Zimmerman was a notoriously slow punter—he took four steps before he kicked the ball—and this time they came at him with everything they had. The Steagles line could not hold. Bob Masterson infiltrated the right side and blocked the kick. Lou Rymkus, a lumbering 223-pound tackle, scooped up the ball around the three and crawled into the end zone on his hands and knees. Masterson kicked the extra point to give the Redskins a 14-7 lead.

Bobby Thurbon returned the subsequent kickoff to the Steagles 45. A pass to Tony Bova advanced the ball to the Redskins 35. Then Zimmerman lobbed a short pass to Ernie Steele, who was standing near the left sideline. Steele caught the ball and streaked downfield behind a wall of blockers. He was tackled just as he crossed the goal line. The Redskins complained vehemently that Steele had stepped out of bounds a yard shy of the end zone, but the touchdown stood.

"I caught the pass and made the touchdown and Zimmerman wanted to take all the credit," Steele later joked. "He said, 'I called that play just for you!'"

Zimmerman converted the extra point to tie the score.

The Redskins threatened to take the lead in the game's waning moments, but Ray Graves intercepted a Baugh pass on the Steagles 12 to extinguish the threat. Fifteen seconds later the final gun sounded, ending the game at 14-14. The Redskins' 13-game winning streak was over.

The Redskins hadn't lost but they had been beaten. Bob Seymour took a knee in the ribs. Dick Farman picked up an ugly black eye. Early in the fourth quarter running back Andy Farkas was tackled so viciously that his pants were ripped off, forcing Washington to expend a valuable timeout so he could change into a new pair while his teammates huddled around him. It had been a hellacious game, "a slam-bang brawling affair from start to finish, with a lot of roughhouse tactics tossed in," according to the *Washington Times-Herald*'s Vincent Flaherty. The animosity between the teams was palpable. Much of it stemmed from Zimmerman's feud with Redskins owner George Preston Marshall, but Ray Graves said it went deeper than that: "There were players on both teams who had played against each other in college and didn't like each other." And with only four officials to police the action (as opposed to seven today)—and no facemasks to get in the way—scores were easy to settle.

The Steagles' tactic of ruthlessly harassing Sammy Baugh was a smashing success. Although he still managed to pass for 147 yards, Baugh did not resemble the passer who had thrown a record six touchdown passes just a week earlier. He spent much of the game running for his life. Steagles guard Rocco Canale broke through the Washington line and ripped Baugh's burgundy No. 33 jersey off his back—twice. (The jerseys were made of tightly woven wool and did not tear easily.) Baugh played much of the first half in tatters, his left arm exposed to the shoulder and his white undershirt visible on his back.

"Baugh . . . was roughed, slammed and walloped," wrote Vincent Flaherty. The Steagles had definitely done a job on Baugh, but Roy Zimmerman did not escape unscathed. The Redskins roughed him up at every opportunity, and he suffered a deep gash in the back of his left leg when Bob Masterson spiked him late in the game.

Like their teams, Baugh and his former understudy played to a standoff. Each threw one touchdown pass and three interceptions. Both punted brilliantly. And both were on the field nearly the entire game: Baugh played 55 minutes, Zimmerman 59. Despite the new rule allowing unlimited substitution, most coaches still kept their 11 starters in the game as much as possible.

"They didn't really take advantage of it," Steagles tackle Ted Doyle said of the new rule. "I guess it's because it was foreign to the coaches. They didn't recognize it as an opportunity—which it really was, a big opportunity—but they didn't recognize it as such."

After the game, Zimmerman limped into the Redskins locker room to shake hands with his former teammates. The hatchet was buried—but when the teams met again in three weeks it was sure to be dug up. The Redskins already had retribution on their minds.

Greasy Neale, who turned 52 two days before the game, considered the tie something of a birthday gift, but tie games were one of the NFL's nagging bugaboos. On the same day the Steagles and Redskins tied, the Giants and Lions played to a 0-0 draw on a hopelessly muddy field at Briggs (later Tiger) Stadium in Detroit—the last scoreless game in league history.

Tie games frustrated players and fans alike. Between 1920 and 1932, 11 percent of all games ended without a winner (or a loser). After the 1932 season, the league moved the goalposts from the back of the end zone, where they had been since 1927, up to the goal line, to encourage more field goal attempts and, in the process, reduce the number of ties. To some extent it worked. The number of tie games dropped from ten to five in a year. But throughout the 1940s, 4.3 percent of all games still ended inconclusively, and in 1943 the figure was 7.5 percent. What's more, the league did not count tie games in the standings until 1972. Before then, a tie was disregarded. Since then, it has counted as half a win and half a loss. So, after a bruising 60 minutes on the gridiron, the game between the Steagles and the Redskins simply never happened, at least as far as the standings were concerned. (The NFL finally added one extra period of sudden-death overtime in 1974, and in the ensuing 30 years there were only 15 ties— an average of one every two seasons, or 0.2 percent of all games.) Still, a tie was better than a loss, and the Steagles had regained sole custody of second place:

	W	L	T	Pct.
Redskins	4	0	1	1.000
Steagles	3	2	1	.600
Giants	2	2	1	.500
Dodgers	1	6	0	.143

The Steagles' odds of winning the division were still long, but surmountable. For one thing, the schedule was in their favor. The Redskins still had to play the Lions, the Bears, the Steagles, and the Giants (twice), opponents with a cumulative record of 14-8. The Steagles only had to face the Dodgers, the Lions, the Redskins, and the Packers, who were a combined 12-12. Looking ahead to the next two weeks, the *Pittsburgh Post-Gazette*'s Jack Sell could not resist daydreaming: "The ideal set of results for local fans . . . would have the favored Steagles repeat over Brooklyn with the underdog Detroit upsetting the Redskins. That would place emphasis on the meeting of the Steagles and Lions in Forbes Field on Sunday, November 21, and, with the Chicago Bears invading Washington that afternoon, might eventually have the Steagles boosted into a tie for the Eastern lead by nightfall on the twenty-first."

Sell's math was a little off: if the Steagles won their next two games and the Redskins lost theirs, Phil-Pitt would actually claim sole possession of first place by mere percentage points (0.714 to 0.667). It was a preposterous notion.

Two days after the Redskins game, Bill Hewitt quit the Steagles. The ostensible reason for his departure was patriotism.

"I presume he felt he could not do justice to his war job and still play with us," Bert Bell said. But the truth was, the Offside Kid was washed up. In six games he had caught just two passes and scored no touchdowns.

"It was a shame, but that's the way it was," said tackle Vic Sears. "Nobody beats old age." At 34, Bill Hewitt just couldn't play anymore—and he didn't want to, not even for $400 a game.

"Candidly," he wrote a year later of his abortive comeback, "I wasn't worth the money. Nobody would be at the age of thirty-three [*sic*], after three years away from the game. But in my poorest season as a player I enjoyed the one big financial year I have had since I left college. Maybe there's a kind of poetic justice in that."

Bill Hewitt never did find meaningful, well-paying employment outside football. After the war he took a job as a purchasing agent for a milk company, but that didn't work out. Then he decided to open his own automobile dealership, to take advantage of the postwar boom in car sales.

On the afternoon of Tuesday, January 14, 1947, he was driving home alone from a business meeting when his car skidded off the road and crashed into a culvert along Route 309 in eastern Pennsylvania, about halfway between Bethlehem and Philadelphia. A passing motorist found the football great unconscious behind the wheel and drove him to Grandview Hospital in Sellersville, Pennsylvania. There Hewitt regained consciousness. He asked the doctors to "go easy" when telling his wife of the accident. Although he had suffered a broken rib and punctured lung, Hewitt minimized the extent of his injuries. A few minutes later he was dead. He was 37. The cause of the accident was never discovered. At the time, police said, the road was "not unduly slippery."

In 1971, Bill Hewitt was inducted into the Pro Football Hall of Fame in Canton, Ohio.

BRUISED AND BATTERED, the Steagles began preparing for their upcoming game against the Dodgers in Brooklyn. Roy Zimmerman, who had injured his groin and hip earlier in the season, was now nursing a wounded leg. It had taken six stitches to mend the gash he'd suffered in the Redskins game. When he showed up for practice on Tuesday, he was on crutches. It scarcely seemed possible he could play the following Sunday, though the Dodgers probably didn't know that. At the time teams were not required to publicly disclose player injuries. (The NFL changed that in 1947, mainly to prevent gamblers from exploiting inside information.)

Zimmerman wasn't the only aching Steagle. The locker room resembled an infirmary. Jack Hinkle was still suffering the lingering effects of a concussion he'd sustained in training camp. Vic Sears was playing with a broken finger. Bobby Thurbon had a pulled muscle in his leg. Ben Kish had a bruised knee.

In pro football's early days, players were left to treat their injuries on their own time and at their own expense. A few enterprising and sympathetic owners made arrangements with local doctors to provide care, such as Art Rooney, whose early Hope-Harvey team in Pittsburgh was named in part for one Dr. Harvey, who treated injured players. But most owners were not nearly so accommodating.

"We didn't even have a trainer," Tuffy Leemans recalled discovering upon joining the Giants in 1936. "In those days, if you wanted to get rid of a charley horse, there was only one method they knew of. They would take a broom handle and roll it out. They would lay you down on a table and roll that broom handle over your thigh. You'd have tears in your eyes as big as lemons."

By the 1940s most teams kept a doctor on call to tend to major injuries, often in exchange for free tickets. The Steagles' doctor "wasn't the greatest in the world," said halfback Ernie Steele: "Mostly he'd just talk to you and try to make you feel good. Moral support. If we really had a problem we'd go to the hospital." Sprains, contusions, and other less serious ailments were treated by the trainer, Fred Schubach, who doubled as the team's equipment manager. The treatments were rudimentary, often nothing more than a warm bath followed by a rubdown. Some players lathered their body in pungent liniments, as Bill Hewitt had. Halfback Jack Hinkle would "get in the tub with the Epsom salts and stay there for hours and hours." The player shortage, not to mention machismo, compelled many injured players to try to "walk it off" or simply play through the pain, however excruciating.

"We had a saying," tackle Bucko Kilroy said. "Don't get hurt, because if you get hurt you have to play anyway."

Al Wistert remembered limping to the sideline in the middle of a game: "Greasy Neale looked at me and he's puzzled and he says, 'What's the matter?' And I said, 'I think I've broken my leg.' And he says, 'Well get back in there until you're sure!' That's the way it was in those days." (Wistert's leg, it turned out, was not broken.)

Neale kept warning the Steagles not to take the Dodgers lightly. He was worried about a "letdown" after their "brilliant performance" against the Redskins. Neale also knew Brooklyn had improved vastly since getting steamrolled by the Steagles on October 2. After opening the season with four straight shutout losses, the Dodgers managed to post 21 points against the Bears and ten against the Redskins in laudable losing efforts. Then, just a week before facing the Steagles again, they finally broke into the win column with a 7-0 victory over the Cardinals.

Injuries had plagued the Dodgers early in the season. In his first game back after recovering from the torn muscle he'd suffered when he tripped over his helmet in training camp, Dean McAdams, the team's ace passer, broke three bones in his hand. Merlyn Condit, another passer, tore a muscle in his leg. Considering the circumstances, head coach Pete Cawthon had done a remarkable job simply keeping the team afloat.

"What with the injuries on top of a general lack of material," Cawthon said, "we have to do a bit of juggling to keep all eleven positions filled for the sixty minutes of a game."

But now the Dodgers were finally healthy. McAdams and Condit had played well against the Cardinals. So had Andy Kowalski, a rookie end from Gloucester, New Jersey, by way of Mississippi State. Kowalski had appeared unannounced at the Dodgers' training camp and asked for a tryout. Against the Cardinals he caught five passes and "was quite a busybody" on defense. Even Cawthon's Texas Tech alums were much improved. To ready the Dodgers for the Steagles' T formation, Cawthon had them scrimmage Brooklyn College at Ebbets Field. The Kingsmen were still running the T that Allie Sherman had helped head coach Lou Oshins install two years earlier. On the eve of the Steagles game, Cawthon pronounced the Dodgers "better prepared for this game than for any other contest" all season.

The Steagles couldn't be faulted for feeling overconfident, though. After all, they'd held the Dodgers to minus 33 yards rushing in their first encounter. The Steagles were still ranked second in the league in overall defense and first in rushing defense. On offense, the line was blocking so effectively—and the backs were running so efficiently—that four of the top 16 rushers in the league were Steagles: Johnny Butler, Ernie Steele, Jack Hinkle, and Bobby Thurbon. The mood of the team was good, too. In the *Post-Gazette*, Havey Boyle noted the "friendly atmosphere" among the players in the wake of the Redskins game.

If only their starting quarterback was healthy.

On Friday night Roy Zimmerman was still on crutches. Allie Sherman, who had practiced with the first team all week, was named Zimmerman's replacement. Sherman was confident. Although he had played only sparingly, his statistics compared favorably with Zimmerman's. In fact, Sherman had a higher completion percentage (40%) than Zimmerman (33%). At the same time Sherman, a 20-year-old rookie from Brooklyn, couldn't help but feel nervous and excited. Not only would he be starting his first NFL game, he would be doing it in his proverbial backyard, at a ballpark he'd always dreamed of playing in: Ebbets Field.

Ebbets Field secured its place in pro football history on October 22, 1939, when the Dodgers hosted the Eagles. It was one of the most monumental football games ever played—though hardly anybody who was there knew it at the time. The Dodgers won, 23-14, with Brooklyn's veteran fullback Ace Gutowsky making a brief appearance and rushing for seven yards—just enough to make him the league's all-time leading rusher with 3,399 yards. But what made the game historic was the fact that it was the first NFL game to be shown on television. NBC station W2XBS, which had broadcast a baseball game from Ebbets Field earlier that year, carried the game as an experiment. The 13,000 fans watching the game in person probably outnumbered the television audience. There were only about 1,000 TV sets in all of New York City. A few hundred curious visitors to the World's Fair in Queens also watched, on monitors set up at the RCA Pavilion. The announcer was Allen "Skip" Waltz, a former NYU football star who covered sports for W2XBS. Two cameras were used, one next to Waltz in the mezzanine and one on the field.

"It was . . . a cloudy day," Waltz later said, "and when the sun crept behind the stadium there wasn't enough light for the cameras. The picture would get darker and darker and eventually it would be completely blank and we'd revert to a radio broadcast."

But W2XBS deemed the experiment a success. At least football was easier to follow on television than baseball. The fledgling station decided to carry more Dodgers games that season. None of the players who took part in the game had any idea it was being televised, even many years later, and the papers made no mention of the fact the next day. But out of those first faint, flickering black-and-white images grew a colossus. In 1949 the league's television revenue totaled $75,000. By 2005 the NFL had signed contracts with CBS, DirecTV, ESPN, FOX, and NBC collectively worth more than $3 billion annually.

Even for the woeful Dodgers, the attendance for the Steagles game on November 14 was disappointing: 7,614. It was the league's smallest crowd of the season. One reason was the bitterly cold weather. Another was Sid Luckman. Just 15 miles from Ebbets Field, the Polo Grounds was packed with more than 56,000 fans eager to see Luckman and his Chicago Bears square off against the Giants.

Of all the league's scheduling problems, the New York situation was the most intractable. Dodgers owner Dan Topping was also the president of the baseball Yankees, and when he bought the football team in 1934 he'd hoped to move it into Yankee Stadium. But Giants owner Tim Mara blocked the move because he felt it would infringe on his franchise's territory. (The Polo Grounds and Yankee Stadium were less than a mile apart and within sight of each other.) As a result of their feud, Topping and Mara frequently scheduled their teams at home on the same date, to the detriment of both, but mostly the Dodgers.

On Sunday morning, Greasy Neale took Allie Sherman aside and told him he would not be the starting quarterback after all. Roy Zimmerman said he felt well enough to play at least part of the game, so Neale had decided to use him—but only on passing plays. Halfback Johnny Butler would move under center and take the snaps on running plays. Sherman was not happy. He thought Neale had made a bad decision. It was, in fact, a staggeringly bad decision, certainly one of the worst of Greasy Neale's long and storied coaching career. He completely undermined the cornerstone of the T formation—or any formation for that matter: the element of surprise.

It didn't take long for the Dodgers to figure out exactly what was going on: When Zimmerman limped gingerly onto the field, the Steagles were going to pass. When Butler lined up at quarterback, they were going to run. The Dodgers adjusted their defense accordingly and, except for a three-yard touchdown run by Bobby Thurbon midway through the first period, they completely shut down the Steagles. Brooklyn scored touchdowns on a one-yard run in the second quarter and a 65-yard pass in the third and won the lackluster game 13-7. The result even surprised Dodgers owner and Marine captain Dan Topping, who had just returned from action in the Pacific and was attending his first game of the season.

"Why, this Brooklyn team isn't as bad as I had pictured it to be," Topping said afterwards. "I did not learn the results until after the first four games had been played, so when the bad news came all at once I expected the worst. But now that I've had a look at them, I'd say the boys are pretty fair." It was the first time Topping had seen his team win a game in person since December 7, 1941, when the Dodgers spoiled Tuffy Leemans Day at the Polo Grounds.

The Steagles had once again played stellar defense, holding the Dodgers to just 176 total yards, but on offense Neale's strategy had failed miserably. Roy Zimmerman completed just one pass. He also threw an interception that led to the first Brooklyn touchdown. The feeling in the locker room after the game was one of utter dejection. Coming so soon after the ecstasy of the Redskins game made the loss doubly hard to take. There was no lack of second-guessing in the papers the next day, and although the criticism was mild compared to today's vituperative sports radio shows, for the time it was quite pointed. In the *Pittsburgh Press,* Cecil Muldoon wrote, "There was little doubt today—or all yesterday afternoon for that matter—that the Steagles could have won from the Dodgers if Neale hadn't kept sending the injured Zimmerman into the game."

"It was a heartbreaker for the crippled Steagles to lose," wrote Jack Sell in the *Post-Gazette,* ". . . it would have been better had Zimmy been kept on the sidelines."

The fans who went to the Polo Grounds instead of Ebbets Field that day made the right choice. Sid Luckman completed seven touchdown passes to break Sammy Baugh's two-week-old record as the Bears mauled the Giants 56-7. Not to be upstaged, Baugh set a different record that day: He made four interceptions in the Redskins' 42-20 declawing of the Lions. Both records have since been equaled, but neither has been broken. By virtue of the Giants loss, the Steagles maintained possession of second place. However, their odds of winning the division had been reduced to the dreaded "mathematical possibility." Under the headline "DODGERS KNOCK LOCALS OUT OF RACE," the *Philadelphia Daily News* erroneously reported the next day that the Steagles had "lost their chance" for the title. It wasn't true, but unless the

Steagles won their remaining three games—and the Redskins fell apart—it would be. The new standings:

	W	L	T	Pct.
Redskins	5	0	1	1.000
Steagles	3	3	1	.500
Giants	2	3	1	.400
Dodgers	2	6	0	.250

Thanksgiving

ONE HOT SUMMER DAY IN 1939, somewhere on the outskirts of Youngstown, Ohio, University of Georgia assistant football coach Bill Hartman pulled his Plymouth into a filling station and asked the attendant to fill the tank and check the oil. Hartman was on his way home from a fruitless recruiting trip. Head coach Wally Butts had sent him north to convince the best high school back in Ohio to play for the Bulldogs, but by the time Hartman reached the kid he'd already decided to go to Ohio State. Now Hartman had a day and a half to figure out how to break the news to Butts. That's how long the drive back to Athens would take.

Noticing his Georgia plates, the attendant asked Hartman what had brought him up to Ohio. When Hartman told him, the attendant said, "Well, the best back in the state really lives right down the street here, about three or four blocks."

"Who is that?" Hartman asked.

"Well," said the attendant, "that's Frank Sinkwich."

Two and a half years later, on New Year's Day 1942, five-foot-ten, 185-pound Frank Sinkwich, now a junior at Georgia, passed for three touchdowns and ran for another as the Bulldogs demolished Texas Christian 33-7 to win the Orange Bowl. Exactly one year after that, Sinkwich scored the only touchdown in a 9-0 Georgia win over UCLA before 90,000 fans in the Rose Bowl.

"Fireball" Sinkwich ended his college career with 2,331 yards passing and 2,271 yards rushing—4,602 total yards, 322 more than Red Grange had amassed at Illinois. Sinkwich also passed for 30 touchdowns and rushed for 30 more. He won the 1942 Heisman Trophy—the first player from the Southeastern Conference so honored.

On April 8, 1943, the Detroit Lions made him the first overall pick in the NFL draft, but Frank Sinkwich had a prior engagement—with the Marine Corps. On Thursday, July 15, he reported for boot camp at Parris Island. By the following Monday his feet were blistered and sore from all the marching.

"I'm not surprised," said Sinkwich. "I knew it was tough." If he survived another six and a half weeks, he'd be sent to Quantico for officer training school. His goal, Sinkwich said, was to get the war over "as soon as possible" so he could play pro football. It wouldn't be soon enough for Lions owner Fred Mandel. His team desperately needed Frank Sinkwich.

The Lions joined the NFL in 1930 as the Portsmouth Spartans. Portsmouth sits on the north side of the Ohio River in southernmost Ohio, just across from Kentucky. In 1930 it was an industrial town of 42,000 with a passion for football. Led by coach George "Potsy" Clark, the Spartans finished second in the league in 1931 and barely missed capturing the title the following season, losing the famous and controversial (in Portsmouth, anyway) indoor championship game to the Bears.

By the 1933 season the Spartans and the Green Bay Packers were the only two "town teams" left in a league that just seven years earlier included franchises in Pottsville, Duluth, Dayton, Racine, Canton, and Hammond (Indiana). The Spartans and the Packers had something else in common: Both clubs were hemorrhaging cash. In Green Bay local residents kicked in $15,000 to save the Packers, reorganizing the team as a publicly owned nonprofit corporation with a local board of directors. (It is still the only publicly owned pro sports team in North America.) To raise cash the team could periodically sell stock. If the team was sold, the profits were to go to the local American Legion post. (In 1997 the beneficiary was changed to the team's charitable arm, the Green Bay Packers Foundation.) Portsmouth, although its population was slightly larger than Green Bay's, was much harder hit by the Depression and simply couldn't raise that kind of money. The city's love of football was undiminished, but few could afford the luxury of paying fifty cents to watch it, much less buy shares in a team.

"Hell," recalled Earl "Dutch" Clark, the team's star passer, "we'd get 4,000 or 5,000 people out to watch practice and at game time we'd be lucky if we had 2,000." By the end of the 1933 season the team couldn't meet its payroll.

Early the following year, a radio executive named George A. "Dick" Richards swooped in and bought the franchise, moving it to Detroit and renaming it the Lions, a nod to the city's baseball team, the Tigers. The change of scenery did not diminish the team's performance. With Potsy Clark still at the helm, the Lions won the 1935 championship. In 1940, Richards sold the team to Fred Mandel, a Chicago department store magnate, for $200,000. Nineteen forty was also Potsy Clark's last year as head coach and the Lions finished 5-5-1. In 1941 they finished 4-6-1—the team's first losing season since its inaugural campaign in Portsmouth. In 1942 the bottom fell out: 0-11. Age and war had taken their toll. With their best players retired and no replacements available, the Lions were hapless. They scored only five touchdowns all season and never scored more than seven points in a single game. Even worse, their average attendance fell 40 percent from the previous season, to 14,000 a game.

In 1943, Mandel asked Charles "Gus" Dorias to right the ship. Dorias was something of a football revolutionary. Playing for Notre Dame against Army on November 1, 1913, he completed 14 of 17 passes for 243 yards and three touchdowns. One completion went for 40 yards—the longest passing play in football history to that time. Never before had the forward pass been used so effectively. In 1925 Dorias became the head coach at the University of Detroit, a position he held for 18 seasons (17 of them winning).

When the school suspended its football program for the duration, Fred Mandel immediately hired him to coach the Lions.

Dorias was a proponent of what (for the time) was considered wide-open football. Although his preferred formation was the Notre Dame box (naturally), his teams threw a lot of passes—even deep in their own territory, a risk that most coaches considered insane.

Although Dorias faced a major rebuilding effort when he took over the team, the Lions were not completely bereft of talent. They had Harry "Hippity" Hopp, a decent back who could run as well as pass. They also had Alex "Wojie" Wojciechowicz, who had been one of Fordham University's famed "Seven Blocks of Granite." Quick and versatile, the five-eleven, 217-pound Wojciechowicz played center on offense and linebacker on defense. He was renowned for his vicious hits on pass receivers. Still, it would take more than Hippity Hopp and Wojie to make the Lions roar again.

Then, quite unexpectedly, Gus Dorias got some very good news.

As boot camp progressed, Frank Sinkwich's feet never got better. They were always sore. It didn't seem unusual at first: Recruits' feet always hurt. But after a month, Sinkwich was still in agony. One morning he fell out on sick call and limped to the dispensary, where an examination revealed something missed in his induction physical: flat feet. As they prevented a marine "from properly performing his duty"—i.e., marching—the Marine Corps considered flat feet a disqualifying condition. On September 11, 1943, less than two months after his induction, Sinkwich was given an honorable discharge for physical disability. It was an ironic and slightly humiliating turn for the Heisman Trophy winner and first overall pick in the NFL draft, and Sinkwich promised himself he would somehow find a way to get back into the service. In the meantime, he would play pro football.

On September 14, three days after his discharge, Sinkwich signed a contract with the Lions. Five days after that, Sinkwich made his professional debut against the Chicago Cardinals. Although he had practiced with the team for just two days, Sinkwich threw a 17-yard touchdown pass in Detroit's 35-17 victory. In their first game of the season the Lions had managed to score as many touchdowns as they had in all of the previous campaign.

The schedule-makers were kind to the Lions. The following week they played Brooklyn and dispatched the Dodgers with ease, 27-0. Reality intervened on October 3 in the form of the Chicago Bears, though the loss was not as substantial as might have been expected: 27-21. By the time they met the Steagles in Pittsburgh on November 21, Detroit's record was 3-5-1—not spectacular, but a drastic improvement over the previous season. (Due to the league's unusual scheduling, their game against the Steagles would be the Lions' tenth and final contest of the season. By contrast, the Redskins and Giants had played just six each.)

Frank Sinkwich had lived up to his advance billing. He led the Lions in rushing and passing. Harry Hopp was the team's leading scorer, primarily as the beneficiary of Sinkwich's passes. If you discounted that 0-0 game against the Giants in the quagmire, the Lions were averaging three touchdowns a game. Not bad for a team that had not scored more than seven points in a single game the previous season. Improved, too, was attendance: at 30,750 per game, the Lions were averaging more than twice as many fans as in 1942.

The Steagles were not taking the Lions lightly, particularly after the previous week's fiasco in Brooklyn. They still had a lot to play for. If they lost, all hope of catching the Redskins and winning the division would be lost as well. There was also second place to think about. The third-place Giants were only percentage points behind the Steagles, and this week they were playing the Chicago Cardinals, practically an automatic win.

Second place was not just a moral victory. The runner-up in each division got a share of the championship game pot. A year earlier, each of the Steelers had collected $108.06 for finishing second in the East. That was nothing to sneeze at. The Steagles were also eager to maintain their standing as the best defensive team in the league, having yielded to their opponents an average of just 182.1 yards per game. There were personal goals to achieve as well. Heading into the game, Jack Hinkle was the sixth leading rusher in the league with 263 yards, and Johnny Butler was right behind him in seventh place with 256. A rushing title was not out of the question for either player.

Just before the game, the Steagles got some good news: Lions center/linebacker Alex Wojciechowicz would not be able to play due to an injured knee. As far as the Steagles were concerned, his timing was perfect. Their receivers could breathe a little easier. The Steagles, on the other hand, would be at full strength. The gash in quarterback Roy Zimmerman's leg had healed so well that he was expected to play the entire game. Only Ernie Steele, who had suffered a bad charley horse in the Dodgers game, was questionable.

Steelers co-owner Art Rooney was hoping even harder than usual for a big crowd for what would be the Steagles' final appearance at Forbes Field. Bert Bell had been ribbing him mercilessly about the record-breaking attendance at the Redskins game in Philadelphia two weeks earlier. Ever since the two men had become partners after the 1940 season, Bell, the Philadelphian, had chided Rooney, the Pittsburgher, about Philadelphia's superiority as a football city. When he saw the crowds waiting to get into Shibe Park before the Redskins game, Rooney had moaned sarcastically, "I was hoping for a nice little rain, but look how the sun is shining. I can hear Bell poppin' off already." Rooney even joked about going door to door to ensure an impressive turnout for the Lions game. He didn't need to. Interest in the game was high in Pittsburgh, mainly because it marked the local debut of Frank Sinkwich, who hailed from just across the border in Youngstown. At least a thousand fans from Sinkwich's hometown were expected to attend the game.

Rooney couldn't have asked for better weather on Sunday, November 21. It was an unusually clear, crisp day in Pittsburgh, and when the Lions kicked off to the Steagles at 2:30 that afternoon the stands were filled with more than 23,000 fans, 7,000 more than had seen the Steagles' previous game at Forbes Field. They were treated to what one sportswriter called "one of the wildest games ever played in the National Football League." High up in the University of Pittsburgh's 42-story Cathedral of Learning building, the school's basketball coach, Henery "Cliff" Carlson, was settling in for an afternoon's work when he went to a window and glanced down at Forbes Field. The game was just getting under way:

> *There was the kickoff and another play, I believe. Then suddenly a backfield man was streaking out in the open. Afterwards I learned that was Jack Hinkle loose on a 56-yard run with Frankie Sinkwich tackling him from behind. Somehow, I sensed that this was to be "the ball game" of the year. I made a beeline for the elevator, borrowed an overcoat from a friend and rushed to the ballpark. My hunch was right, too. That was some battle.*

The Lions scored touchdowns on a 98-yard kickoff return, a two-yard run, an 88-yard pass-and-lateral, a 71-yard pass, and a one-yard run—five in all. The Steagles' touchdowns were less spectacular but equally numerous: a four-yard run, a one-yard run, a two-yard run, a seven-yard pass, and another two-yard run. It was an offensive display rarely seen before in pro football. The ten total touchdowns were just one short of the league record at the time. The lead changed hands four times. It was a game that either team could have won. And it all came down to an extra point.

THE IMPORTANCE OF KICKING IN FOOTBALL has waxed and waned. Before 1900 a field goal was actually worth more points (five) than a touchdown (four). (A kicked goal after a touchdown was worth two points.) Players were prized for their kicking abilities, a vestige of the game's hazy origins in soccer and rugby. Most players employed the dropkick, where the ball is dropped and booted at the moment it hits the ground. Since the ball was shaped like a watermelon, it bounced true and was easy to kick. Stories of early pros dropkicking field goals of 50 yards or more are common (though difficult to verify). But by the time the National Football League was formed in 1920, the touchdown (six points) had long supplanted the field goal (three points) as the preferred mode of scoring, and by 1932 kicking had fallen so out of favor that just six field goals were made all season—an average of only one every ten games!

Kicking enjoyed a brief renaissance when the goalposts were moved forward to the goal line in 1933, but it took a big step backward the following year, when the shape of the ball was changed to encourage more forward passing.

The maximum circumference around the short axis—the middle of the ball—was reduced to 21.25 inches. That was 1.75 inches slimmer than the ball that was used in the 1920s. (The maximum circumference around the long axis was unchanged at 28.5 inches.) The new, bullet-shaped ball—the familiar prolate spheroid—was much easier to throw, but it was nearly impossible to dropkick. Dropkicking specialists faded from the game. Detroit's Dutch Clark was the last player to dropkick a field goal in the NFL, in a game against the Cardinals on September 19, 1937. And until Doug Flutie of the New England Patriots did it as a stunt in a game on New Year's Day 2006, the last player to dropkick an extra point successfully was the Bears' Ray McLean in the 1941 championship game.

By 1943, the familiar placekick—where the ball is snapped to a kneeling holder who places it upright on the ground for the kicker—was the only means employed to score points by foot. Not that it was employed very often. Green Bay's Don Hutson led the league in field goals in 1943—with three. And with coaches underutilizing free substitution and rosters reduced by the war, there was no room for a kicking specialist. The duty fell to players as a secondary responsibility. It was an afterthought.

Some of the most renowned kickers in league history played other positions primarily. Don Hutson was an end, the Cleveland Browns' Lou Groza was a tackle, and George Blanda, who played for four teams between 1949 and 1975, was a quarterback. And they kicked the ball straight on, with their toes. It was a practical, unpretentious style. It wasn't until rosters were expanded in the 1960s that teams began hiring kicking "specialists," often Europeans who kicked the football the same way they kicked a soccer ball. Pete Gogolak, who was signed by the Buffalo Bills in 1964, was the first soccer-style kicker in the pros. The son of Hungarian refugees, Gogolak played football only because his high school in Ogdensburg, New York, had no soccer team. Soccer-style kickers proved so accurate that in 1974 the goalposts were returned to the back of the end zone.

WITH THE STEAGLES LEADING 14-7 late in the second quarter, the Lions mounted an 11-play, 64-yard drive that culminated with Elmer Hackney plunging over the goal line from the two. The two teams lined up for the extra point. Detroit's kicker was a six-foot, 234-pound lineman named Augie Lio, who, despite his bulk, was fairly accurate. He converted 21 of 23 extra point attempts in 1943, a success rate of 91 percent, not far off the league average of 93 percent. (Today the success rate is 99 percent—and the goalposts are ten yards farther away.) The ball was snapped. Ernie Steele—who wasn't even expected to play because of a charley horse—slipped through a gap in the Detroit line. He raised his meaty right hand and the ball deflected off it.

"I remember blockin' that kick," Steele said. "I remember goin' up and getting the ball." The half ended with the score 14-13 Steagles.

Halfway through the third period the Lions were leading 20-14 when the Steagles engineered a 67-yard drive that ended with a two-yard Bobby Thurbon touchdown run. Roy Zimmerman converted the extra point, but the Steagles were offside. The ball was moved five yards back and Zimmerman had to try again. His second attempt sailed wide of the uprights, but this time it was the Lions who were offside. The ball was moved five yards forward to its original position. Zimmerman's third kick was perfect, neither team was offside, and the score was 21-20 Steagles. Each team scored two more touchdowns in the fourth quarter, successfully converting the extra points each time. The Steagles won the game, 35-34. William "Red" Friesell, a retired NFL referee who'd officiated the Bears' 73-0 win in the 1940 championship game, watched the game in the press box.

"I guess I've seen everything now," Friesell said as the final gun sounded.

Art Rooney couldn't have asked for a better way to end the season in Pittsburgh.

"I've waited ten years for a game like that," he said, "and I'm certainly glad it happened this season."

Jack Hinkle had his best game of the season, rushing for 132 yards, enough to move him into third place among the league leaders. But Johnny Butler stayed right on his tail, rushing 55 yards to move up to fourth place. On defense, the Steagles surrendered 379 total yards and their ranking dropped from first to third behind the Redskins and the Bears. Still, they held Frank Sinkwich to negative yards rushing, and he completed just seven of 11 passes for 125 yards, no touchdowns, and two interceptions.

It was an exhilarating victory. The feeling in the steamy locker room afterwards was the opposite of the previous week at Ebbets Field. But there was disappointing news from Washington: Even with Sammy Baugh sidelined with an abscessed tooth and a bruised knee, the Redskins still managed to upset the Bears 21-7. It was Chicago's first regular season defeat in 23 games. The star of the game was Baugh's substitute, George Cafego, whom the Redskins had purchased from the Dodgers for $100 a week earlier. If he hadn't been traded, it would have been Roy Zimmerman's chance to shine in Washington. But he would get that opportunity the following Sunday, when the Steagles played the Redskins at Griffith Stadium.

As expected, the Giants easily dismissed the Cardinals, 24-13, to keep pace with the Steagles in the battle for second place:

	W	L	T	Pct.
Redskins	6	0	1	1.000
Steagles	4	3	1	.571
Giants	3	3	1	.500
Dodgers	2	7	0	.222

The following Thursday, November 25, was Thanksgiving Day. In Cairo, Roosevelt and Churchill met with Chiang Kai-shek to coordinate operations in South Asia. Roosevelt and Churchill also spent part of the day preparing for their upcoming meeting with Stalin in Tehran. That night Roosevelt hosted a feast for Churchill that included two huge turkeys.

"Let us make it a family affair," Roosevelt said as he carved the birds, which he had brought from Washington for the occasion. After dinner, the president offered a toast.

"Large families are usually more closely united than small ones," he said, raising his glass, "and so this year, with the peoples of the United Kingdom in our family, we are a large family, and more united than ever before. I propose a toast to this unity, and long may it continue!"

Then a military band entertained the guests and played the requests of Roosevelt ("Home on the Range") and Churchill ("Carry Me Back to Old Virginny"). Roosevelt even sang "a little ditty of his own composition," the Associated Press reported. It was in the key of E flat but the words and music were unrecorded.

"I had never seen the President more gay," Churchill later recalled.

"All in all," historian Doris Kearns Goodwin writes, "it was a delightful evening, one that would remain a high point in Churchill's mind for years."

Around the world, America's ten million servicemen marked the holiday much less extravagantly. The Office of the Quartermaster General had promised every soldier, sailor, and marine "at least a pound of turkey" on Thanksgiving. Nearly two million birds were procured to keep that promise. On battleships and in submarines, on battlefields and in boot camps, America's troops—"the best fed fighters in the world," as the War Department liked to brag—enjoyed roasted turkey with all the trimmings, including cranberry sauce, mashed potatoes, and pumpkin pie (though the side dishes were often of the canned or dehydrated variety).

Even on the central Pacific island of Tarawa, which had been captured just two days earlier after four days of brutal combat and at the cost of 1,000 American lives (and more than 4,000 Japanese and Korean lives), the exhausted and bedraggled troops were fed turkey dinners, which were ferried ashore on landing boats.

"We even got ice cream," marveled one marine.

The turkey promise was impossible to fulfill absolutely, of course. On board the U.S.S. *Wake Island,* newly commissioned and docked for supplying at Astoria, Oregon, sailors had to settle for Virginia baked ham. But, in a remarkable and commendable logistical achievement, practically every serviceman was served a special meal.

Back home, turkeys were almost impossible to find. The OPA had banned all sales of the birds in August to allow the military to stock up for Thanksgiving. The ban was lifted in late October, but by then all supplies were depleted. Turkeys, the *Philadelphia Inquirer* reported on the day before Thanksgiving, simply "weren't to be had." Across the country homemakers descended on meat and poultry markets, vainly searching for the birds. The owner of a Philadelphia market said he had put in an order for 500 turkeys. He received just 12, which he reserved for family and friends. On the black market turkeys in the city were selling for up to 85 cents a pound, well above the OPA ceiling of 53 cents. In Pittsburgh, black market birds were fetching 78 cents a pound and the OPA was powerless to stop the sales, since the city's federal judges had gone home early for the holiday and temporary injunctions were unobtainable.

Lacking turkey, most families substituted chicken or ham. To conserve ration coupons, the trimmings were frequently the product of Victory Gardens, assiduously preserved in Mason jars for the occasion. In that respect, it was much like the first Thanksgiving, in that much of what was consumed was produced by the people who consumed it.

Around the table, the talk inevitably turned to General George Patton. It had recently been reported that Patton had slapped three hospitalized soldiers in August, saying to one suffering from a severe case of shell shock, "You ought to be lined up against a wall and shot." Public opinion was fiercely divided. One congressman called for Patton's dismissal, saying the "despicable incident" had "destroyed the general's usefulness as commander of the Seventh Army or any other division." But others said Congress should "let the Army handle its own problems." In the end, Eisenhower reprimanded Patton and ordered him to apologize.

Many Thanksgiving dinners were served later than usual in 1943, since most factories were operating at full capacity at the behest of the War Production Board. (Workers were paid time and a half.) In observance of the holiday, however, no men were drafted and those scheduled to depart for induction centers were allowed to delay their leaving one day to spend Thanksgiving with their families. There was no pro football either. The Detroit Lions, who had started the tradition of playing a home game on the holiday when they moved from Portsmouth in 1934, had suspended the practice for the duration.

Although the country was engaged in history's bloodiest war, Americans still had many reasons to give thanks in the fall of 1943. For one thing, despite persistent fear and paranoia, the war had not touched the homeland directly. American advances since the last Thanksgiving instilled confidence that the war would be won, sooner or later.

"Things have come a long way in a year," said an editorial in the *Pittsburgh Press* on the day before the holiday.

> *And while it cannot be said too often that the war is far from won, the tide has turned. . . . Africa has been freed of Nazis, the Mediterranean is under our control, the submarine menace has been greatly diminished, the continent of Europe has been invaded, the Russians have gained their greatest victories and air raids on Germany are taking a tremendous toll on the enemy.*
>
> *We can see daylight ahead.*

For most of the Steagles, Thanksgiving Day was no different from any other. They put in a full day at the factories and ship-yards, then reported for practice at Shibe Park at 6:00 p.m. After practice, however, Greasy Neale dispensed with his usual "skull session" and hosted a Thanksgiving dinner for the team at the Hotel Philadelphian. Afterwards, Neale and the Steagles played bridge while Genevieve and the wives listened to a star-studded holiday special on the CBS radio network featuring, among others, George Burns and Gracie Allen.

The players had much to be thankful for. The Steagles had already exceeded all expectations. If they won one of their last two games, they would clinch a winning season. If they won both, there was still an outside chance they could end up tied for first place. Not least of all, though, the players were thankful for having escaped the front lines. Tens of thousands of Americans were already dead or wounded. Four NFL veterans had been killed in the service of their country so far:

- Keith Birlem, an end for the Redskins and Cardinals in 1939, was killed attempting to land a crippled bomber returning to England after an air raid on May 7, 1943. (Birlem was a teammate of Steagles quarterback Roy Zimmerman at San Jose State.)

- Eddie Doyle, an end for Frankford and Pottsville in the 1920s, was killed in the invasion of North Africa, November 8, 1942.

- Len Supulski, an end for the Eagles in 1942, died when

his plane crashed during a training mission outside Kearney, Nebraska, on August 31, 1943. Several Steagles had been Supulski's teammate in 1942, and his death hit them especially hard. "It was very sad because he meant a lot to the club," said halfback Ernie Steele.

■ Don Wemple, a Brooklyn end in 1941, was killed in the crash of an Army transport plane in India on June 23, 1943. (Wemple was a teammate of Steagles end Larry Cabrelli at Colgate.)

The carnage was not invisible on the home front. That fall the Office of War Information permitted for the first time the publication of photographs depicting dead U.S. troops. This was done partly to placate Americans who had grown skeptical and weary of relentlessly upbeat coverage of the war. But it was also done to combat growing apathy on the home front. After two years of war, the government believed Americans needed to be reminded of its cost. The pictures of the dead, it was hoped in a kind of perverse logic, would renew enthusiasm for the war. It would also prepare Americans for the heavy casualties sure to come. The images, however, were carefully screened. The bodies were to appear whole. There was to be no gore.

In its September 20 issue, *Life* magazine published a full-page photograph of three Americans gunned down on a beach on the Pacific island of Buna. Their bodies are sprawled in the sand, their faces not visible. Their wounds are not apparent. A half-submerged Japanese landing craft is visible in the water nearby.

"And so here it is," reads an accompanying editorial. "This is the reality that lies behind the names that come to rest at last on monuments in the leafy squares of busy American towns." In the photograph, the editorial continues, "We can still sense the high optimism of men who have never known oppression—who, however scared, have never had to base their decisions upon fear. We are still aware of the relaxed self-confidence with which the leading boy ran into the sudden burst of fire—almost like a halfback carrying the ball down a football field."

"When photographs of dead servicemen were printed," writes Christina S. Jarvis in *The Male Body at War,* "their bodies became privileged symbols of sacrifice from which the goals of nation and the war could be discerned."

The photographs and their implicit messages were especially poignant to the millions of American men who could not fight. Of the 22 million men who registered for the draft between September 1940 and August 1945, five million were rejected as physically or mentally unfit. Many (if not most) of those classified 4-F felt deep guilt and even shame at having been denied the opportunity to serve and spared the horrors of war. They were also subjected to ridicule and scorn.

There were stories of men committing suicide after being classified 4-F (suicidal tendencies, however, were a disqualifying condition; the overall suicide rate in fact plummeted during the war). On college campuses, women often refused to date them since there was obviously "something wrong with them." They were mocked. A popular song among GIs was "Four-F Charlie," in which the protagonist is "a complete physical wreck" who is both cowardly and impotent:

> Men won't sing of his wild daring
> Girls won't praise his marital daring . . .
> And his blood is thin as water
> He can never be a father.

The Steagles were not immune to this kind of derision. On the contrary, as professional athletes, they were sometimes the targets of bitter vitriol. At games, fans often wondered, loudly and profanely, what the hell they were doing on a football field instead of a battlefield.

They even got hate mail, recalled end Tom Miller.

"We used to get letters from people who used to say, 'You big husky guys are out there playin' football and my son is out there fightin' in the war!' We used to get a lot of that. I didn't feel bad about it because I'd been in the service. But I know it did bother some of the guys quite a bit."

"It was weird," said center Ray Graves. "It was just hard for the fans to realize they could go to a football game while we were fighting. It was rough."

Professional athletes were also the object of special (and sometimes unfair) scrutiny by draft boards. Steagles tackle Vic Sears was called before his draft board in Eugene, Oregon, four times.

"The son of the head of the draft board was deferred," Sears recalled. "I guess they felt that I'd fill the gap, so they kept asking me to go in." Each time, Sears was rejected due to his stomach ulcers.

When Frank Sinkwich was honorably discharged from the Marines because of his flat feet, Senator Kenneth Spicer Wherry of Nebraska said he thought the armed forces ought to be able to "find a place" in which they could use Sinkwich.

"What's the matter with him?" the senator demanded. "Haven't we got a place for him? Can't he take the place of some man we can send across the water?"

Gene Tunney, the former heavyweight boxing champion who was a Navy commander overseeing recreation programs in the South Pacific, couldn't understand how a man deemed unfit for military service could play professional football.

"If a man is physically fit to play football," Tunney growled, "then he is physically fit for this bigger game."

Professional athletes had their defenders, too. In December 1943 the syndicated sports columnist Joe Williams published an interview with an unnamed doctor at a New York induction center. The doctor told Williams,

> *Your readers should bear in mind that a champion in civilian life might easily be a complete drawback in action. A punctured eardrum, for instance, may appear to be a trivial physical*

defect, which, under ordinary circumstances, no one will question; but when the punctured eardrum is considered in terms of front line action, the medical approach must be different. If we could be certain the enemy would refrain from using poison gas, a punctured eardrum would not be looked upon as a serious defect—but how can our authorities be certain of the enemy's intentions? Subjected to a gas attack, a man with a punctured eardrum couldn't hope to survive serious and possibly fatal damage to his brain. Thus right off he would be a detriment to his outfit.

Grantland Rice also counseled his readers to go easy on 4-F athletes. He wrote,

It is only natural that a lot of non-athletes, clerks, filling station attendants, soda water jerkers, farm kids, etc., who can neither run nor jump, block or tackle . . . should gripe, after a fashion, because they are rated fit to be fighting men—with athletes left out, rated as unfit to fire a gun or work on a ship. But they should remember these are Army and Navy regulations through the draft. The individual has nothing to say about it.

Complicated emotions surrounded life as a 4-F athlete. While they were sometimes vilified, the public, paradoxically, consistently supported the continuation of sports. In a poll conducted by *Esquire* magazine, 80 percent of all respondents said they wanted to keep sports running during the war. When the magazine polled soldiers, the results were even more overwhelming: 96.5 percent supported sports. Servicemen were philosophical about 4-F athletes.

"One time I was having a couple drinks with a soldier," said Vic Sears. "I said, 'Do you wonder why I'm not in the service? Strong, healthy, plays football?' He says, 'I know you got a helluva reason or you'd be in.'"

Although President Roosevelt never publicly proclaimed his support for professional football (as he had for major league baseball), the sport had its defenders in the highest reaches of the government. On June 23, 1943, Senator James M. Mead of New York went on record in favor of continuing sports as "part of the American way of life and unless they affect the war effort adversely. . . . Both professional baseball and football furnish recreation and relaxation for thousands of war workers and servicemen and women. . . . From the spectator and the competitor standpoint they are an integral part of the war effort. In addition to the morale features, sports events of all kinds have stimulated the sales of war bonds and have raised funds for the Army and Navy relief societies and Red Cross." (It should be noted that Mead held stock in the Buffalo Bisons minor league baseball team.)

But pro football's biggest fan in Congress by far was Samuel A. Weiss, a Democratic representative from Pittsburgh who, on Sundays, officiated National Football League games.

Born in Poland in 1902, Weiss was not yet two years old when his family emigrated to the United States and settled in Glassport, Pennsylvania, just outside Pittsburgh. At Duquesne University, Weiss tried out for the football team. Although he stood just five-four and weighed only 145 pounds, he became the starting quarterback. In 1924, his senior year, he was voted team captain, an unprecedented honor for a Jew at the Catholic school. After college Weiss played two seasons for his hometown's highly regarded and wonderfully named semipro team, the Glassport Odds. Then he went back to Duquesne, earned a law degree, and in 1935 was elected to the Pennsylvania House. Five years later he won a seat in the U.S. House. Weiss had refereed high school games in Pittsburgh and he wished to continue refereeing after his ascension to Washington. He approached Elmer Layden about the possibility of officiating National Football League games on Sundays. The commissioner, thrilled at the prospect of such a powerful political connection, not only made Weiss a referee, he also appointed him deputy commissioner. Beginning in 1942, Weiss's name regularly appeared in NFL box scores.

Weiss lobbied relentlessly for the preservation of professional football and other sports. He liked to point out that the

British had not abandoned their spectator sports. On April 17, 1943, 105,000 fans packed Hampden Park in Glasgow to watch England beat Scotland, 4-0, in an international soccer match. A week later, crowds of 50,000 or more filled four different stadiums in London to watch League Cup matches, including 54,000 at the historic Stamford Bridge stadium, where Arsenal whipped Queen's Park Rangers, 4-1.

"If the British who are within a half hour of the real danger of the Luftwaffe can enjoy a soccer-football game," he asked rhetorically of those who opposed sports, "for goodness sake what has happened to the good old U.S.A.?" In the spring of 1943 Weiss beseeched President Roosevelt to appoint a "sports czar" to ensure the continuation of sports without hampering the war effort. He told the president that the "boys out there in the jungles and in the foxholes" wanted sports to continue.

"I've had letters from lads out there—in the steaming jungles of Guadalcanal and New Guinea—who plead for the continuation of sports," Weiss said. "Their greatest joy is a shortwave broadcast or a six-weeks-old newspaper with news of some sporting event."

Roosevelt was not unsympathetic. One of his top aides, Marvin McIntyre, agreed that some sort of "declaration of policy" was in order. But the proposal seems to have been quashed by Paul McNutt, the head of the War Manpower Commission. McNutt feared a sports czar would encroach on his turf. Roosevelt was having a hard enough time keeping McNutt and Selective Service director Lewis Hershey from strangling each other; he didn't need somebody else pissing in the soup. Besides, the president had much more important things to worry about.

On Sunday, November 28, Roosevelt, Churchill, and Stalin convened in Tehran, and the Steagles and the Redskins staged their rematch in Washington. The results of the former meeting, at which the future conduct of the war was outlined, are still much disputed. The results of the latter meeting, though, are incontrovertible.

12

Survival

A S THEY PREPARED TO MEET THE STEAGLES AGAIN, the Redskins
had more than revenge on their minds. If they won the game,
they would clinch the Eastern Division, rendering inconsequential their final two regular season games against the Giants. That
essentially would give them three weeks off until the championship game on December 19. Sammy Baugh, Washington's sen-
sational passer, was still nursing a toothache and a bruised knee,
but he considered a win so imperative that he was determined to
play all 60 minutes.

The Steagles were motivated too. They were aroused by the
possibility—however remote—of finishing first in the Eastern
Division. If they beat the Redskins this week and the Packers
next—and if the Giants beat the Redskins next week and again
the week after that—the Steagles and Redskins would finish the
season with identical 6-3-1 records, necessitating a playoff for the
division title. (The Giants also had a shot at finishing 6-3-1.) The
Pittsburgh Press's Cecil Muldoon said the Steagles had "about as
much chance of winning the Eastern Division title as a Republican has of being governor of Mississippi." (The Magnolia State
hadn't had a Republican in the governor's mansion since
Reconstruction and wouldn't have another until Kirk Fordice was

elected in 1991.) But in the *Pittsburgh Post-Gazette,* Jack Sell was more optimistic, saying, "[W]here there's life there's hope."

And then there was the Zimmerman factor. Sammy Baugh's erstwhile backup would be making his first appearance in Washington since Redskins owner George Preston Marshall shipped him to Philadelphia the previous August. Zimmerman's feud with Marshall had not abated.

"Zimmerman would call it his happiest day in football if he could beat the Redskins in Washington," wrote Merrell Whittlesey in the *Washington Post.* When asked if he regretted trading Zimmerman, Marshall said of course not. Since their much publicized animosity was largely responsible for a record crowd in Philadelphia and would help make the rematch in Washington a sellout, Marshall insisted that the "loss of Zimmerman has been a good investment." It was an excellent example of Marshallian logic.

On Saturday afternoon the Steagles went through a light workout at Shibe Park, then headed *en masse* to North Philadelphia station, where they boarded a train for Washington. Normally the team wouldn't have stayed overnight in the capital, but Greasy Neale and Walt Kiesling considered this game important enough to justify the expense. The team stayed at the Willard Hotel on, appropriately enough, Pennsylvania Avenue. In Suite 301 that night, Lex Thompson hosted a small party. Lieutenant Thompson, who seems to have had a supernatural ability to secure furloughs to watch his team play, said he was "certain" the Steagles would win the next day, and Neale and Kiesling agreed—they said they "fully expected the Redskins to be pushed over." Their opinion was not shared by the bookies: the Steagles were 14-point underdogs. After all, they had not yet won a game away from their two homes, getting crushed by the Bears in Chicago and the Giants in New York, and embarrassed by the Dodgers in Brooklyn. And the Redskins were coming off their stunning 21-7 vanquishing of the Bears. On the morning of the game, Merrell Whittlesey confidently predicted in the *Washington Post,* "Anything but a Redskin victory with two touchdowns to spare seems highly unlikely today."

The game kicked off at 2:00 p.m. and Griffith Stadium was indeed sold out. Among the crowd of 35,826 were a few hundred Philadelphians and even a smattering of Pittsburghers. The sun was shining and the air was clear. The pleasant aroma of fresh-baked bread wafted over the ballpark from the Bond Bakery just up Georgia Avenue. But baking bread was not what the men on the field had in mind.

The game was scoreless until the penultimate play of the first quarter, when Steagles halfback Bobby Thurbon burst through a hole at right tackle "like a shot out of a cannon" and scored on a seven-yard run. Incredibly, it was the first rushing touchdown surrendered by the Redskins all season. Until then, their opponents had scored only on passes, kicks, and returns. Zimmerman added the extra point to make it 7-0.

In order to beat the Redskins, Greasy Neale knew the Steagles would have to play flawlessly. That's what he'd told them all week. So when Jack Hinkle missed a block in the second quarter, Neale yanked him from the game. Hinkle, who had rushed for more than 100 yards against the Lions a week earlier and was on his way to rushing for 100 more on this day, was incredulous.

"Why didn't you take that man out?" Neale barked when Hinkle reached the sideline.

"But Greasy, I wasn't supposed to take that man out—or was I?"

"Of all the . . ." Neale began before switching gears. "How do you manage to remember what you're supposed to do at that factory you work in? How does your boss stand you around without suffering a nervous breakdown?"

After a minute all was forgiven and Hinkle returned to the game.

As they had in their first encounter, the Steagles ambushed Sammy Baugh at every opportunity. He was "smeared several times" in the first half and forced to hurry many passes. It was also apparent that his knee was still bothering him, and on several occasions he was relieved by George Cafego, the hero of the Bears game.

The Steagles went ahead 14-0 in the middle of the third quarter when Bobby Thurbon scored again, this time on a four-yard run. The touchdown culminated a dazzling, 62-yard drive during which the Steagles executed the T to perfection, mixing runs and passes over 13 plays and thoroughly befuddling the Redskins, whose frustration was rising to dangerous levels.

When the Redskins got the ball back, Sammy Baugh uncorked a long pass to Bob Masterson, who was tackled near midfield by Ray Graves. Redskins tackle "Wee" Willie Wilkin (who was six-four, 265 pounds) objected to the vigor with which Graves wrestled Masterson to the ground. Wilkin jumped on the prostrate Graves, kneeing him in the ribs. Steagle Ben Kish rushed to his teammate's defense and threw a punch at Wilkin. Redskins guard Clyde Shugart joined the fracas, though he later claimed he was merely trying to separate Wilkin and Kish. Players from both teams converged on the scene and exchanged angry words. Hoots and hollers and not a few empty bottles rained from the stands. The hostilities threatened to explode into a full-scale brawl. Miraculously, referee Carl Rebele was able to restore order. Wilkin, Kish, and Shugart were ejected.

"What happened was all Wilkin's fault," Shirley Povich wrote in the *Washington Post* two days later. "Graves of the Steagles had just tackled Bob Masterson on a pass play. There didn't seem to be anything vicious about it. The whistle had blown, the play was long since over, when 265-pound Wilkin came galloping up to pile on. It was uncalled for, and so Kish, who was standing by, took a poke at Wilkin that was almost justifiable."

Ultimately the Steagles profited from the altercation. The ejections of Wilkin and Shugart weakened an already dispirited Redskins line. Kish was a good running back, but the Steagles had plenty of those. The league coffers profited, too: an ejection carried an automatic $50 fine. Kish later appealed his fine to Elmer Layden, claiming he'd done nothing more than "push" Wilkin, but the commissioner was unmoved.

Shortly after the fight, the Redskins blocked a Zimmerman punt and recovered the ball on the Steagles 33. That led to a four-yard touchdown pass from Baugh to Masterson, making the score 14-7. Five minutes into the final period the Redskins had the ball and were driving for the tying touchdown when Zimmerman intercepted a Baugh pass on the Steagles 32. Seven plays later halfback Ernie Steele took the snap directly from center, busted through "a hole a mile wide being opened by the Steagle line," and sprinted 47 yards for a touchdown. Zimmerman's extra point was blocked.

Andy Farkas received the ensuing kickoff on the five but was immediately smothered by a swarm of Steagles. Pinned deep in his own end, Baugh attempted one of his famous "quick kicks" on second down. It was supposed to put the Steagles on their heels. It didn't. Vic Sears bolted through a crack in the Redskins line and blocked the punt. Tom Miller recovered the ball on the one. On the next play Jack Hinkle waltzed into the end zone un-touched, extending the Steagles lead to 27-7.

With five minutes remaining in the game, George Cafego, temporarily substituting for Baugh, threw a 37-yard strike to Frank Seno on the Steagles 12. As Baugh trotted back onto the field to reclaim his position, he was, for the first time in Griffith Stadium, booed. A "thoughtless jeer," the *Washington Post* called it. "The people booed Babe Ruth, too," wrote Shirley Povich, who also offered an alternate explanation for the fans' outburst: "You could read into their boos a deep compliment to Cafego."

It didn't take Baugh long to silence the boobirds. On the very next play he threw a touchdown pass to Joe Aguirre.

With the final seconds ticking down and the Redskins trailing 27-14, Baugh tossed a long pass to Andy Farkas around the Steagles five. Ernie Steele, playing defensive back for the Steagles, intentionally let Farkas catch the ball, then tackled him.

"I knew if I batted down the pass, that would stop the clock," explained Steele, who lay on top of Farkas until the hands of the giant Longines clock in right-centerfield finally came to rest on zero. Linesman Charley Berry fired his starter pistol and the game was over.

It was the Redskins' first loss in more than a year, and their first at the hands of a team from Philadelphia or Pittsburgh since 1937. It was by far the biggest upset of the season. The *Inquirer* called it an "almost unbelievable" win for the Steagles. Once again it was the line that made the difference: the Steagles outrushed the Redskins 297-58. Jack Hinkle alone rushed for 117 yards, moving him into second place among the league leaders. Johnny Butler rushed for 36, good enough to maintain fourth place. It wasn't the flawless performance that Greasy Neale had hoped for: the Steagles fumbled four times, and Roy Zimmerman was far from perfect, completing just four of ten passes for 44 yards and no touchdowns. But Zimmerman, who played all but five minutes, managed the offense brilliantly and played stellar defense as well. Late in the game, as Sammy Baugh was leaving the field, Zimmerman had rushed over to shake his hand. It was a gracious gesture by the former pupil who, on this day at least, had bested the master, and the crowd applauded appreciatively.

"It was the happiest day of my life," Zimmerman said after the game, just as Merrell Whittlesey had predicted he would. Zimmerman added that he "didn't have any grudge against the swell guys on the Redskins, but I got even with one man"—George Preston Marshall.

The Redskins did even the score on one count: the body count. This time it was the Steagles who took a beating. Johnny Butler's thumb was broken when a Redskin stepped on his hand. Tony Bova lost two teeth. Bobby Thurbon's lower lip was busted open, and four stitches were required to mend it. Ray Graves, of course, had very sore ribs. Winning, however, was a potent balm.

"What a ball game!" exulted Bert Bell the day after. Looking ahead to the season finale against Green Bay the following

Sunday at Shibe Park, Bell admitted it wouldn't be easy to stop the Packers' star receiver, Don Hutson.

"Still," Bell said, "we stopped Baugh. Maybe we can pull up with the answer for Hutson. . . . Be a funny thing, wouldn't it, if we would stop Hutson and knock off Green Bay Sunday and the Giants could beat Washington twice and let the Steagles tie for the Eastern title. It would be a very funny thing. That George Marshall would be fit to be tied. I would love to see that. I sure would."

The Giants had stayed in the race by defeating the Dodgers at the Polo Grounds, 24-7. Rookie Bill Paschal, who was coming on strong late in the season, scored two touchdowns for the Giants and rushed for 69 yards, moving him into tenth place among the leading rushers.

The Eastern Division standings were in turmoil. Since the Giants still had to play the Redskins twice, there was now the possibility of a three-way tie for first, if the Steagles beat the Packers and the Giants took both games from the Redskins. That would force the first three-team playoff in league history. Just about all that was certain was that the eventual winner of the division would meet the Bears in the championship game. The Bears had clinched the West by beating the Cardinals, 35-24. Now things were getting interesting:

	W	L	T	Pct.
Redskins	6	1	1	.857
Steagles	5	3	1	.625
Giants	4	3	1	.571
Dodgers	2	8	0	.200

After the Redskins game, an ecstatic Lex Thompson once again treated the team to dinner. And, since Washington observed "meatless Sundays," lobster was once again on the menu. Afterwards the celebration continued in the lounge of the Willard

Hotel, where Greasy Neale granted the entire squad permission to imbibe, which they did liberally. It was quite a party.

"I celebrated a little too much after the game," remembered tackle Ted Doyle. "I had to catch a train out of Washington [that night] and I went to sleep and missed my train!" He showed up late at the Westinghouse plant the next day, but his bosses went easy on him.

"By then they understood it all. I'd made enough trips. I got off the train in East Pittsburgh and went to work."

THE REDSKINS AND THE GIANTS weren't originally supposed to meet on consecutive weekends at the end of the season. When the schedule was finally hammered out after long and tedious negotiations among the owners in June, the two teams were slated to open the season against each other in Washington on October 3. What George Preston Marshall didn't realize was that Griffith Stadium was already booked on that date: The Washington Senators were playing their season finale against the Detroit Tigers. The Polo Grounds was also booked, as was Municipal Stadium in Baltimore. Lacking other options, Marshall petitioned Commissioner Elmer Layden to reschedule the game to December 12, a week after the other six clubs had already completed their schedules, and only a week after the Redskins and Giants were scheduled to play in New York. It was also the date on which the championship game had been scheduled. Reluctantly Layden acquiesced. The title game was pushed back one week to December 19, which elicited howls of protest from sportswriters who felt the season was already much too long.

"An eight-team organization should be able to complete a forty-game schedule by the first Sunday in December," wrote Dale Stafford in the *Detroit Free Press*.

The Redskins needed only a win or a tie in either game against the Giants to clinch the Eastern Division. If they lost both games, however, a playoff would be needed to crown a winner. And if the Steagles ended their season with a win over Green Bay, the playoff would involve three teams, necessitating a round-robin format that could push the championship game all the way back to January 9.

So, on December 5 at the Polo Grounds, the Redskins and Giants began what was essentially a two-game series for the Eastern title, with the Steagles a very interested third party. The Redskins were 14-point favorites, and at first it looked like they would take care of business without much ado. They took a 3-0 lead in the first quarter when a "horribly wobbly, half-scuffed" kick by Bob Masterson somehow managed to clear the crossbar from 26 yards out. They made it 10-0 six minutes into the third quarter when Andy Farkas capped a 64-yard drive with a one-yard plunge. But with Bill Paschal leading the way, the Giants came roaring back. The flashy rookie scored on a one-yard run late in the third quarter to cut Washington's lead to 10-7. Then, with less than five minutes left in the game, Paschal brought the crowd of 51,308 to its feet with an electrifying 53-yard touchdown run, which Rud Rennie described in the next day's *New York Herald Tribune:* "[T]he Giants opened the right side of the Redskins' line and Paschal went careening through, into the clear, with only Baugh chasing him. For a fraction of a moment Baugh kept pace. But Paschal turned on the steam and ran away from him, winning the game in 10:42 of the quarter."

The final score was Giants 14, Redskins 10. Paschal finished the day with 188 yards rushing, the best single-game performance in the league all season. The Redskins had now lost two straight games in which they could have clinched the Eastern Division. In the *Washington Post,* Merrell Whittlesey said their title hopes had reached "the panicky stage."

A week later, on December 12, in the game that should have been played on October 3, the Redskins' title hopes reached the terminal stage. The Giants defeated them again, 31-7, at Griffith Stadium before 35,540 disgruntled and disbelieving fans, many of whom exited the ballpark in disgust long before the final gun. Bill Paschal had another outstanding day, rushing for 92 yards. That gave him 572 for the season, of which 280—nearly half—were accrued in the final two games. It was the first time the Redskins had lost three consecutive games since 1937. In New York, Giants head coach Steve Owen was hailed as a genius for guiding a club that at one point in the season was 2-3-1 into a playoff for the divisional title. In Washington, there was only angst. The heading over the box score in the *Washington Evening Star* the next day read, "Giants vs. Pygmies."

The Redskins and the Giants had finished the season with identical records of 6-3-1. A playoff would be needed to determine the Eastern Division champion. But would it include the Steagles? That depended on what the Steagles had done a week earlier, in their final regular season game.

13

Win and In

O N SUNDAY, DECEMBER 5, 1943, the Steagles arrived at Shibe
Park around noon, two hours before the kickoff of their game
against the Green Bay Packers. Inside the home team locker
room, a cramped and damp concrete cube underneath the first
base stands, they changed into their football attire, like knights
donning armor: pants, cleats, shoulder pads, and, finally, the kelly
green jersey, its many tears and rips meticulously repaired by
equipment manager cum trainer Fred Schubach. They dressed in
silence. The only sound in the locker room was that of white athletic tape being ripped from its spool to stabilize creaky joints and
bind aching muscles. The players' bodies were worn out, not only
by the punishing football season, but also by the long hours they
put in at their war jobs. They were weary, yes, but they were also
excited. For most of them this was to be the most important football game they had ever played, certainly professionally.

It was remarkable that they had gotten even this far. Thrown
together by necessity and chance, they were a motley bunch, the
unwanted remnants of two mediocre teams, with a host of ailments: ulcers, perforated eardrums, trick knees. There had been
animosities, but they had been overcome, and now they were truly
a team, a team on the verge of a championship no less.

"When you're on a team," explained center Ray Graves, "you're part of the team whether you like it or not. You can have fights among yourselves, but you're still a team. That's the way football is."

Once in uniform, the players went out to the field to warm up, stretch, do calisthenics, run a few drills, and check out the condition of the turf, which by this point in the season resembled a bombing range. They were surprised by how many people were already in the stands.

Around 1:15 p.m., Greasy Neale and Walt Kiesling called the team together in the locker room. The 25 players took seats on the long benches that ran in front of the lockers on three sides of the room. They were "wound up and ready to fight." Don't worry about what the Giants and Redskins are doing up in New York, the coaches told them. Just do your job. There were no hysterical, hyperbolic speeches, no spittle-emitting harangues or tear-jerking pep talks. Neither coach was like that.

"There was never any idle talk," Vic Sears said of Greasy Neale. "It just never occurred to him to waste any time." Ted Doyle said Kiesling wasn't a "fire-'em-up" kind of coach either: "He just pointed out some of the things you should do and some of the things you shouldn't, that type of thing. In fact, there weren't many people that were fire-'em-up in the league then."

Neale and Kiesling carefully went over the game plan one more time, the pass patterns, the running plays, the defensive alignments. Each player's assignments were reviewed, who blocked whom, who covered whom. Above all, the coaches emphasized the need to stop Don Hutson, Green Bay's lithe receiver. Hutson, who planned to retire after the Steagles game, was leading the league in scoring and pass receptions. The Steagles were fortunate in that Hutson would not be in top shape: he had accidentally slammed his hand in the door of a taxicab a few days before the game. His right index finger was in a splint. But Greasy Neale knew a one-handed Don Hutson was still more dangerous than most two-handed receivers in the league. Neale once called him "the only man I ever saw who could feint in three different directions at the same time." Just as the key to beating the Redskins was stifling Sammy Baugh, the key to beating the Packers was stifling Don Hutson. To that end, the Steagles would employ the same tactic that had been so successful against Baugh: They would try to rough up Hutson at every opportunity. Knock him off his game. In a time when receivers were afforded few of the protections from interference they enjoy today, it was a perfectly logical and licit strategy.

Emotionally, the two teams were worlds apart. The Steagles were coming off their stunning and ferocious victory in Washington. The Packers hadn't even had a game scheduled the previous Sunday, but, as was customary, they filled the open date with an exhibition contest. At a ballpark in Bristol, Connecticut, they crushed a semipro outfit called the New London Diesels, 62-14. The Packers arrived in Philadelphia on Wednesday afternoon and worked out at Shibe Park the rest of week. Another difference between the two teams was that, while the Steagles had everything to play for (namely a chance to tie for the Eastern Division title), the Packers had nothing at stake in this game. Win, lose, or draw, they were guaranteed to end the season in second place behind the Bears in the West (and to pocket their share of the championship pot).

The game would pit Green Bay's high-powered offense against Phil-Pitt's smothering defense. The Packers were second in the league in total yards gained per game (341.5) and passing yards per game (200.7). The Steagles meanwhile had given up the second-fewest total yards per game (224.8) and the fewest rushing yards (68.7). The Steagles, however, would not be at full strength. Their second-leading rusher, Johnny Butler, was sidelined by a broken thumb. The bookies rated the Packers slight favorites.

The Steagles' pregame skull session took about 30 minutes. Neale and Kiesling wished the players luck and sent them into the long tunnel that led to the field. Neale was the last man out of the locker room. It was one of his many superstitions. Once he spotted a player running back to the locker room to use the bathroom before a game.

"We better win today or else," he growled.

Neale also wore the same suit and hat when his team was winning.

"I even drive to the park by the same route, if we won the last time I took that route," he once confessed.

As they walked through the concrete tunnel, the players' hard rubber cleats made a loud clickety-clack sound that echoed in their heads. The tunnel opened into the baseball dugout along the first base line. When they reached the top step of the dugout, the Steagles were amazed by what they saw: Shibe Park was absolutely packed.

The lines had started forming outside the ticket windows at nine o'clock that morning, two-and-a-half hours before they opened and five hours before kickoff. It was the first NFL game ever played in Philadelphia for which the demand for tickets exceeded the supply. The weather helped: it was an unseasonably mild day. But there was more to it than that. Not since the days of the Frankford Yellow Jackets had the city's pro football fans seen a team as good as this one. Their Eagles—well, their Steagles— were completing the most successful season in the history of the franchise, with a chance of winning it all. Their enthusiasm foretold the fervor that would come to grip the team's fans in the generations to come.

By game time the stands were overflowing. Even way, way up, in the far reaches of the upper deck behind home plate, not an empty seat could be seen. Everywhere there were people. The players had never seen anything like it. More people, in fact, had assembled to watch this game than had ever before witnessed a professional football game anywhere in the state of Pennsylvania. Lex Thompson, there on his usual weekend pass, was "flabbergasted" by the size of the crowd. The attendance of 34,294 shattered the record set against the Redskins four weeks earlier. Back in Pittsburgh, thousands more were tuned into radio station WWSW to hear Joe Tucker and Bill Cullen call the game. In the *Pittsburgh Press,* Cecil Muldoon wrote, "The big complaint from Pittsburgh fans was the scarcity of games there but the combined team's showing [has] more than made up for the deficiency and provided a successful season instead of a possible blackout." The *Post-Gazette*'s Havey Boyle agreed: "[T]he merger worked out pretty well."

It would work out even better if they beat the Packers.

The Packers were decked out in their classic blue jerseys with gold trim. (Not until the early 1950s would green become the team's primary color.) The crowd roared in anticipation as Don Hutson kicked off, the ball spinning end over end in a high arc, but the Steagles' first drive ended prematurely, as had many all season, with a fumble. Jack Hinkle was the culprit this time. Green Bay recovered the ball on the Steagles 31. From there Tony Canadeo busted through a big hole at right guard and streaked into the end zone. Hutson converted the extra point, and barely two minutes into the game, Green Bay led 7-0. Hinkle atoned for his miscue on the Steagles' next possession, sweeping wide around the left end and dashing 38 yards down the sideline for the tying touchdown. Just a few minutes later the Packers jumped back in front. Irv Comp intercepted a Roy Zimmerman pass on the Packers 25 and returned it 46 yards, all the way to the Steagles 39. Three plays later, Canadeo took the snap and handed off to Lou Brock. As the Steagles converged on Brock, Canadeo slipped undetected into the right corner of the end zone. Just before getting smeared, Brock hit Canadeo with a wobbly pass. Hutson converted again and it was 14-7 Packers.

But once more the resilient Steagles struck right back. On third down from the Green Bay 44, Zimmerman heaved the ball to Tony Bova near the ten. Don Hutson stepped in front of Bova and nearly intercepted the pass, but, encumbered by the splint on his index finger, he bobbled the ball momentarily. Bova snatched it out of Hutson's hands and raced across the goal line. As was the custom, Bova gently placed the pigskin on the ground. The crowd exploded. Shibe Park was literally shaking with excitement. Zimmerman calmly booted the extra point, and the rip-roaring first period ended with the two teams dead even on the scoreboard: 14-14.

While the fans were delirious, Greasy Neale was concerned. He didn't think the Steagles could possibly sustain the frenetic and exhilarating pace of the first period.

In the second period Don Hutson kicked a 25-yard field goal: Green Bay 17, Phil-Pitt 14. In the third, Joe Laws intercepted a Zimmerman pass to set up a four-yard scamper by Irv Comp: Green Bay 24, Phil-Pitt 14. On the last play of the third quarter, Zimmerman was intercepted again, leading to a 12-yard touchdown pass from Comp to Hutson: Green Bay 31, Phil-Pitt 14.

Then Greasy Neale took a gamble. He decided to give Zimmerman, who was exhausted, a rare rest. Twenty-year-old rookie quarterback Allie Sherman went into the game and calmly guided the Steagles on a 60-yard drive that ended when he tossed a perfect 13-yard touchdown pass to Tony Bova. When the Steagles got the ball back, Neale reinserted a refreshed Zimmerman, who masterminded a 63-yard drive that included a 45-yard pass to Bova and ended with a four-yard touchdown run by Ernie Steele. Suddenly, with seven minutes left, the Steagles trailed by just three points, 31-28. The crowd, wrote Red Smith, "looked on with jaw agape and eye glazed."

On Green Bay's next possession, the Packers were forced to punt. With less than five minutes left, Lou Brock booted the ball high into air from his own 26. Jack Hinkle, who was having the best season of his life, camped under the ball. It hit him in the chest with a thud and he bobbled it momentarily. By the time he'd gained full control of it, five Packers were bearing down on him. Hinkle was buried in an avalanche of blue and gold jerseys and the ball came loose for another fumble. Green Bay's Charley Brock collapsed on the ball on the Steagles 38. Four plays later, Irv Comp fired a 24-yard touchdown pass to Don Hutson, who managed to make the catch with his left hand—his only "good" hand. It was the spectacular final act of Hutson's spectacular career. It was also the final nail in the Steagles' coffin: Green Bay won, 38-28.

Despite their best efforts, the Steagles had not been able to stop Hutson. He caught six passes for 56 yards, scoring two touchdowns. He also kicked a field goal and five extra points, giving him 20 points for the game and 117 for the season, most in the league by far.

The Steagles' line had played a good game, with Phil-Pitt outrushing Green Bay 318-278. But turnovers, their Achilles' heel all season, killed them. The Steagles fumbled four times and Roy Zimmerman threw six interceptions, three of which led to Packer touchdowns. He also missed two field goal attempts.

"We made mistakes" is how a disappointed Greasy Neale summed up the team's performance after the game.

Nevertheless, the Steagles had much to be proud of. Theirs was the first winning season in the history of the Philadelphia franchise and just the second for Pittsburgh. Their defense ended the season ranked second to the Bears in fewest total yards allowed per game (230.1) and first against the rush, ceding opponents just 79.3 yards per game on the ground. On offense they led the league in rushing yards per game (173), ending the Bears' four-season hold on that title.

Jack Hinkle rushed for 59 yards against the Packers, ending the season with 571. In the papers the next day he was hailed as the league's new rushing king, but the Giants' Bill Paschal still had one more game to play. In that game Paschal would surpass Hinkle by a single yard to win the closest ground-gaining race in league history (subsequently equaled in 2004). Hinkle's total, of course, does not include the 37-yard run he made against the Giants on October 9 that was mistakenly attributed to Johnny Butler. Contemporaneous newspaper accounts confirm that Hinkle, not Butler, made that run. Rightfully, Jack Hinkle was the NFL's leading rusher in 1943, but he has never pursued the matter with the league.

"In my mind I know I won it," Hinkle said.

Hinkle's achievement did not go unrewarded, however. Owner Lex Thompson gave him a raise (subject to wage-control guidelines, of course).

Ernie Steele rushed for 96 yards against the Packers to finish the season with 409, good enough for sixth place on the rushing list. Steele surpassed teammate Johnny Butler, who sat out the game with a broken thumb, though Butler still finished seventh in the league with 362 yards. With 291 yards, Bobby Thurbon finished eleventh, giving the Steagles four of the league's top 11 rushers, a testament not only to the talents of the running backs themselves, but also to the dexterity of the linemen who blocked for them. Steele and Thurbon led the team in scoring with 36 points each. Half-blind Tony Bova was the team's leading receiver with 17 catches for 419 yards, a whopping average of 24.6 yards per catch, best in the league.

After the season, seven Steagles were named to the various all-pro teams selected by the wire services: Tony Bova, Ray Graves, Jack Hinkle, Elbie Schultz, Vic Sears, Ernie Steele, and Roy Zimmerman. Perhaps most surprisingly—and certainly most important, as far as Messrs. Bell, Rooney, and Thompson were concerned—the Steagles were a box office smash. Their cumulative paid home attendance of 129,347 was a record for both franchises. A "combination official" confided to the *Inquirer* that it was "the most successful season financially either Philadelphia or Pittsburgh ever had." Bert Bell said, "We took in more in the six home games this year than the Eagles and Steelers did together in ten games last year."

On the whole the players were satisfied with the season.

"I think we surprised ourselves," said Al Wistert. "We did pretty well in spite of the fact that we were a hybrid team." Vic Sears credited Greasy Neale for the Steagles' unexpected success.

"We got better all the time," Sears said. "Nobody stays the same with Greasy Neale."

A farewell banquet was held for the team at the Hotel Philadelphian the night of the Packers game. The next morning the players scattered. Although they were not required to, many players kept working at their war jobs in Philadelphia. Bobby Thurbon joined a Teamsters basketball team in Pittsburgh. Walt Kiesling went back to his off-season job in the Office of the Register of Deeds in St. Paul. Vic Sears' draft board ordered him to return to Oregon for yet another physical, which, due to his ulcers, he again flunked. Rocco Canale reported back to Mitchell Field. Bucko Kilroy returned to convoy duty on the North Atlantic. Roy Zimmerman went back to his California farm. Ernie Steele went home to Seattle and found work in a shipyard. Ray Graves, who like Allie Sherman aspired to be a head coach someday, went back to his alma mater, the University of Tennessee, where he was hired as an assistant. (He wouldn't return to the Eagles until 1946.) Ted Doyle, of course, just kept working on the Manhattan Project at the Westinghouse plant in East Pittsburgh.

Ironically, when the Giants played the Redskins in the final game of the regular season a week later, the Steagles were rooting for the Redskins to win. Having already been eliminated from the title chase, the Steagles still hoped to finish tied for second with the Giants. Alas, the Giants won and the Steagles missed out on the portion of the championship pot that would have come with sharing second place: $52.83 each.

	W	L	T	Pct.
Redskins	6	3	1	.667
Giants	6	3	1	.667
Steagles	5	4	1	.555
Dodgers	2	8	0	.200

On December 19, on their fourth attempt, the Redskins finally clinched the division by defeating the Giants 28-0 in a one-game playoff at the Polo Grounds. Sammy Baugh threw for 220 yards and one touchdown. He also intercepted a pass to set up a touchdown and got off a 65-yard punt, one of the longest in playoff history.

In the championship game a week later at Wrigley Field, the exhausted Redskins took on the Bears, who hadn't played a game in four weeks. The contest was billed as a showdown between football's two greatest passers, Baugh and Sid Luckman, but early in the game Baugh suffered a concussion (while tackling Luckman, ironically) and never regained form. Luckman threw five touchdown passes as the Bears won handily, 41-21. Thirty-five-year-old Bronko Nagurski scored a touchdown for Chicago in what would be his last NFL game.

The game's most memorable moment occurred shortly before halftime, when Redskins owner George Preston Marshall was spotted sitting on the Bears bench. Marshall claimed he'd only come down from his box to visit and thought the half would be over by the time he arrived. But Bears general manager Ralph Brizzolara suspected Marshall was trying to steal the Bears' plays and asked police to remove him. Marshall, dressed in a full-length raccoon coat, was briefly detained beneath the stands before being allowed to return to his box.

"You can say for me that Brizzolara is not a gentleman," Marshall shouted to reporters. "And I'll never speak to him again."

The game was a sellout, and each Bear took home $1,135.81 for winning the title. Each Redskin's take was $754.60. Sid Luckman was named the league's most valuable player.

The National Football League had not merely survived in 1943, it had actually thrived. Not only had average per-game attendance hit an all-time high; according to *Pittsburgh Post-Gazette* sports editor Havey Boyle, "every club made a nice profit except Brooklyn and the Cardinals." Nineteen forty-four would present its own challenges—namely the Father Draft—but the future, in the long run anyway, looked quite bright. So bright, in fact, that Branch Rickey, the forward-thinking president of the Brooklyn Dodgers baseball team, was worried. On the last day of 1943 Rickey warned his fellow baseball executives that pro football was on the verge of becoming America's new national pastime.

"I see post-war pro football expanding into six or eight leagues," Rickey predicted. "They will have two games a week. With all this progress in air travel, it will be simple for a team to play on Sunday in San Francisco and the following Wednesday in New York." He was off on the particulars, of course—but Branch Rickey was definitely on to something.

Epilogue: V-J Day

▌ | | | | ▌

ALTHOUGH THE STEELERS-EAGLES MERGER technically ended at the conclusion of the Packers game on December 5, 1943, the Steagles did not formally dissolve until the following month, when the two teams announced they would be going their separate ways.

"Last fall," explained Steelers co-owner Bert Bell, "in our very cordial relationship with the Eagles, most of the home games were played in Philadelphia, but in 1944 we feel we owe it to our fans to give Pittsburgh the fuller season." How this would be accomplished was an open question: The Steelers still had only six players under contract.

In Philadelphia, Eagles owner Lex Thompson promised to "keep faith with Philadelphia fans and give them the team and the home games to which they are entitled." Thompson, who had entered into his partnership with the Steelers somewhat reluctantly in the first place, and wouldn't even let his radio announcer utter the word "Steagles" on the air, was happy enough to see the merger end. Besides, the Eagles had about 20 players under contract, enough, probably, to go it alone in the fall.

With the Father Draft ramping up, players would be harder

to find than ever, but Commissioner Elmer Layden was determined to forge ahead. He instituted an "anti-pessimism" policy.

"The best thing to do in these uncertain times is to adopt a policy of 'go on living' instead of being pessimistic," Layden said. "We are going ahead with plans for a 1944 schedule." On April 6 those plans were dramatically bolstered when the Army announced that it had reached its goal of 7.7 million men. Two days later, Selective Service director Lewis Hershey ended the induction of most men 26 or older. While the NFL would still lose some players to the service, Hershey's order was a welcome reprieve.

Other changes were afoot in the NFL that spring. At a meeting in Philadelphia in late April, the owners finally voted to allow coaching from the sidelines. They also voted to retain unlimited substitution for the duration. (It would be repealed in 1946, but reinstated permanently in 1950, officially beginning the era of two-platoon football in the NFL.) As usual, the one thing the owners were unable to agree on was a schedule. With the Cleveland Rams deciding to return to the league after their one-year hiatus, and a new franchise in Boston (known as the Yanks), the league now had 11 teams, an especially unwieldy number for scheduling purposes. On April 22, after many hours of tiresome negotiations, Lions owner Fred Mandel made a motion:

> *The League requests the Chicago Cardinals and the Pittsburgh Steelers to merge for the season of 1944. This request is based on the fact that the League being composed of eleven clubs, it is found that many difficulties face the League in the making of the schedule. The League realizes the problems imposed upon these two members, but faced with this urgent condition, they [sic] ask in the interest of the League that these members so merge.*

Steelers co-owners Bert Bell and Art Rooney were not enamored of the proposal; after all, they had split with the Eagles in pursuit of more home games in Pittsburgh. But they went along with it anyway, mainly out of deference to Elmer Layden, who had supported their merger application a year earlier. Besides, the Steelers were still desperately shorthanded.

"Since the close of the past campaign we have tried to line up new material with absolutely no success," Rooney lamented. Bell and Rooney would probably have preferred to merge with the Eagles again, but Lex Thompson was adamant that his team fly solo. So the Steelers merged with the Cardinals, who had gone winless in 1943. Bell and Rooney were, at least, able to get three regular season games scheduled in Pittsburgh, one more than in 1943. As for Charlie Bidwill, the Cardinals owner, he was simply grateful for any help he could get. The combine, which was officially christened with the distinctly unpleasant-sounding name "Card-Pitt," was based in Chicago and was placed in the Western Division with the Bears, Packers, Lions, and Rams.

To put it mildly, the results of this merger were disastrous. Practices were haphazard at best. The team went 0-10 and held a lead just twice all season. Part of the problem was the coaches—though it wasn't that they didn't get along. While Walt Kiesling and Greasy Neale were barely on speaking terms, Kiesling and his compatriot in 1944, the Cardinals' Phil Handler, actually hit it off—maybe a little too well. They both enjoyed going to the track, and at times it seemed they were more interested in the horses than in their football team. Rooney complained that Kiesling "carried the *Racing Form* more than the playbook." After Card-Pitt's third game of the season, a 34-7 embarrassment at the hands of the Bears, Kiesling and Handler fined three players, including halfback Johnny Butler, $200 each for "indifferent play." Butler, who had performed so admirably for the Steagles a year before, refused to pay the fine and was kicked off the team. That same week, a disgruntled fan wrote the *Pittsburgh Post-Gazette,* suggesting the combine be called the "Carpits," since "every team in the league walks over them." On the eve of Card-Pitt's final game of the season, the team's leading rusher, John Grigas, quit. Grigas, who had played for the Cardinals in 1943, was fed up with losing.

After all, he had played 19 games in the National Football League without winning even one.

Walt Kiesling was fed up too. After the Card-Pitt debacle, he left the Steelers to take a job closer to home, as Curly Lambeau's assistant in Green Bay.

"That wasn't a very good year," remembered Ted Doyle, one of five former Steagles on the team. (Besides Johnny Butler, the others were Tony Bova, Elbie Schultz, and Bobby Thurbon.)

Why was Card-Pitt so bad?

"Talent," explained Doyle. "The Cardinals didn't have much. And we didn't have a helluva lot left over either. So there just wasn't the ability there."

"The whole bunch from Chicago were fine fellows," Art Rooney said after the season, "but we all know now that these combines just won't work out."

"The season couldn't have turned out any worse than this one," added Bert Bell bluntly. The Steelers and the Cardinals went their separate ways at the conclusion of the season.

The Eagles' season, on the other hand, couldn't have turned out much better. Greasy Neale cut his own salary from $12,000 to $3,000 because he believed he "couldn't produce an improved team with the material on hand." He was wrong. The Eagles finished the season 7-1-2 and missed winning the Eastern Division by a whisker. Many Steagles were instrumental to the Eagles' success, including Jack Hinkle, Bucko Kilroy, Ernie Steele, Al Wistert, and Roy Zimmerman. But the team's biggest star was Steve Van Buren, a rookie halfback from Honduras by way of Louisiana State University. Van Buren, the team's No. 1 draft choice, led the Eagles in rushing in 1944. He would go on to become one of the greatest running backs in NFL history and the first Eagle player to be enshrined in the Pro Football Hall of Fame. Only a 28-7 loss to their longtime nemesis, the Chicago Bears, prevented the Eagles from winning the Eastern Division in 1944. They finished second to the Giants, who went 8-1-1. What made it all the more remarkable was the fact that owner Lex Thompson once again required the players to work full time in defense plants.

The war finally took its toll on the Bears in 1944. Of the 28 players on the 1943 championship team, 19 were lost to the armed forces, including Harry Clark, Hampton Pool, and Clyde "Bulldog" Turner, three of the players investigated by the War Manpower Commission for leaving war jobs to play for the Bears.

"We tried to get replacements," co-coach Luke Johnsos recalled. "We held tryouts at Cubs Park [Wrigley Field] and signed up anybody who could run around the field twice. We had players forty, fifty years old. We had a very poor ball club." Johnsos exaggerated, of course. Despite the massive personnel losses, the Bears still managed to finish the season 6-3-1, tied with Detroit for second place in the West behind Green Bay.

The Brooklyn Dodgers changed their name in 1944 but not, as the saying goes, their stripes. Owner Dan Topping hired a new general manager, a former fight promoter named Tom Gallery, who quickly tired of fielding phone calls and getting mail intended for the baseball Dodgers.

"It drove me nuts," Gallery said. "So one day I decided to change the team name. I looked up and saw a framed design on the office wall—the snarling tiger drawn by Walt Disney for Topping's air wing. Why not the Brooklyn Tigers?" The change gave the NFL, for the first time, Lions and Tigers and Bears. These Tigers, however, had no teeth. They matched Card-Pitt by going winless and finishing the season 0-10. (Fortunately for fans, the two teams did not play each other.) The Tigers even managed to finish behind the newly-minted Boston Yanks, who went 2-8.

In the 1944 championship game, the Packers beat the Giants 14-7. Although he didn't score a touchdown, one of the stars of the game was none other than Don Hutson. It turned out Hutson's game against the Steagles was not his last after all.

"I kept announcing that I was going to retire from football and devote my entire time to my business interests," Hutson explained. "But I kept coming back, until 1945 anyway. It was damn near impossible for me to quit football in Green Bay. You know what the Packers meant to the town and I'd been having some good years. I got the feeling they wanted me to play forever.

But the time had come. Before the 1945 season, I told Curly I'd play that year only if he promised not to ask me to play again the next year. He said all right, and he was good to his word. And that was it."

Because the Giants double-teamed Hutson throughout the championship game, Green Bay used him as a decoy and passed the ball to other receivers, who were usually wide open. Hutson only caught two passes, but his mere presence was instrumental in Green Bay's victory.

On December 9, 1944, the drafting of men 26 and older was resumed. With the fighting still raging on two fronts and preparations under way for a possible invasion of Japan, the Army's appetite for able-bodied men once again turned ravenous. Attendant with the renewed demand for manpower was an even greater scrutiny of 4-F athletes. James F. Byrnes, the head of the Office of War Mobilization and Reconversion (and later secretary of state), asked Lewis Hershey to re-examine all professional athletes who were deferred for physical reasons.

"It is difficult for the public to understand, and certainly it is difficult for me to understand, how these men can be physically unfit for military service and yet be able to compete with the greatest athletes of the nation in games demanding physical fitness," Byrnes said.

What ensued was blatantly discriminatory. A professional athlete—a "P.A." in Selective Service jargon—was likely to be inducted whatever his infirmities. On January 15, 1945, Philadelphia Phillies outfielder Ron Northey was ordered to report for induction, even though he was 4-F with a perforated eardrum, a heart ailment, and high blood pressure. Frank Sinkwich, the Detroit Lions' star halfback, beat Selective Service to the punch. As he'd hoped, Sinkwich found a way back into the military. He joined the Army Air Forces, which, being more concerned about flying than marching, didn't consider flat feet to be an issue. Sinkwich, however, didn't spend much time in the air. He played football for the AAF team in Colorado Springs, where he suffered a serious knee injury that ended his promising football career.

On April 12, 1945, Franklin Roosevelt died of a cerebral hemorrhage at the winter White House in Warm Springs, Georgia. He was succeeded by his vice president, Harry Truman, who as a senator had occasionally attended Redskins games at Griffith Stadium. Truman authorized the dropping of atomic bombs on Hiroshima and Nagasaki, and on Tuesday, August 14, 1945, Japan surrendered unconditionally. World War II was over. The headline in the next day's *Philadelphia Inquirer* read, simply, "PEACE." Immediately the nation began the painful process of reconverting to a peacetime economy. The armed forces began demobilizing. Over the next year, more than seven million men and women would be discharged. Conscription continued, but inductions were slashed nearly in half and all men 26 or older were made exempt. The military cancelled contracts worth more than $23 billion. Unemployment soared overnight. In the four days after the surrender, more than 70,000 workers were laid off from war plants in Philadelphia alone. The government-funded day-care centers were closed. Manpower controls were lifted. Rationing ended for most goods (though some, including sugar, would continue to be rationed until 1947, when the Office of Price Administration was finally disbanded).

Three days after the surrender, the Office of Defense Transportation lifted all travel restrictions affecting athletic events. ODT director J. Monroe Johnson thanked sports organizations for their cooperation during the war. He said, "The example set by athletic leaders, both professional and amateur, in voluntarily cutting travel was probably the strongest single factor in impressing upon the general public the urgency of the wartime transportation situation." Monroe thanked in particular the commissioner of the National Football League, Elmer Layden.

On August 22, in a sign of professional football's growing prominence and influence, Layden called on Harry Truman at the White House. Layden presented Truman with a gold-engraved lifetime pass, which the smiling president promised to use. (Truman, as it turned out, was too busy. A sitting president wouldn't attend an NFL game until 1966, when Lyndon Johnson took in a preseason affair at D.C. Stadium.)

The Philadelphia Eagles did some reconverting of their own in the days after the war ended. General manager Harry Thayer announced that players could quit their day jobs if they so desired.

"It is not necessary," Thayer said. "But the club itself will no longer demand they keep outside jobs."

Art Morrow, who covered the Eagles for the *Philadelphia Inquirer*, lamented the end of compulsory moonlighting.

"Players did not have so much leisure between games for the type of extracurricular activities that make for Sunday fumbles," Morrow wrote, apparently forgetting that the Steagles had led the league in fumbles in 1943.

When Japan surrendered, NFL training camps were just getting under way. Players who'd gone off to war began trickling back. Sometimes they went right to work. Ken Kavanaugh played two seasons with the Bears before joining the Army Air Forces in 1942. He flew 25 missions over Germany. Kavanaugh was mustered out shortly after V-J Day and reported back to the Bears the day before they played the Eagles in an exhibition game in Bethlehem, Pennsylvania.

"George Halas made me play, and I scored three times," Kavanaugh recalled with a laugh.

Among the returning servicemen was Jack Sanders, a lineman who had played for the Steelers in 1942. Sanders lost part of his left arm in the fighting at Iwo Jima. While recuperating at the Naval Hospital in South Philadelphia, he decided to try out for the Eagles. He appeared in three games in 1945.

Many former soldiers were unable to reacclimatize themselves to professional football. Physically and psychologically, it was a difficult transition. After missing three seasons while in the Navy, Eagles tackle John Eibner reported to training camp in 1946. He knew he was out of shape, so he asked his friend and teammate Vic Sears for help. When Eibner was playing defense in scrimmages, Sears would give him a signal to let him know which play was going to be run. The coaches were impressed with Eibner's seemingly telepathic ability to find the ball carrier, and he made the team.

"This was the only time I ever did anything like that," said Sears. "I just loved the guy and never was sorry for it."

In 1945, Tommy Thompson, who'd been the Eagles starting quarterback before the war, returned from the service only to find his position already occupied by Roy Zimmerman. Thus began the first quarterback controversy in Eagles history. It ended after the 1946 season, when the Eagles traded Zimmerman to the Detroit Lions.

Zimmerman retired from football after the 1948 season to pursue his first love: pitching. He became one of the country's top fast-pitch softball hurlers. He once struck out 30 batters in a 14-inning game, and his team, the Fresno Hoak Packers, won the International Softball Congress championship in 1950 and 1952. On August 22, 1997, Zimmerman died of cancer. He was 79.

The waves of returning servicemen did not displace all the 4-Fs who'd replaced them during the war. That's because professional football was one sector of the postwar economy where jobs were plentiful. Not only had the NFL increased the maximum roster size to 33 again; there was a whole new league looking for players.

In 1946, Arch Ward, the *Chicago Tribune* sports editor and sports impresario, launched the All-America Football Conference with franchises in eight cities. At first, NFL Commissioner Elmer Layden did not take the new rival seriously. When AAFC officials approached Layden before their inaugural season to discuss issues of mutual concern, including territorial rights, Layden dismissed them out of hand.

"Let them get a football and play a game," Layden quipped, "and then maybe we'll have something to talk about." He miscalculated badly. Arch Ward promoted the league relentlessly, in the *Tribune* and elsewhere, and when Dan Topping announced he was moving his Brooklyn Tigers (nee Dodgers) from the NFL to the

AAFC, the upstart gained instant credibility. (By switching leagues, Topping was finally able to achieve his goal of playing in Yankee Stadium. To further confuse sports historians, he renamed his team the New York Yankees.)

Players were offered big raises to jump to the AAFC. Salaries went up overnight, and a full-fledged war broke out between the two leagues. One of its first casualties was Layden himself. Partly because of his weak response to the new competitor, Layden's contract was not renewed in 1946. His replacement was none other than Bert Bell, founder of the Philadelphia Eagles and co-owner of the Pittsburgh Steelers. Before taking the job, Bell sold his interest in the Steelers to Art Rooney, who once again became the team's sole proprietor. The two leagues finally made peace before the 1950 season, when three AAFC franchises (the Baltimore Colts, the Cleveland Browns, and the San Francisco 49ers) were admitted to the NFL.

A welcome postwar development in pro football was integration. In 1946, former Ohio State University and Great Lakes Naval Station head coach Paul Brown signed two African-Americans, Marion Motley and Bill Willis, for his Cleveland Browns franchise in the AAFC. The new league, like the early NFL, had no "gentlemen's agreement" barring blacks, and no way to enforce one if it did. As sports historian Alan H. Levy writes, "Brown was a meticulous individual who, in his desire to bring the game of football to a more precise scientific level, cared little about the pigment of a man's skin." Brown knew good football players when he saw them. Both Motley and Willis ended up in the Hall of Fame.

The National Football League also integrated in 1946, though under less noble circumstances. When the Rams moved into the Los Angeles Coliseum, the city's African-American leaders made an interesting argument: Since the Coliseum was a public facility, and the NFL was segregated, wasn't the city required to build a "separate but equal" stadium for blacks? Los Angeles had no intention of building a second 90,000-seat stadium, of course, and city leaders pressured the Rams to integrate, which they did, much to the chagrin of George Preston Marshall. (Coincidentally, a similar tactic would be used to force Marshall to integrate his Redskins 16 years later.) The Rams signed two former UCLA stars, Kenneth Washington and Woodrow "Woody" Strode. Neither performed exceptionally well. Washington was 28 and had bad knees. Strode was 32 and lasted just one season. Like Jackie Robinson, who integrated major league baseball the following year, pro football's black pioneers were forced to endure cheap shots and verbal abuse on the field.

"If I have to integrate heaven," Strode once mused, "I don't want to go." To say they opened doors would be an understatement. In 2004, 69 percent of the players in the NFL were black.

In 1947—just four years after merging as two of the weakest teams in the league—the Philadelphia Eagles and the Pittsburgh Steelers tied for first place in the Eastern Division. The Eagles won the playoff at Forbes Field, 21-0, but lost the championship game to the Chicago Cardinals, another surprisingly resurgent team. The Steelers would not appear in another playoff game for 25 long years and they wouldn't win their first title until January 12, 1975, at the conclusion of the franchise's forty-third season. By then, of course, the championship game was known as the Super Bowl (and had been since 1967). The Steelers would win three more Super Bowls for Art Rooney before their beloved owner died in 1988 at age 87. They won another Super Bowl in 2006.

In 1948 the Eagles won their first NFL championship, defeating the Cardinals in a blizzard at Shibe Park, 7-0. Five former Steagles were on the roster: tackle Bucko Kilroy, fullback Ben Kish, tackle Vic Sears, halfback Ernie Steele, and tackle Al Wistert. A year later the Eagles won the title again, beating the Rams 14-0 in a pouring rain at the Los Angeles Coliseum. At Greasy Neale's insistence, the team returned to Philadelphia by train.

Despite their success on the field, the Eagles still struggled financially. Lex Thompson claimed the team lost more than $30,000 in 1947 and $80,000 in 1948, mainly due to the bidding war with the AAFC.

"Salaries have gone crazy," Thompson complained in a 1948 article in *Sport* magazine:

> *My payroll in '41 was $41,000. Last year it inflated to $225,000. Now it's up past $250,000 and still climbing. The average starting wage for a first-year man in the National [Football] League used to be $1,500. . . . After December, we operated job-placement bureaus that provided good off-season employment. Today, ballplayers laugh at you if you suggest they work in the off-season. . . . Tackles and guards have no drawing power, but I'm paying mine $7,000 a season.*

On January 15, 1949, Thompson sold the Eagles to a syndicate of 100 Philadelphia businessmen for $250,000. A little less than six years later, on December 20, 1954, Thompson, 40, was found dead of a heart attack outside the door of his suburban New York apartment.

The syndicate that bought the Eagles was known as the "100 Brothers." It was headed by James P. Clark, a trucking company tycoon and inveterate meddler. Clark got along with Greasy Neale about as well as Walt Kiesling had. After a 7-3 loss to the Giants near the end of the 1950 season, Clark burst into the locker room and berated Neale in front of his players.

"The team made plenty of mistakes," Clark exclaimed, "and you made mistakes." Typically, Neale's response included a copious amount of colorful profanity. Clark fired Neale after the season. At 59, Greasy Neale, one of the greatest football coaches of all time, was unemployed.

"I had a reputation for being a great handler of men," Neale said. "The only one I couldn't handle was Jim Clark." When he'd taken the job in Philadelphia, Neale had promised his much-traveled wife Genevieve—his "driving force," as he called her—that it would be his last. Two months after he was unceremoniously fired, Genevieve died. Neale was shattered. But, true to his word, he never coached again. In 1969 Greasy Neale was inducted into the Pro Football Hall of Fame. He died on November 2, 1973, three days shy of his eighty-second birthday. He held the Eagles' record for most wins by a head coach (66) until Andy Reid surpassed him in 2004.

After four seasons in Green Bay, Walt Kiesling returned to the Steelers in 1949 as an assistant coach. Before the 1954 season, Art Rooney fired head coach Joe Bach and, once again, asked Big Kies to take over. After three losing seasons Kiesling stepped down as head coach but stayed with the Steelers as an assistant, the job he always preferred. Kiesling remained with the team until he passed away on March 2, 1962, at age 58. At the time of his death, Kiesling's tenure in the National Football League was second only to George Halas's. In recognition of his longevity, Kiesling was posthumously elected to the Hall of Fame in 1966. The Steagles, therefore, were coached by two Hall of Famers, albeit two who never got along. In Canton their busts sit just a few feet apart.

As commissioner, Bert Bell presided over the National Football League's phenomenal growth after the war. He assumed control of scheduling, ending the owners' tiresome practice of endlessly haggling over the particulars of each and every game. The owners, weary themselves, trusted Bell and were glad to hand him the task. Bell drew up each season's schedule by labeling his sons' dominoes with the various team names, then arranging them on a giant cardboard calendar on his dining room table. His philosophy was simple.

"Weak teams should play other weak teams while the strong teams are playing other strong teams early in the year," he said. "It's the only way to keep more teams in contention longer into the season." The result was to become the league's hallmark: parity. (Bell is often credited as the source of the famous quote, "On any given Sunday, any team can beat any other.") The stranglehold that the Bears, Redskins, Giants, and Packers had on the championship game was broken. Even the Cardinals and the Eagles had a shot at the title now.

Bell also ushered football into the television age, shrewdly exploiting the medium to both promote and protect the league. By 1956, CBS was broadcasting every regular season game, and paying more than $1 million for the privilege, while NBC had the rights to the championship game. But the networks weren't showing injuries or fights. Bell, ever protective of the game's image, prohibited that.

"We don't want kids sitting in the living room to see their heroes trading punches," he explained. "That doesn't teach good sportsmanship." Bell was also known to call play-by-play announcers after games to critique their performance. (Runners were not to be "tripped up" or "wrestled to the ground"; they were always to be "tackled.") His attention to detail paid off handsomely. Ratings skyrocketed. The famous 1958 championship game, in which the Colts beat the Giants 23-17 in overtime, was watched in 10.8 million homes, establishing professional football as the nation's preeminent televised sport.

But Bell was wary of the young medium as well.

"Television creates interest and this can benefit pro football," he said. "But it's only good as long as you can protect your home gate. You can't give fans a game for free on television and also expect them to pay to go to the ballpark to see the same game." Why buy the cow when you can get the milk for free? So Bell banned the free milk. In 1951 he decreed that a team's home games could not be televised locally. The blackout policy angered many fans and was challenged by the Justice Department as an illegal restraint of trade. But Bell stood firm and a federal court upheld the policy. Attendance rose by 72 percent through the 1950s, from 25,356 per game in 1950 to 43,617 in 1959. (In 1972 Congress passed a law lifting blackouts for home games that are sold out 72 hours before kickoff. The legislation was said to be the result of frustrated congressmen who couldn't get Redskins tickets and wanted to watch the games on TV.)

Yet even as he helped build the National Football League into the wealthiest sporting enterprise in the nation, Bell never lost his passion for the game itself. On an autumn Sunday afternoon there was only one place he wanted to be, and that was at a football game. As a man of power and privilege, he could have sat, for free, in the most expensive box in the stadium. But he always preferred to buy his own tickets and sit in the stands, among the "working stiffs," as he called the league's bread and butter. That's where he was on Sunday, October 11, 1959, when he suffered a massive heart attack that killed him almost instantly.

"It was almost as though he were allowed to choose time and place," wrote the sports columnist Red Smith.

Bert Bell died at Franklin Field in Philadelphia, where he'd starred at quarterback for the University of Pennsylvania four decades earlier. He was watching the Eagles play the Steelers.

Postscript: 2003

▮ ▯ ▯ ▯ ▯ ▮

HEINZ FIELD, THE PITTSBURGH STEELERS' CURRENT HOME, overlooks the confluence of the Allegheny and Monongahela rivers, not far from the very spot where General Forbes wrested Fort Duquesne from the French. The stadium exemplifies all that the National Football League has become since World War II: enormous, flashy, and rich. Built at a cost of $281 million (of which taxpayers contributed $158 million), Heinz Field is a spectacular venue, a glistening glass-and-steel horseshoe with impeccable sightlines and breathtaking views of downtown. Each of its 64,450 seats is the color of yellow mustard, and the three-story-tall video screen at the open end of the stadium is topped by two giant bottles of Heinz ketchup.

Heinz Field could scarcely be more different from Forbes Field, the Steelers' first home. It is thoroughly modern in every way, from its state-of-the-art sound system to its turf, a blend of natural grass and synthetic fibers called DD GrassMaster. But when the Steelers hosted the Philadelphia Eagles in a preseason game on August 16, 2003, the atmosphere inside the stadium was decidedly retro. No garish logos adorned the field. Big band music, not rock, blared from the sound system. On the giant video screen, all the pictures were in black and white. For on that muggy Saturday night, the Steelers turned the clock back to 1943 to commemorate the sixtieth anniversary of the Steagles.

The event was the brainchild of Steelers owner Dan Rooney, who was 11 when what was then his father's team merged with the Eagles.

"It was a time in America that was so meaningful," Rooney said.

At halftime, faded images of the Steagles were shown on the video screen while the public-address announcer, Randy Cosgrove, briefly explained to the incredulous throng the hybrid team's strange saga. Then Cosgrove read the names of the three former Steagles who were unable to attend the evening's festivities.

"Tackle Ted Doyle."

Ted Doyle retired from the Steelers after the 1945 season. Or rather he wasn't invited back. A new coach, Jock Sutherland, had taken over.

"I never heard from him so I guess he didn't want me," Doyle said. "I didn't go back." Doyle never pursued the matter with Art Rooney because he "didn't want to interfere with anything." So he and Harriet and their two children moved back to Nebraska. Doyle managed a bowling alley in the town of Fairbury for a time, then went to work for an agricultural products company. He retired for good in the mid 1980s. He and Harriet live in Gretna, Nebraska. Doyle still thinks he would've been better off taking that job with Hormel back in 1938.

"Halfback Jack Hinkle."

Jack Hinkle would never have another season like 1943. Steve Van Buren replaced him as the Eagles' No. 1 running back the following season. Hinkle was switched back to a blocking back, a position he filled quite adeptly until his retirement after the 1947 season. In 1951 he became an assistant football coach at the Drexel Institute of Technology (now Drexel University) in Philadelphia. In 1958 he was named head coach. After three losing seasons he resigned to take a sales job with a brass and copper company. He and his wife Joane, who still calls him "Honey," live outside Philadelphia.

"End Tom Miller."

Shortly before the 1945 season, the Eagles traded Tom Miller to the Redskins. The following summer, Miller went to visit his in-laws, who happened to live in Green Bay. In a barbershop he bumped into Packers head coach Curly Lambeau, who was surprised to learn that Miller's wife was a local girl. A month later, Lambeau, apparently convinced Miller's relations with his in-laws were sound, bought his contract from Washington.

"Not that I was very good," Miller joked. "The Redskins were glad to get rid of me." Miller ended up playing just two games for the Packers, but in 1955 he was appointed the team's publicity director. He was promoted, first to assistant general manager under Vince Lombardi, then to assistant to the president. He retired from the Packers in 1988 and was inducted into the team's Hall of Fame in 1999. After a lengthy illness, Tom Miller died on December 2, 2005. He was 87.

At this point in the ceremonies, six old men, all stooped but sturdy, emerged from a tunnel beneath the stands and slowly made their way to midfield as the PA announcer called their names.

"Center, No. 52, Ray Graves!"

After retiring from pro football for good following the 1946 season, Ray Graves took a job as an assistant coach at Georgia Tech, where he worked under the legendary Bobby Dodd. In 1960 he became the head coach at the University of Florida. He coached the Gators to five bowl appearances, winning four, including a 27-12 victory over his mentor Dodd in the 1967 Orange Bowl. Graves retired from coaching after the 1969 season with a record of 70-31-4. He was the winningest coach in Florida history until 1996, when he was surpassed by one of his former players, Steve Spurrier. But his most lasting contribution to the school came in 1965, when he was approached by four university researchers who wanted to test a concoction they'd developed for alleviating dehydration.

"One of the reasons I have respect for Coach Graves was that when we explained to him what we had found he professed no ability to really understand what we were saying, but he accepted it," Robert Cade, one of the researchers, later recalled. "But he hedged his bets a bit. He said we could try it only on the freshman team." So far the University of Florida has collected more than $80 million in royalties from sales of the resulting product, which the researchers, in honor of the school's football team, named Gatorade.

"Tackle, No. 76, Frank 'Bucko' Kilroy!"

A knee injury ended Bucko Kilroy's playing career after the 1955 season but he never left the NFL. He became a scout, first for the Eagles, then for the Washington Redskins, Dallas Cowboys, and New England Patriots. Kilroy was instrumental in developing many of today's standard scouting techniques.

"I used to go out and time people and measure them, and some of the other scouts used to ridicule me," he said. "When we started giving them IQ tests, they really started in on me. We were the first to do any of that, and the other scouts would say, 'Aw, why the hell are you doing that? Just look at the guy.'"

Kilroy joined the Patriots as director of player personnel in 1971. He was twice promoted, first to general manager, then to vice president. He helped assemble the teams that won three Super Bowls in four seasons from 2001 to 2004, and he still works for the Patriots as a consultant. The year 2005 was his sixty-third in the National Football League, equaling George Halas's record of longevity.

"Tackle, No. 79, Vic Sears!"

Even after two-platoon football became the norm with the permanent implementation of unlimited substitution in 1950, soft-spoken tackle Vic Sears still played both ways for the Eagles. During most games he never left the field; he even covered kickoffs and punts. As a result, he probably put in more actual playing time than any other player in Eagles history and was truly one of the last of the "60-minute men." (Eagles legend Chuck Bednarik played "only" 58 minutes in the 1960 championship game.) Sears finally retired after the 1953 season but stayed in the Philadelphia area, working as a manufacturer's representative.

"I did a lot of traveling along the East Coast," Sears said. "It was a good way to make a living and I enjoyed it."

"Quarterback, No. 10, Allie Sherman!"

Allie Sherman never did get a chance to be a first-string quarterback, but his time on the sidelines with Greasy Neale paid off in 1949, when longtime New York Giants coach Steve Owen finally decided to switch to the T formation.

"Take Allie Sherman to help you," Neale said to his old friend Owen. "He's the smartest young man in football." After five seasons as an assistant with the Giants, Sherman became the head coach of the Winnipeg Blue Bombers in the Canadian Football League. In 1957 he returned to the Giants as a scout. Two years later he was promoted to offensive coordinator, replacing Vince Lombardi, who had left to take the top job in Green Bay. In 1961, at age 38, Sherman was named head coach of the Giants. Greasy Neale would often come out to watch his protégé run practices, standing silently on the sidelines, his white poodle Bianco tucked under one arm. Sherman coached the Giants to the Eastern Division title in each of his first three seasons but lost the championship game each time, twice to Green Bay and once to the Bears. As stars like Frank Gifford and Y.A. Tittle retired, however, the Giants slumped into mediocrity. Fans began serenading Sherman with choruses of "Goodbye Allie," sung to the tune of "Good Night, Ladies." On the eve of the 1969 season Sherman was dismissed. He never coached again. Instead he pursued lucrative business ventures on Wall Street. Now comfortably retired in New York, Sherman frequents the Friars Club, where he is known, simply, as "Coach."

"Defensive back and halfback, No. 37, Ernie Steele!"

Pre-Pearl father Ernie Steele was finally drafted in 1945 but was classified 4-F. He'd accidentally cut his left wrist while chopping wood as a teenager, severely damaging the tendons. He was left with limited mobility in his left hand. To this day he is unable to open it all the way. That didn't prevent him from carrying a football, however, and in 1948 he averaged 7.6 yards per rushing attempt to help the Eagles win their first championship. He retired after that season and moved back to Seattle, where he opened a cocktail lounge in the Capitol Hill neighborhood. Ernie Steele's, as it was known, became a Seattle landmark and was one of the favorite haunts of the grunge scene in the late 1980s and early 1990s. Steele sold the business in 1993 and Ernie Steele's is, sadly, no more, though it lives on in a song by the band The Presidents of the United States of America called "Candy Cigarette":

> *Three p.m. and we're slow to recover*
> *We're hangin' out and well hungover*
> *'Cause Ernie Steele's makes a mean martini*
> *So pass the fire and light me sweetie.*

"Tackle, No. 70, Al Wistert!"

Al Wistert never did develop osteomyelitis, the bone disease for which he was rejected by the military. He did, however, develop a deep and abiding affection for Greasy Neale, the coach he couldn't stand in his rookie season.

"He was a wonderful man when I finally got to know him," Wistert said. "My opinion of him is very high. I'd lost my dad when I was just a kid and I'd often searched for somebody else to take my dad's place—and I feel that man was Greasy Neale."

In 1947 Wistert was named the Eagles' team captain, an honor he held until his retirement after the 1951 season. He was an all-pro every season but his first and he was the first Eagle to have his number retired. He is widely regarded as the best lineman not in the Pro Football Hall of Fame, an opinion that he does not disavow.

"I'd like to be in there," Wistert said. "I'm still ticked off about that." After football he sold life insurance. Wistert now lives on a farm outside Grants Pass, Oregon.

"Steeler fans," the PA announcer thundered, "please welcome home the 1943 Pittsburgh Steagles!" The crowd, standing now, erupted in long, warm, appreciative applause. The six Steagles stood beaming at midfield, weathered octogenarians basking one last time in the adulation of football fans. Some of them had tears in their eyes—as did a lot of other people in the stadium.

Notes

■ | | | | ■

Unless otherwise noted, all quotes attributed to Harriet Doyle, Ted Doyle, Ray Graves, Jack Hinkle, Frank "Bucko" Kilroy, Tom Miller, Vic Sears, Ernie Steele, and Al Wistert were drawn from the author's conversations with them.

Preface: 1941

ix   **The Tuffy Leemans biographical information** comes from Carroll, et al., *Total Football II* (pp. 326–327) and Cope, *The Game That Was* (pp. 151–157). Leemans' performance against Alabama was described in the *Washington Star,* October 6, 1935.

x   **"Fans, teammates . . ."** (Leemans): *New York Times,* December 8, 1941.

xii   **My account of Pearl Harbor Day** is based on contemporaneous newspaper reports, as well as Goldstein, "Football Sunday, Dec. 7, 1941: Suddenly the Games Didn't Matter," Maiorana, "Battle Cry: 'Infamy.' A Day to Remember," Povich, "At Redskins-Eagles Game, Crowd Was Kept Unaware That War Had Begun," and Prange, et al., *December 7, 1941.*

xiii   **"For a few . . ."** (Povich): Povich, "At Redskins-Eagles Game, Crowd Was Kept Unaware That War Had Begun."

xiii   **"We don't want . . ."** (Espey): *Washington Post,* December 8, 1941.

xiii   **"I didn't want . . ."** (Marshall): Povich, "At Redskins-Eagles Game, Crowd Was Kept Unaware That War Had Begun."

xiv   **"By the end . . ."** (Povich): Povich, "At Redskins-Eagles Game, Crowd Was Kept Unaware That War Had Begun."

xiv   **"We didn't know . . ."** (Baugh): Maiorana, "Battle Cry: 'Infamy.' A Day to Remember."

xiv   **Fans listening to the games on the radio** were better informed than those in the stands. In New York, for example, WOR abruptly cut away from the

Dodgers-Giants game with this announcement: "We interrupt this broadcast to bring you this important bulletin from the United Press: Flash. Washington. The White House announces Japanese attack on Pearl Harbor."

xiv **"The American people . . ."** (Roosevelt): Goodwin, *No Ordinary Time* (p. 295).

xv **"I don't know . . ."** (Owen): Goldstein, "Football Sunday, Dec. 7, 1941: Suddenly the Games Didn't Matter."

xv **The statistics concerning NFL players in the armed forces** are taken from Claassen, *The History of Professional Football* (pp. 80–81). In addition to the nineteen players killed, John O'Keefe, who worked in the front office of the Eagles, and Jack Chevigny, a former head coach of the Chicago Cardinals, also died in the service of their country.

xvi **My valuation of the 32 NFL franchises** is based on *Forbes* magazine's estimate that the average value of an NFL franchise in 2005 was $819 million. Estimated valuations for each franchise are posted on the *Forbes* website: *http://www.forbes.com/business/2005/09/01/sports-football-gambling-cz_05nfland.html.*

One: A Bad Break

1 **I based my account of Al Wistert's ill-fated rushing attempt** on interviews with him, as well as reports in the *Chicago Tribune,* October 18–19, 1941.

2 **Information about the Wistert family** came from interviews with Al Wistert, as well as Spoelstra, "The Michigan Tackle That Time Forgot." It's worth noting that the middle Wistert brother, Alvin, also was an all-American tackle at Michigan–but after his baby brother, Al. After a four-year hitch in the Marines, Alvin was working in a Massachusetts soap factory when his brothers encouraged him to go to college on the GI Bill. He was 31 when he enrolled at Michigan in 1947. He was an all-American at 33.

3 **"I must confess . . ."** (Crisler): Spoelstra, "The Michigan Tackle That Time Forgot."

5 **For more information about Arch Ward,** see Littlewood, *Arch.*

5 **Al Wistert recounted the story of his contract negotiations** in interviews with the author.

6 **My account of the 1943 *Chicago Tribune* college all-star game** is based on reports in the *Tribune,* August 25–26, 1943.

7 **The examination a typical draftee faced** is described by Christina S. Jarvis in *The Male Body at War.* "From his feet to his ears, he was poked, prodded, and measured. His height, weight, chest size, and other physical statistics were recorded, and blood and urine samples were taken for tests. He encountered opthalmoscopes, stethoscopes, chest x-ray machines, and other diagnostic aids, which allowed the gaze of the doctors to penetrate beneath the skin. . . . [He was] examined by a psychiatrist who asked him if 'he liked girls' and screened for problems of the nervous system."

8   **My account of the draft lottery** is based on reports in the *New York Times,* October 30, 1940, as well as Flynn, *The Draft, 1940–1973.* My history of conscription is largely drawn from Flynn, *The Draft, 1940–1973* and Flynn, *Lewis B. Hershey.*

9   **"The men themselves . . ."** (Roosevelt): Goodwin, *No Ordinary Time* (p. 144).

9   **"some form of selection"** (Roosevelt): Flynn, *The Draft, 1940–1973* (p. 10).

10   **"Chinaman's chance"** (Byrnes): Flynn, *The Draft, 1940–1973* (p. 16).

10   **My description of Selective Service regulations** is based on Petersen and Stewart, *Conscription Manual;* as well as Flynn, *The Draft, 1940–1973*; Flynn, *Lewis B. Hershey;* and United States Selective Service System, *Selective Service as the Tide of War Turns.*

Two: Keystoners

12   **My account of the blue laws** is based largely on Warrington, "The Fight for Sunday Baseball in Philadelphia." The *Philadelphia Evening Bulletin* clip files at the Urban Archives at Temple University were also a valuable source of information.

12   **"We cannot meet . . ."** (Mack): Warrington, "The Fight for Sunday Baseball in Philadelphia."

13   **My histories of the Frankford Yellow Jackets and the Pottsville Maroons** are based on Carroll, et al., *Total Football II* (pp. 99–109).

14   **Art Rooney's early years** are described in Cope, *The Game That Was* (pp. 121–139). The legendary $20 bet at Saratoga is described in Anderson, "An Old Gambler Finally Collects."

14   **"Racing's not the same . . ."** (Rooney): Anderson, "An Old Gambler Finally Collects."

14   **"I bought the franchise . . ."** (Rooney): Cope, *The Game That Was* (pp. 127–128).

14   **The Bert Bell biography** is drawn largely from material contained in the *Philadelphia Evening Bulletin* clip files, especially Day, "Bert Bell Collapses and Dies At Eagles Football Game." Also helpful was Pro Football Hall of Fame, "Bert Bell: The Commissioner."

14   **"If I can lick . . ."** (Bell): Didinger and Lyons, *The Eagles Encyclopedia* (p. 6).

15   **"Bert will go . . ."** (elder Bell): MacCambridge, *America's Game* (pp. 41–42).

15   **My accounts of the first legal Sunday professional football games in Pennsylvania** are based on reports in the *Philadelphia Inquirer* and the *Pittsburgh Post-Gazette,* November 8–13, 1933. Art Rooney told of inviting police superintendent Franklin T. McQuade to the game in Cope, *The Game That Was* (p. 128).

15   **For Connie Mack,** the man who led the fight against the blue laws in Pennsylvania, their repeal was a hollow victory. By the time the 1934 baseball season came around his team's finances had been so thoroughly decimated by the Depression that there weren't enough Sundays on the

calendar to make up the difference. He'd been forced to sell off his best players—including future baseball Hall of Famers Mickey Cochran, Lefty Grove, and Al Simmons—to help pay off a $700,000 loan. The A's finally limped to Kansas City in 1954. Today the franchise is based in Oakland.

16 **All team records throughout the book** are drawn from Carroll, et al., *Total Football II,* Neft, et al., *The Football Encyclopedia,* and Liu and Marini, *2005 NFL Record & Fact Book.*

16 **The Lex Thompson biography** is based on material contained in the *Philadelphia Evening Bulletin* clip files, as well as Stump, "Get Smart—or Go Bust?" Thompson described his search for a "sports hobby" in Kauffman, "Football a Hobby of Eagles' Prexy."

16 **The swapping of the Philadelphia and Pittsburgh franchises** is superbly described in Braunwart, et al., "Pennsylvania Polka." My account is based largely on that article, as well as contemporaneous newspaper reports.

17 **"I certainly hated . . ."** (Rooney): Braunwart, et al., "Pennsylvania Polka."

18 **"Rooney and I have been . . ."** (Bell): *Philadelphia Evening Bulletin,* December 9, 1940.

18 **"He can sell . . ."** (Marshall): *Philadelphia Evening Bulletin,* December 9, 1940.

18 **"Then I got . . ."** (Rooney): Braunwart, et al., "Pennsylvania Polka."

19 **"I know we've . . ."** (Rooney): Braunwart, et al., "Pennsylvania Polka."

19 **Rooney's exchange with Bell** about "changing coaches" is from MacCambridge, *America's Game* (p. 45).

Three: New Priorities

20 **"In dramatic lore . . ."** (Rice): Heisler, *Echoes of Notre Dame Football* (p. 222).

20 **Amos Alonzo Stagg's anti–pro football quote** comes from Peterson, *Pigskin* (p. 6).

21 **Al Ennis' lament** about the lack of local coverage is contained in a fascinating booklet on file at the Pro Football Hall of Fame in Canton, Ohio. The booklet was written by Ennis (and, certainly, Greasy Neale) and distributed to members of the Eagles during training camp in 1948. It contains long lists of rules for training camp and road trips, as well as frank assessments of everything from the team's public relations efforts to the quality of various hotels in NFL cities. ("For the 1947 Championship Game at Chicago, we elected to stay at the Hotel Sherman, in downtown Chicago, and had a most unpleasant experience there. At no time did any member of the management . . . evince the slightest interest in our behalf.")

21 **My account of Elmer Layden's reign** as NFL commissioner (and his sometimes peculiar preoccupations) is based largely on MacCambridge, *America's Game* and Peterson, *Pigskin.*

21 **Layden's efforts** to move pro football to a "high, dignified plane" are described in MacCambridge, *America's Game* (p. 9) and Peterson, *Pigskin* (pp. 136–137).

22   **"Material will be scarce . . ."** (Layden): *Philadelphia Inquirer,* December 9, 1941.

22   **Roosevelt's Green Light Letter** has been widely published, including in Bloomfield, *Duty, Honor, Victory* (p. 69), Gilbert, *They Also Served* (pp. 41–42), MacCambridge, *America's Game* (p. 11), and Mead, *Even the Browns* (pp. 35–36). A copy of the original letter is posted on the website of the National Baseball Hall of Fame: *http://www.baseballhalloffame.org/education/primary_sources/world_war_ii/letter_01.htm.*

23   **"But everything we decide . . ."** (Layden): Peterson, *Pigskin* (p. 138).

23   **I calculated the number of players** lost to the armed forces based on contemporaneous newspaper accounts, as well as data contained in Neft, et al., *The Football Encyclopedia* and Peterson, *Pigskin.*

24   **The Ted Doyle biography** is based on interviews with him and his wife, Harriet Doyle.

25   **Rooney's signing of Whizzer White** is described in Cope, *The Game That Was* (p. 129).

25   **My description of Johnny Blood** is based on Cope, *The Game That Was,* Peterson, *Pigskin,* and Whittingham, *What a Game They Played.* Blood explained the origin of his pseudonym in Whittingham, *What a Game They Played* (p. 32).

26   **"He liked an unusual . . ."** (Hinkle): Cope, *The Game That Was* (p. 99).

26   **"I've always had . . ."** (Blood): Whittingham, *What a Game They Played* (p. 38).

27   **"I would not say . . ."** (Blood): Cope, *The Game That Was* (p. 69).

27   **Ted Doyle's letter to Bert Bell** was published in the *Pittsburgh Post-Gazette,* June 15, 1943.

Four: Making Changes

29   **My account of the April 1943 league meeting** is based on contemporaneous newspaper reports, as well as the minutes of the meeting, which are on file at the Pro Football Hall of Fame.

29   **"I don't believe . . ."** (Layden): NFL meeting minutes, April 6, 1943.

30   **"It'll be a miracle . . ."** (unnamed coach): *Chicago Daily Times,* April 6, 1943.

30   **"We're going to operate . . ."** (Marshall): *Chicago Daily Times,* April 7, 1943.

30   **"we can and will play football"** (Layden): *Philadelphia Inquirer,* April 6, 1943.

30   **The "war clause" in Layden's contract** and his salary were reported in the *Pittsburgh Press,* June 23, 1943.

32   **"If a squad . . ."** (Layden): *Stars and Stripes,* April 8, 1943.

32   **"I don't want . . ."** (Neale): *Philadelphia Evening Bulletin,* November 1, 1948.

34   **"It's just a matter . . ."** (unnamed official): *Chicago Daily Times,* April 8, 1943.

35   **"At no time . . ."** (Thayer): *Chicago Tribune*, April 8, 1943.

35   **"I believe we'll . . ."** (Layden): *Chicago Daily Times*, April 6, 1943.

35   **For my account of African-Americans in professional football,** I am deeply
      indebted to Levy, *Tackling Jim Crow.*

36   **Judge Landis' declaration** that "any major league club is entirely free
      to employ Negroes" was reported on December 3, 1943, in newspapers
      nationwide, including the *Pittsburgh Press.*

38   **Marshall's racism** is well documented in Levy, *Tackling Jim Crow.*

38   **The minutes of the 1933 league meeting** make no mention of race.
      However, as Levy writes, "it is abundantly clear that at the end of the 1933
      season [the owners] chose to ban African-Americans from the league."
      The fact that Joe Lillard, the Chicago Cardinals' leading scorer in 1933,
      was not invited back to the team in 1934 is prima facie evidence that a ban
      had been implemented.

39   **Myron Cope's interview with Art Rooney** is in Cope, *The Game That Was*
      (p. 7).

39   **"We'll start signing . . ."** (Marshall): Levy, *Tackling Jim Crow* (p. 120).

Five: Hatching the Steagles

41   **My account of the negotiations** that led to the merger of the Steelers and
      the Eagles is based on contemporaneous newspaper reports, particularly in
      the *Pittsburgh Post-Gazette,* the *Pittsburgh Press,* and the *Philadelphia Inquirer,*
      as well as the minutes of league meetings, which are on file at the Pro
      Football Hall of Fame.

41   **"The prospects . . ."** (Rooney): *Pittsburgh Press,* May 27, 1943.

42   **"contribute substantially"** (Thompson): *Philadelphia Inquirer,* June 16,
      1943.

44   **My description of Lewis Hershey** is based on Flynn, *Lewis B. Hershey.*

44   **I based my account of the Father Draft debate** on contemporaneous news-
      paper accounts, as well as Flynn, *The Draft, 1940–1973,* Flynn, *Lewis B.
      Hershey,* and United States Selective Service System, *Selective Service as the
      Tide of War Turns.*

44   **Public opinion regarding the Father Draft** is discussed in Flynn, *Lewis B.
      Hershey* (p. 117).

45   **"the preservation of the family"** (Kilday): Flynn, *The Draft, 1940–1973*
      (p. 72).

45   **The exchange between Senator Wheeler and General McNarney** was
      reported in the *Philadelphia Inquirer,* September 16, 1943.

45   **"We certainly can't . . ."** (unnamed draft board chairman): *Philadelphia
      Inquirer,* October 1, 1943.

45   **"one-half million fathers"** (Hershey): United States Selective Service
      System, *Selective Service as the Tide of War Turns* (p. 20).

46   **My account of the June 1943 league meeting** is based on contemporaneous
      newspaper reports, as well as the minutes of the meeting, which are on file

at the Pro Football Hall of Fame.

46 **"There is a more optimistic . . ."** (Layden): *Pittsburgh Press,* June 15, 1943.

48 **Arch Ward's anti-merger column** was published in the *Chicago Tribune* on June 18, 1943.

49 **"To allow Pittsburgh and Philadelphia . . ."** (Bell): NFL meeting minutes, June 19, 1943.

50 **"When the Bears and Cardinals' . . ."** (Thayer): *Pittsburgh Press,* June 20, 1943.

50 **"Without it . . ."** (Bell): *Pittsburgh Press,* July 7, 1943.

52 **"We believe football . . ."** (Layden): *Chicago Daily Times,* June 21, 1943.

52 **"I think that . . ."** (Marshall): NFL meeting minutes, June 20, 1943.

53 **The Bill Hewitt biographical information** comes from Hewitt, "Don't Send My Boy to Halas," Davis, *Papa Bear,* and material contained in the *Philadelphia Evening Bulletin* clip files. Unless otherwise noted, all Hewitt quotes are taken from Hewitt, "Don't Send My Boy to Halas."

54 **"one of the great ends" and "flaming spirit"** (Halas): Davis, *Papa Bear* (pp. 132–133).

54 **My account of the 1932 championship game** is based on Neft, et al., *The Football Encyclopedia* (pp. 92–93) and Peterson, *Pigskin* (pp. 107–108).

54 **"I never saw . . ."** (Grange): Roberts, *The Chicago Bears* (p. 139).

Six: Greasy and Walt

57 **"Why, we wouldn't see Thorpe . . ."** (Neale): Holland, "Greasy Neale: Nothing To Prove, Nothing To Ask."

58 **The Neale biographical information** comes from Holland, "Greasy Neale: Nothing To Prove, Nothing To Ask," Neale and Meany, "Football Is My Life," and material contained in the *Philadelphia Evening Bulletin* clip files. Unless otherwise noted, all Neale quotes in this chapter come from Neale and Meany, "Football Is My Life."

59 **"Yale or no Yale . . ."** (Neale): *Philadelphia Evening Bulletin,* November 3, 1973.

62 **The Kiesling biographical information** comes from Pro Football Hall of Fame, "Hall of Fame Profile: Walt Kiesling," Tucker, *Steelers' Victory After Forty* (pp. 56–59), and his obituary published in the *Pittsburgh Post-Gazette,* March 3, 1962.

63 **My account of the Duluth Eskimos** is based on Cope, *The Game That Was* (pp. 71–81) and Carroll, et al., *Total Football II* (pp. 103–104).

64 **"I chased him . . ."** (Haugsrud): Cope, *The Game That Was* (p. 78).

65 **"I plan no . . ."** (Kiesling): *Pittsburgh Post-Gazette,* October 4, 1939.

66 **The Steagles' summer practices** and training camp were covered extensively in the *Philadelphia Inquirer,* probably because the newspaper's charitable arm sponsored the team's September 16 exhibition game against the Bears at Shibe Park. After that game, the *Inquirer*'s coverage of the Steagles diminished.

67 **Today River Field** is part of a University of Pennsylvania athletic complex. None of the Steagles' other homes for practices and games (Forbes Field, Parkside Field, Shibe Park, and the field at 54th Street and City Line Avenue) is extant.

68 **My description of football formations** is based on Carroll, et al., *Total Football II* (pp. 474–490).

68 *"Football became . . ."* (Halas): Peterson, *Pigskin* (p. 134).

69 **"If that wouldn't . . ."** (Neale): *Philadelphia Evening Bulletin*, November 7, 1948.

69 **Greasy Neale recounted his purchase of the 1940 championship game film** in Holland, "Greasy Neale: Nothing To Prove, Nothing To Ask" and Daley, "High Flying Eagle."

70 **"I don't think the T . . ."** (Bierman): *Pittsburgh Post-Gazette*, December 8, 1943.

70 **"On the whole . . ."** (Neale): *Philadelphia Inquirer*, August 8, 1943.

71 **Elmer Layden's decision** to increase team rosters to 28 players was reported in the *Philadelphia Inquirer*, August 26, 1943.

71 **"We're going to . . ."** (Ennis): *Pittsburgh Press*, August 26, 1943.

71 **"Pittsburgh gridders-workers . . ."** (Bell): *Pittsburgh Post-Gazette*, July 8, 1943.

72 **"Why couldn't our professional squads . . ."** (Bell): *Philadelphia Inquirer*, January 8, 1942.

73 **The "non-deferrable" and "essential"** lists were published in the *New York Times* on August 15, 1943.

73 **"The time has come . . ."** (McNutt): *New York Times*, August 15, 1943.

73 **McNutt and Hershey's contentious relationship** is discussed in Flynn, *Lewis B. Hershey.*

73 **"I will not transmit . . ."** (Hershey): Flynn, *Lewis B. Hershey* (p. 90).

74 **"The usefulness of the sport . . ."** (McNutt): Mead, *Even the Browns* (p. 90).

74 **The wages of workers at the Budd factory** were published in the *Philadelphia Daily News*, July 29, 1943.

75 **The war production figures** come from Dear and Foot, *The Oxford Companion to World War II* and Polmar and Allen, *World War II: The Encyclopedia of the War Years, 1941–1945.*

75 **Executive Order 8802** is discussed in Goodwin, *No Ordinary Time* (pp. 252–253).

75 **The African-American employment statistics** are cited in Goodwin, *No Ordinary Time* (p. 540).

75 **The Raymond Clapper column** was published in the *Pittsburgh Press*, December 15, 1943.

75 **For my account of women in the workplace** during the war, I am deeply indebted to Anderson, *Wartime Women* and Erenberg and Hirsch, *The War in American Culture.*

76 **"lacks the glamour"** (female worker): Anderson, *Wartime Women* (p. 29).

76   **Wartime day-care programs** are discussed in Goodwin, *No Ordinary Time* (pp. 416–417).

76   **The Dorothy Dix column** about women wearing "tubular britches" was published in the *Philadelphia Evening Bulletin*, August 3, 1943.

76   **"We're here to work . . ."** (Penczak): *Philadelphia Evening Bulletin*, August 3, 1943.

77   **"You'd think . . ."** (male worker): Anderson, *Wartime Women* (p. 47).

77   **The Pauline Rugh story** was widely reported in Pennsylvania newspapers in August and September 1943. The Red Smith column appeared in the *Philadelphia Record*, September 9, 1943. The Havey Boyle column appeared in the *Pittsburgh Post-Gazette*, September 1, 1943. Unfortunately, my attempts to locate Rugh and her former players were unsuccessful.

Seven: Unfit for Military Service

78   **My description of the Steagles training camp** is based on contemporaneous newspaper reports as well as player interviews. The conflict between Greasy Neale and Walt Kiesling is well documented. For example, see Dervarics, "When Steagles Walked the Earth" and Spadaro, "Remembering the 'Steagles.'"

80   **Greasy Neale's favorite profane sayings** were collected by the author in player interviews.

80   **"I loved Greasy . . ."** (Hinkle): *Philadelphia Evening Bulletin*, February 8, 1968.

80   **"It is to be doubted . . ."** (Daley): *New York Times*, February 16, 1969.

80   **The anecdote about Walt Kiesling sabotaging Art Rooney's play** appears in Cope, "Pro Football's Gashouse Gang."

81   **"Seldom did Kiesling . . ."** (Tucker): Tucker, *Steelers' Victory After Forty* (p. 58).

81   **"You can't get into condition . . ."** (Kiesling): *Pittsburgh Post-Gazette*, August 30, 1943.

81   **"He was a tremendous . . ."** (Rooney): Cope, *The Game That Was* (pp. 136–137).

81   **"The thing about Walt . . ."** (Haugsrud): Pro Football Hall of Fame, "Hall of Fame Profile: Walt Kiesling."

81   **"Greasy had a sense . . ."** (Kilroy): Infield, "When the Steagles Roamed the Gridiron."

81   **"Kies was a great . . ."** (Rooney): Cope, *The Game That Was* (p. 137).

83   **The Allie Sherman biography** is based on Asinof, "Big Shrimp of Pro Football," Sherman, *Book of Football*, and material contained in the *Philadelphia Evening Bulletin* clip files.

84   **The Roy Zimmerman biography** is based on interviews with his wife, Dena Mary Zimmerman, and his sons, Donald Zimmerman and Rex Zimmerman, as well as contemporaneous newspaper accounts.

85 **"Zimmerman made few . . ."** (Whittlesey): *Washington Post,* November 25, 1943.

85 **The circumstances surrounding Zimmerman's** trade to the Eagles were reported in the *Pittsburgh Post-Gazette,* November 9, 1943.

86 **For information about the physical standards for inductees** I am indebted to Anderson, *Physical Standards in World War II.* I ascertained each player's draft status based on contemporaneous newspaper reports, later articles about the team, player interviews, and Selective Service records.

88 **"He was a legitimate receiver . . ."** (Rooney): Longman, *If Football's a Religion, Why Don't We Have a Prayer?* (p. 64).

88 **"Let's face it . . ."** (Sears): Longman, *If Football's a Religion, Why Don't We Have a Prayer?* (p. 64).

89 **"I was doing mostly . . ."** (Kilroy): Leuthner, *Iron Men* (p. 144).

89 **Hank Soar discussed playing football** while on active duty in Peterson, *Pigskin* (p. 140). Tony Canadeo did likewise in Whittingham, *What a Game They Played* (pp. 217–218).

91 **For my description of wartime Pittsburgh,** I am indebted to Burlbaugh, *The War, the Steagles and the Card-Pitts.* For my description of Forbes Field, I am indebted to Didinger and Lyons, *The Eagles Encyclopedia.*

94 **Throughout the book, my game accounts** are based on contemporaneous newspaper reports and player interviews.

94 **"Hotel reservations . . ."** (Canadeo): Barnett, "When the Packers Went to War."

96 **"The mistakes we made . . ."** (Neale): *Philadelphia Inquirer,* September 13, 1943.

96 **"Any team that . . ."** (Neale): *Philadelphia Inquirer,* September 16, 1943.

96 **My description of wartime Philadelphia** is based on Miller, et al., *Philadelphia Stories.* My description of Shibe Park is based on Kuklick, *To Every Thing A Season* and Westcott, *Philadelphia's Old Ballparks.* My description of bond drives is based on Lingeman, *Don't You Know There's a War On?*

99 **"If all the clubs . . ."** (Bell): *Philadelphia Evening Bulletin,* September 10, 1943.

Eight: Birds of Steel

101 **"You worked all day . . ."** (Hinkle): Ecenbarger, "The Steagles Hybrid Team Zany Moments in Steelers' Past."

101 **"With the pick of both . . ."** (Neale): *Pittsburgh Post-Gazette,* June 25, 1943.

102 **Lewis Hershey's letter** to local draft boards was published in United States Selective Service System, *Selective Service as the Tide of War Turns* (pp. 165–166).

102 **"We found that . . ."** (unnamed draft board official): *Philadelphia Record,* October 1, 1943.

102 **The induction shortfall** is described in Goralski, *World War II Almanac, 1931–1945* (p. 283).

103 **"ignoring the considered judgment"** (McNarney): Flynn, *The Draft, 1940–1973* (p. 74).

103 **"What kind of . . ."** (Roosevelt): Flynn, *The Draft, 1940–1973* (p. 74).

104 **Pete Cawthon's efforts** to cobble together the Dodgers are recounted in Lynch, *Tender Tyrant* (pp. 127–130).

104 **"I'm out of shape . . ."** (Jones): Lynch, *Tender Tyrant* (p. 128).

105 **"We simply do not . . ."** (Cawthon): *New York Herald Tribune,* October 21, 1943.

105 **Dennis Shea's disparaging comments** about the Steagles were published in numerous papers, including the *Pittsburgh Post-Gazette,* July 21, 1943.

106 **"a serious student" and "had real possibilities"** (Neale): Holland, "Greasy Neale: Nothing To Prove, Nothing To Ask."

108 **"deeply impressed"** (Owen): *Philadelphia Inquirer,* October 4, 1943.

108 **The story of how Bill Paschal** came to play for the Giants was told in a Grantland Rice column that was published on December 8, 1943 in the *Pittsburgh Post-Gazette.*

109 **Greasy Neale discussed his long friendship with Steve Owen** in Neale and Meany, "Football Is My Life."

110 **"They clocked me . . ."** (Hinkle): *Philadelphia Evening Bulletin,* February 8, 1968.

111 **"When he gets in a game . . ."** (Neale): *Milwaukee Journal,* December 1, 1943.

111 **Hinkle explained the "41 Outside" play** in an interview with the author. The story of the misattributed 37-yard run appears in Ecenbarger, "Steagles" and Infield, "When the Steagles Roamed the Gridiron."

111 **"I didn't realize . . ."** (Hinkle): *The Times Herald* (Norristown, PA), undated clipping on file at the Pro Football Hall of Fame.

113 **My account of Allie Sherman's late-game touchdown** against the Giants is based on an interview with Ted Doyle.

114 **Bucko Kilroy discussed Walt Kiesling's defensive coaching** acumen in Infield, "When the Steagles Roamed the Gridiron."

114 **"I didn't like it . . ."** (Graham): Ross, "The White, Night Football."

114 **"about ten years"** (Luckman): *Pittsburgh Post-Gazette,* July 8, 1943.

115 **"30 and 40 percent weaker"** (Kiesling): *Pittsburgh Post-Gazette,* November 9, 1943.

115 **"The caliber of play . . ."** (Kilroy): Didinger, "War Baby in 1943, Eagles and Steelers Were Steagles."

115 **"The 4-F boys . . ."** (Mara): *Pittsburgh Post-Gazette,* September 15, 1943.

115 **The story of Allie Sherman encountering the Giants** at the North Philadelphia train station appeared in the *New York Times,* November 7, 1963.

116 **My description of life at the Hotel Philadelphian** is based primarily on my interviews with Ray Graves, Tom Miller, Vic Sears, and Ernie Steele, all of whom lived there in 1943. Also helpful was Infield, "When the Steagles Roamed the Gridiron."

116 **Philadelphia's wartime housing shortage** is described in Miller, et al., *Philadelphia Stories* (p. 134).

Nine: Chicago

120 **The matchstick story** appeared in the *Chicago Tribune*, April 9, 1943. The stocking story appeared in the *Philadelphia Daily News,* August 27, 1943. My account of wartime rationing is drawn from Bentley, *Eating for Victory,* Lingeman, *Don't You Know There's a War On?,* and Goodwin, *No Ordinary Time.*

122 **For more about homemakers** on the home front, see Anderson, *Wartime Women,* Goodwin, *No Ordinary Time,* and Lingeman, *Don't You Know There's a War On?*

122 **Harriet Doyle reminisced** about her wartime responsibilities in an interview with the author.

123 **"Equipment was very scarce . . ."** (Rooney): Robinson, "Remembering When the Eagles and Steelers Were Teammates."

123 **Al Wistert recounted his encounter with Fred Schubach** in an interview with the author.

124 **"Democracy makes us . . ."** (Conzelman): Peterson, *Pigskin* (p. 139).

125 **Attendance statistics** come from Liu and Marini, *2005 NFL Record & Fact Book.*

125 **"Fans had found . . ."** (Halas): Halas, *Halas by Halas* (p. 216).

125 **"Look, this is a good line . . ."** (Sears): *Chicago Tribune*, October 16, 1943.

125 **"Hell, I don't even . . ."** (Bell): *Philadelphia Record,* October 15, 1943.

126 **"Their spirit . . ."** (Bell): *Philadelphia Record,* October 15, 1943.

126 **Greasy Neale's fondness for rail travel** and his rules for road trips are described in the booklet that was distributed to members of the Eagles during training camp in 1948 and is now on file at the Pro Football Hall of Fame.

128 **My account of the WMC investigation** of the Bears is based on contemporaneous newspaper accounts, specifically the *Philadelphia Evening Bulletin* and the *Pittsburgh Press,* September 23, 1943, and the *Philadelphia Inquirer* and the *Philadelphia Record,* September 24, 1943.

128 **"If rules have . . ."** (Spencer): *Pittsburgh Press,* September 23, 1943.

129 **"If there has been . . ."** (Brizzolara): *Philadelphia Evening Bulletin,* September 23, 1943.

129 **"The league clubs . . ."** (Layden): *Philadelphia Inquirer,* September 24, 1943.

129 **"If the players . . ."** (Spencer): *Philadelphia Record,* September 24, 1943.

129 **"We turned our practices . . ."** (Thayer): *Philadelphia Inquirer,* September 24, 1943.

130 **"The division . . ."** (Johnsos): Halas, *Halas by Halas* (p. 204).

130 **The story of Bronko Nagurski's 1943 comeback** is well told in Dent, *Monster of the Midway.*

131 **"He couldn't throw . . ."** (Turner): Cope, *The Game That Was* (p. 209).

131 **"They've got a tough ball club . . ."** (Driscoll): *Chicago Tribune,* October 13, 1943.

132 **The opening of Chicago's first subway** was reported in the *Chicago Tribune,* October 17, 1943.

132 **The WMC ruling** was reported in the *Chicago Tribune* and the *New York Times,* October 17, 1943.

133 **The Bears' tenancy at Wrigley Field** is discussed in Halas, *Halas by Halas* and Davis, *Papa Bear.*

135 **Al Wistert discussed his play** in the Bears game and his relationship with Greasy Neale in an interview with the author.

135 **"You can't win . . ."** (Neale): *Philadelphia Inquirer,* October 20, 1943.

136 **"Boys, we lost . . ."** (Zimmerman): *Philadelphia Inquirer,* October 20, 1943.

136 **"The Steagles have . . ."** (Owen): *New York Herald Tribune,* October 22, 1943.

137 **The evacuation instructions for the Polo Ground** were published in the Steagles-Giants game program, October 24, 1943.

137 **My descriptions of Neale and Kiesling on the sidelines** are based on player interviews.

139 **"We would be better off . . ."** (unnamed spokesman): *Philadelphia Record,* October 26, 1943.

Ten: Strikes

142 **James W. Cururin's letter** was published in the *Pittsburgh Post-Gazette,* November 26, 1943.

142 **For my account of Pittsburgh's industrial development,** I am indebted to Freese, *Coal* (from which the "Muskeetose" quote is taken).

143 **Edmund Bacon's uncomplimentary comment about his hometown** was published in his obituary in the *Washington Post,* October 16, 2005.

143 **The relationship between Pittsburgh and Philadelphia** is discussed in Soskis, "Tale of Two Cities."

144 **Havey Boyle's Charley Case quip** was published the *Pittsburgh Post-Gazette,* October 30, 1943.

144 **Clint Wager's self-inflicted skull fracture** was reported in the *Chicago Tribune,* October 9, 1943. A more complete history of the Cardinals can be found in Carroll, et al., *Total Football II* (pp. 39–41) and Peterson, *Pigskin.* The report that Handler was reduced to recruiting personnel from the Great Lakes Naval Station appears in Dent, *Monster of the Midway* (p. 270).

147 **My account of the 1943 coal strikes** is based on contemporaneous newspaper reports, as well as Dubofsky and Van Tine, *John L. Lewis,* Freese, *Coal,* Goodwin, *No Ordinary Time,* and Wechsler, *Labor Baron.*

147 **"Our nation is at war . . ."** (Lewis): Dubofsky and Van Tine, *John L. Lewis* (p. 302).

148 **"Two months ago . . ."** (Kerlik): Wechsler, *Labor Baron* (p. 208).

149 **"Speaking for . . ."** (*Stars and Stripes*): Dubofsky and Van Tine, *John L. Lewis* (p. 314).

149 **"a jailed miner"** (Ickes): Dubofsky and Van Tine, *John L. Lewis* (p. 312).

150 **"Lewis bargained for eight months . . ."** (unnamed commentator): Wechsler, *Labor Baron* (p. 250).

150 **An excellent history of the NFL's labor relations** can be found in MacCambridge, *America's Game.*

151 **The Sammy Baugh "Which eye?" anecdote** has been often told. This version comes from Boswell, et al., *Redskins* (p. 40).

152 **"rush the passer"** (Kiesling and Neale): *Philadelphia Inquirer,* November 13, 1943.

153 **The true inventor of the point spread** is a matter of much debate among sports historians. Several bookies have been credited, including Ed Curd, Billy Hecht, and Charles McNeil.

154 **"Give generously . . ."** (Navy League): Steagles-Redskins game program, November 7, 1943.

155 **While it was not unusual for players to poke,** bite, pinch, punch, or gouge one another in the heat of battle, they also adhered to unwritten rules that placed strictures on the violence. For example, if a player on the visiting team was headed out of bounds, it was perfectly acceptable for a player on the home team to annihilate him, to entertain the home crowd. However, if a player on the home team was headed out of bounds, the visitors were expected to administer nothing more than a polite shove. By this simple understanding, the players spared themselves a bit of brutality.

158 **"I presume he felt . . ."** (Bell): *Pittsburgh Post-Gazette,* November 10, 1943.

158 **Bill Hewitt discussed his departure from the Steagles** in Hewitt, "Don't Send My Boy to Halas." His fatal car accident is described in the *News-Herald* (Perkasie, PA), January 15, 1947.

159 **"We didn't even have . . ."** (Leemans): Cope, *The Game That Was* (p. 154).

159 **For more about the history of sports medicine,** see Berryman and Park, *Sport and Exercise Science.*

160 **"What with the injuries . . ."** (Cawthon): *New York Herald Tribune,* October 21, 1943.

161 **"better prepared"** (Cawthon): *Brooklyn Daily Eagle,* November 13, 1943.

162 **My account of the first televised NFL game** is based on Campbell, "Pro Football's First TV Game—1939" and Whittingham, *What a Game They Played* (pp. 193–194).

162 **"It was . . ."** (Waltz): Campbell, "Pro Football's First TV Game—1939."

163 **"Why, this Brooklyn team . . ."** (Topping): *New York Times,* November 15, 1943.

Eleven: Thanksgiving

166 **Bill Hartman recounted how he discovered Frank Sinkwich** in Lancaster, "Legends: Frank Sinkwich." Sinkwich's early difficulties at boot camp were

reported in the *Philadelphia Evening Bulletin,* July 20, 1943.

167 **The history of the Spartans,** the Packers, and the NFL's other "town teams" is recounted in Peterson, *Pigskin* and Carroll, et al., *Total Football II.*

168 **"Hell, we'd get . . ."** (Clark): Peterson, *Pigskin* (p. 122).

169 **Sinkwich's discharge from the Marines** was reported in the *Pittsburgh Post-Gazette,* September 4, 1943.

171 **"I was hoping for . . ."** (Rooney): *Pittsburgh Post-Gazette,* November 10, 1943.

172 **"one of the wildest games"** (Edgar): *Detroit Free Press,* November 22, 1943.

172 **"There was the kickoff . . ."** (Carlson): *Pittsburgh Post-Gazette,* November 30, 1943.

172 **Much of my history of kicking** is drawn from Stephenson, *The Kicks That Count.* The kicking statistics are based on data in Carroll, et al., *Total Football II,* Neft, et al., *The Football Encyclopedia,* and Liu and Marini, *2005 NFL Record & Fact Book.*

175 **"I guess I've seen . . ."** (Friesell): *Detroit News,* November 22, 1943.

175 **"I've waited ten years . . ."** (Rooney): *Pittsburgh Press,* November 27, 1943.

176 **Roosevelt and Churchill's Thanksgiving in Cairo** is described in Goodwin, *No Ordinary Time* (pp. 474–475).

176 **"Let us make it . . ."** and **"Large families . . ."** (Roosevelt): Goodwin, *No Ordinary Time* (p. 474).

176 **The Associated Press report of Roosevelt's "little ditty"** was published in the *Pittsburgh Press,* December 3, 1943.

176 **"I had never seen . . ."** (Churchill): Goodwin, *No Ordinary Time* (p. 474).

177 **"a pound of turkey"** (Office of the Quartermaster General): *Philadelphia Evening Bulletin,* November 2, 1943.

177 **"We even got . . ."** (Paull): "Memories of War: Personal Histories." Retrieved from *http://microworks.net/pacific/personal/bill_paull4.htm.*

178 **"You ought to be . . ."** (Patton): Goralski, *World War II Almanac, 1931–1945* (p. 275).

180 **The publication of photographs of dead American soldiers** is discussed in Jarvis, *The Male Body at War.*

181 **The most popular version of "Four-F Charlie"** was recorded by Ted Courtney in 1941. In *The Male Body at War,* Christina S. Jarvis says the song equates the 4-F man with "failed masculinity and failed humanity." The lyrics quoted here come from Jarvis's book.

182 **"What's the matter with . . ."** (Wherry): *Philadelphia Inquirer,* October 5, 1943.

182 **"If a man is . . ."** (Tunney): *Milwaukee Journal,* December 2, 1943.

182 **The Joe Williams column** about 4-F athletes was published on December 27, 1943, in many papers, including the *Pittsburgh Press.*

183 **The Grantland Rice column** was published on December 18, 1943, in many papers, including the *Pittsburgh Post-Gazette.*

183 **The results of the *Esquire* polls** were published in the *New York Herald Tribune,* November 25, 1943.

184 **"the American way of life"** (Mead): *Philadelphia Inquirer,* June 24, 1943.

184 **The Sammy Weiss biography** is drawn mainly from his obituary in the *Pittsburgh Post-Gazette,* February 2, 1977.

185 **"If the British . . ."** (Weiss): *Washington Times-Herald,* November 11, 1943.

185 **"I've had letters . . ."** (Weiss): *Pittsburgh Press,* July 30, 1943.

Twelve: Survival

187 **"a good investment"** (Marshall): *Washington Times-Herald,* November 28, 1943.

187 **Lex Thompson's party** the night before the Redskins game was described in the *Washington Times-Herald,* November 30, 1943.

188 **The story of Greasy Neale taking Jack Hinkle out of the game** was told in the *Philadelphia Inquirer,* December 1, 1943.

191 **"I knew if I batted . . ."** (Steele): *Philadelphia Inquirer,* December 1, 1943.

191 **"It was the happiest . . ."** (Zimmerman): *Washington Post,* November 29, 1943.

191 **"What a ball game . . ."** (Bell): *Philadelphia Record,* November 30, 1943.

193 **Ted Doyle recounted how he "celebrated a little too much"** after the game in an interview with the author.

Thirteen: Win and In

196 **My account of the Steagles locker room** before the Packers game is based on player interviews.

197 **"in three different directions"** (Neale): Whittingham, *What a Game They Played* (p. 118).

199 **"We better win . . ."** (Neale): Kram, "Neale People."

199 **"I even drive . . ."** (Neale): Neale and Meany, "Football Is My Life."

199 **My description of Shibe Park** on the day of the Packers game is based on contemporaneous newspaper accounts, as well as photographs at the Urban Archives at Temple University.

202 **"We made mistakes."** (Neale): *Philadelphia Evening Bulletin,* December 6, 1943.

203 **"the most successful season"** (unnamed official): *Philadelphia Inquirer,* December 26, 1943.

203 **"We took in more . . ."** (Bell): *Philadelphia Record,* December 10, 1943.

205 **My account of George Preston Marshall's visit to the Bears bench** during the 1943 championship game is based on contemporaneous newspaper reports, as well as Dent, *Monster of the Midway* (p. 285) and Davis, *Papa Bear* (pp. 188–189). Commissioner Elmer Layden fined both Marshall and Brizzolara $500 each for the altercation, a verdict that the *Pittsburgh Post-Gazette's* Jack Sell (among others) deemed "curious."

205 **"You can say . . ."** (Marshall): *Philadelphia Inquirer,* December 27, 1943.

205 **"I see post-war pro football . . ."** (Rickey): *Philadelphia Evening Bulletin,* December 31, 1943.

Epilogue: V-J Day

206 **"Last fall . . ."** (Bell): *Philadelphia Evening Bulletin,* January 2, 1944.

206 **"keep faith with Philadelphia fans"** (Thompson): *Pittsburgh Post-Gazette,* January 14, 1944.

207 **"The best thing to do . . ."** (Layden): *Philadelphia Evening Bulletin,* January 2, 1944.

207 **"The League requests . . ."** (Mandel): NFL meeting minutes, April 22, 1944.

207 **My account of the Steelers-Cardinals merger** is based on Forr, "Card-Pitt: The Carpits," as well as contemporaneous newspaper reports and my interview with Ted Doyle. The minutes of the league meeting at which the merger was consummated, now on file at the Pro Football Hall of Fame, were also helpful.

208 **"Since the close . . ."** (Rooney): *Pittsburgh Post-Gazette,* January 11, 1944.

208 **"carried the *Racing Form*"** (Rooney): Forr, "Card-Pitt: The Carpits."

209 **"The whole bunch . . ."** (Rooney): Forr, "Card-Pitt: The Carpits."

209 **"The season couldn't have . . ."** (Bell): Forr, "Card-Pitt: The Carpits."

209 **Greasy Neale's self-imposed pay cut** was reported in the *Philadelphia Evening Bulletin,* September 8, 1944.

210 **The war's effect on the 1944 Bears** is described in Halas, *Halas by Halas* (pp. 214–215).

210 **"We tried to get replacements . . ."** (Johnsos): Halas, *Halas by Halas* (p. 215).

210 **"It drove me nuts . . ."** (Gallery): Lynch, *Tender Tyrant* (p. 133).

210 **"I kept announcing . . ."** (Hutson): Whittingham, *What a Game They Played* (pp. 127–128).

211 **"It is difficult . . ."** (Byrnes): Mead, *Even the Browns* (p. 219).

211 **The discrimination that professional athletes faced from Selective Service** is described in Mead, *Even the Browns.* The Northey case in particular is discussed on page 220.

212 **"The example set . . ."** (Johnson): *New York Times,* August 18, 1945.

212 **Elmer Layden's visit to the White House** was reported in the *Philadelphia Inquirer,* August 23, 1945.

213 **"It is not necessary . . ."** (Thayer): *Philadelphia Inquirer,* August 16, 1945.

213 **"George Halas made me play . . ."** (Kavanaugh): Peterson, *Pigskin* (p. 141).

213 **Jack Sanders' return to the gridiron** was reported in the *Philadelphia Inquirer,* August 20, 1945.

213 **Vic Sears explained how he helped his friend John Eibner** in an interview with the author.

214 **My account of the war between the NFL and the upstart AAFC** is based on MacCambridge, *America's Game* and Peterson, *Pigskin.*

214 **"Let them get a football . . ."** (Layden): Peterson, *Pigskin* (p. 148).

215 **My account of the postwar integration of professional football** is based on Levy, *Tackling Jim Crow.*

216 **"If I have to . . ."** (Strode): Levy, *Tackling Jim Crow* (p. 95).

217 **"Salaries have gone crazy . . ."** (Thompson): Stump, "Get Smart—or Go Bust?"

217 **"The team made . . ."** (Clark): Didinger and Lyons, *The Eagles Encyclopedia* (p. 127).

217 **"I had a reputation . . ."** (Neale): Didinger and Lyons, *The Eagles Encyclopedia* (p. 103).

218 **"Weak teams should play . . ."** (Bell): MacCambridge, *America's Game* (p. 40).

219 **"We don't want kids . . ."** (Bell): MacCambridge, *America's Game* (p. 105).

219 **"Television creates interest . . ."** (Bell): Pro Football Hall of Fame, "Bert Bell: The Commissioner."

220 **"It was almost as though . . ."** (Smith): MacCambridge, *America's Game* (p. 127).

Postscript: 2003

221 **The figures for the cost of building Heinz Field** come from "Private Financing for a New Penguins Arena," a report by the Allegheny Institute for Public Policy, July 2002.

221 **The account of the Steagles reunion** is based on the observations of the author, who was present.

222 **"It was a time . . ."** (Rooney): *Beaver County Times* (Beaver, PA), July 23, 2003.

223 **"One of the reasons . . ."** (Cade): Kays and Phillips-Han, "Gatorade: The Idea that Launched an Industry."

224 **"I used to go out . . ."** (Kilroy): Leuthner, *Iron Men* (p. 150).

225 **"Take Allie Sherman . . ."** (Neale): *New York Times,* December 26, 1961.

Acknowledgments

❚ ❘ ❘ ❘ ❘ ❚

I WOULD NOT HAVE BEEN ABLE to write this book without the support—moral, practical, and financial—of many people. Some I have known all my life, others I have come to know only recently through correspondence. To them all I am deeply grateful.

For advice, answers, assistance, and accommodations: Jim Algeo, Jr., Tom Algeo, John Roy Anderson, Larry Cabrelli, Jr., Jill Cordes and Phil Johnston, Lynn Cottom, Harriet Doyle, Travis Fox, Jim Gallagher, Jo Hanshaw, Joane Hinkle, Jordy Hinkle, Elise and Rob Kauzlaric, Bruce Kuklick, James Lautenschlager, Paul May, Gigi and Frank McCollum, Dan O'Neil, Kristen and John Petersen, Gino Piroli, Rob Ruck, Grace Sears, Judy Shaubach, Alan Smith, Josephine Steele, Ray Supulski, William T. Supulski, Paula D. Sweeney of the Selective Service System, Martha Teagle and Scott Davis, Mitch Teich, Gary Waleik and the public radio program *Only A Game,* Scott Westcott, Joan and Jim Wilson, Dena Mary Zimmerman, Donald Zimmerman, and Rex Zimmerman.

The staffs at the institutions where I conducted my research were most helpful: the Bowdoin College Library, the Library of Congress Main Reading Room, the Library of Congress Newspaper & Current Periodical Reading Room, the Los Angeles Public Library, the Pro Football Hall of Fame, the Urban Archives at Temple University, and the Van Pelt Library at the University of Pennsylvania.

For going above and beyond, special thanks must be extended to Bob Carroll and the Professional Football Researchers Association, Nancy Farghalli and my colleagues at the public radio program *Marketplace,* Margaret Jerrido and the staff at the Urban Archives, and Matt Waechter at the Pro Football Hall of Fame.

To my agent, Jane Dystel, thank you for your unflagging support and kind encouragement. To my editor, Wendy Holt, and everyone at Da Capo Press, thank you for your wise counsel and good humor.

I am most indebted to the nine members of the Steagles I was fortunate enough to interview. Each was kind enough to speak with me at length: Ted Doyle, Ray Graves, Jack Hinkle, Frank "Bucko" Kilroy, Tom Miller, Vic Sears, Allie Sherman, Ernie Steele, and Al Wistert. Sadly, Tom Miller was unable to witness the completion of this book. He passed away on December 2, 2005.

After publication of the hardcover edition of this book in the fall of 2006, four more Steagles passed away: Ted Doyle, Jack Hinkle, Vic Sears, and Ernie Steele. They were good men and it was an honor for me to have known them.

Finally, to my wife Allyson, mere thanks are not enough. While I was writing this book, Allyson was embarking on a new adventure of her own, as a Foreign Service Officer. That we were able to successfully undertake both projects simultaneously, while moving from Los Angeles to Washington to Mali, is a testament to her infinite patience and grace. Allyson, I couldn't have done it without you. *Merci mon amour!*

Sources

∎ | | | | ∎

THIS BOOK IS BASED PRIMARILY ON MY INTERVIEWS with members of the Steagles, as well as contemporaneous newspaper accounts of the team. The interviews were conducted in person and on the telephone between February 2003 and January 2006.

I am indebted to the sportswriters who covered the team in 1943, particularly Art Morrow of the *Philadelphia Inquirer,* Cecil G. Muldoon of the *Pittsburgh Press,* and Jack Sell of the *Pittsburgh Post-Gazette.* Their work in 1943 made mine in 2005 immeasurably easier.

I am equally indebted to the anonymous men and women who toiled in the basement of the late, great *Philadelphia Evening Bulletin,* assiduously clipping each story that appeared in the paper and filing it according to its subject matter. Before search engines there were clip files. The *Bulletin*'s, consisting of a half million small brown envelopes, now resides at the Urban Archives at Temple University in Philadelphia. To anyone interested in twentieth-century American history, it is a priceless resource.

A complete bibliography follows, but a few sources deserve special mention. Books that were never out of my reach included *Total Football II: The Official Encyclopedia of the National Football League,* edited by Bob Carroll, Michael Gershman, David Neft, and John Thorn; *The Eagles Encyclopedia* by Ray Didinger and Robert S. Lyons; *The Football Encyclopedia: The Complete History of Professional Football from 1892 to the Present* by David S. Neft, Richard M. Cohen, and Rick Korch; and *Pigskin: The Early Years of Pro Football* by Robert W. Peterson.

Finally, no book about any aspect of NFL history could be written without the resources of the Professional Football Researchers Association, a nonprofit organization dedicated to preserving (and often reconstructing) the history of pro football. Since 1979 the PFRA's newsletter, *The Coffin Corner,* has been entertaining and educating both casual football fans and serious students of the game. Many of the articles are posted on the PFRA's website, *www. footballresearch.com*. But beware: That website will suck you in!

Interviews

Larry Cabrelli, Jr., son of Steagles end Larry Cabrelli
Lynn Cottom, daughter of Steagles center Al Wukits
Harriet Doyle, wife of Steagles tackle Ted Doyle
Ted Doyle, Steagles tackle
Jim Gallagher, Philadelphia Eagles executive, 1949–1995
Ray Graves, Steagles center
Jack Hinkle, Steagles halfback
Joane Hinkle, wife of Steagles halfback Jack Hinkle
Frank "Bucko" Kilroy, Steagles tackle
Bruce Kuklick, professor of history, University of Pennsylvania
Tom Miller, Steagles end
Rob Ruck, senior lecturer, Department of History, University of Pittsburgh
Grace Sears, wife of Steagles tackle Vic Sears
Vic Sears, Steagles tackle
Allie Sherman, Steagles quarterback
Ernie Steele, Steagles halfback
Josephine Steele, wife of Steagles halfback Ernie Steele
Al Wistert, Steagles tackle
Dena Mary Zimmerman, widow of Steagles quarterback Roy Zimmerman
Donald Zimmerman, son of Steagles quarterback Roy Zimmerman
Rex Zimmerman, son of Steagles quarterback Roy Zimmerman

Newspapers

Brooklyn Daily Eagle
Chicago Daily Times
Chicago Herald-American
Chicago Tribune
Detroit Free Press
Detroit News
Milwaukee Journal
Milwaukee Sentinel
New York Herald Tribune
New York Times
Philadelphia Daily News
Philadelphia Evening Bulletin
Philadelphia Inquirer
Philadelphia Record
Pittsburgh Post-Gazette
Pittsburgh Press
The Sporting News
Stars and Stripes
Washington Evening Star
Washington Post
Washington Times-Herald

Bibliography

∎ | | | | ∎

Anderson, Dave. "An Old Gambler Finally Collects." *New York Times,* January 13, 1975: 50.

Anderson, Karen. *Wartime Women: Sex Roles, Family Relations, and the Status of Women during World War II.* Westport, CT: Greenwood Press, 1981.

Anderson, Robert S., ed. *Physical Standards in World War II.* Washington, DC: Office of the Surgeon General, Department of the Army, 1967.

Asinof, Eliot. "Big Shrimp of Pro Football." *New York Times Magazine,* December 12, 1965.

Barnett, Bob. "When the Packers Went to War." *Coffin Corner,* Vol. V, No. 2 (1983).

Barnett, Bob, and Bob Carroll. "Kilroy Was There." *Coffin Corner,* Vol. VIII, No. 7 (1986).

Barnhart, Tony. "The '40s: NFL Goes to War." *Coffin Corner,* Vol. IX, No. 8 (1987).

Baumer, William H., and Sidney F. Giffin. *21 to 35: What the Draft and Army Training Mean To You.* New York: Prentice Hall, 1940.

Bentley, Amy. *Eating for Victory: Food Rationing and the Politics of Domesticity.* Urbana, IL: University of Illinois Press, 1998.

Berryman, Jack, and Roberta J. Park, eds. *Sport and Exercise Science: Essays in the History of Sports Medicine.* Urbana, IL: University of Illinois Press, 1992.

"Bill Hewitt Dies After Crash On 309." *News-Herald* (Perkasie, PA), January 15, 1947: 1.

Bloomfield, Gary. *Duty, Honor, Victory: America's Athletes in World War II.* Guilford, CT: The Lyon's Press, 2003.

Boswell, Thomas, et al., *Redskins: A History of Washington's Team.* Washington, DC: Washington Post Books, 2000.

Bibliography

Braunwart, Bob, Bob Carroll, and Joe Horrigan. "Pennsylvania Polka." *Coffin Corner,* Vol. IV, No. 10 (1982).

Brock, Ted. "Scout's Honor." *Pro!,* September 18, 1977: 3C–7C.

Burlbaugh, George. *The War, the Steagles and the Card-Pitts.* Morrisville, NC: Lulu, Inc., 2004.

Campbell, Donald P. *Sunday's Warriors.* Philadelphia: Quantum Leap, 1994.

Campbell, Jim. "Pro Football's First TV Game—1939." *Coffin Corner,* Vol. III, No. 3 (1981).

Carroll, Bob, Michael Gershman, David Neft, and John Thorn, eds. *Total Football II: The Official Encyclopedia of the National Football League.* New York: HarperCollins, 1999.

Celler, Emanuel. *The Draft and You.* New York: Viking, 1940.

Claassen, Harold. *The History of Professional Football.* Englewood Cliffs, NJ: Prentice Hall, 1963.

Cleve, Craig Allen. *Hardball on the Home Front: Major League Replacement Players of World War II.* Jefferson, NC: McFarland & Company, 2004.

Cochran, Blake. *Is Your Number Up? Practical Information for the Future Selectee.* New York: Teachers College, Columbia University, 1941.

Conscription, How Will It Affect You? Or Will It? New York: Arco, 1940 or 1941.

Cope, Myron. *The Game That Was: The Early Days of Pro Football.* Cleveland: The World Publishing Company, 1970.

Cope, Myron. "Pro Football's Gashouse Gang." *True Magazine,* September 1964: 37, 106–107.

Cosentino, Dom. "Playing on the Same Side." *Intelligencer* (Doylestown, PA), November 7, 2004: C1.

Daley, Arthur. "High Flying Eagle." *New York Times,* February 16, 1969: S2.

Danzig, Allison. *The History of American Football: Its Great Teams, Players, and Coaches.* Englewood Cliffs, NJ: Prentice Hall, 1956.

Davis, Jeff. *Papa Bear: The Life and Legacy of George Halas.* New York: McGraw-Hill, 2005.

Day, Anthony. "Bert Bell Collapses and Dies At Eagles Football Game." *Philadelphia Evening Bulletin,* October 12, 1959: 1.

Dear, I. C. B., and M. R. D. Foot, eds. *The Oxford Companion to World War II.* New York: Oxford University Press, 1995.

Dent, Jim. *Monster of the Midway: Bronko Nagurski, the 1943 Chicago Bears, and the Greatest Comeback Ever.* New York: Thomas Dunne Books, 2003.

Dervarics, Charles. "When Steagles Walked the Earth." *Pittsburgh Magazine,* December 1993: 54–57.

Didinger, Ray. "War Baby in 1943, Eagles and Steelers Were Steagles." *Philadelphia Daily News,* August 31, 1993: F8.

Didinger, Ray, and Robert S. Lyons. *The Eagles Encyclopedia.* Philadelphia: Temple University Press, 2005.

Bibliography

Dos Passos, John. *State of the Nation*. Boston: Houghton Mifflin, 1944.

Dubofsky, Melvyn, and Warren Van Tine. *John L. Lewis: A Biography*. Urbana, IL: University of Illinois Press, 1986.

Ecenbarger, William. "Steagles." *Philadelphia Inquirer Magazine,* September 2, 1990: 24–38.

Ecenbarger, William. "The Steagles Hybrid Team Zany Moments in Steelers' Past." *Pittsburgh Post-Gazette Magazine,* October 14, 1990: 26.

Erenberg, Lewis A., and Susan E. Hirsch. *The War in American Culture: Society and Consciousness During World War II*. Chicago: University of Chicago Press, 1996.

Flynn, George Q. *The Draft, 1940–1973*. Lawrence, KS: University Press of Kansas, 1988.

Flynn, George Q. *Lewis B. Hershey: Mr. Selective Service*. Chapel Hill, NC: University of North Carolina Press, 1985.

Forbes, Gordon. *Tales from the Eagles Sidelines: A Collection of the Greatest Eagles Stories Ever Told*. Champaign, IL: Sports Publishing, 2002.

Forr, James. "Card-Pitt: The Carpits." *Coffin Corner,* Vol. XXV, No. 3 (2003).

Foster, William, et al. *Physical Standards in World War II*. Washington, DC: Office of the Surgeon General, Department of the Army, 1967.

Freese, Barbara. *Coal: A Human History*. New York: Penguin Books, 2004.

Frei, Terry. *Third Down and a War to Go: The All-American 1942 Wisconsin Badgers*. Madison, WI: Historical Society Press, 2005.

Gilbert, Bill. *They Also Served: Baseball and the Home Front, 1941–1945*. New York: Crown, 1992.

Goldstein, Richard E. "Football Sunday, Dec. 7, 1941: Suddenly the Games Didn't Matter." *New York Times,* December 7, 1980: 6 (section 5).

Goodwin, Doris Kearns. *No Ordinary Time: Franklin & Eleanor Roosevelt: The Home Front in World War II*. New York: Simon & Schuster, 1994.

Goralski, Robert. *World War II Almanac, 1931–1945: A Political and Military Record*. New York: Bonanza Books, 1981.

Gordon, Robert. *The 1960 Philadelphia Eagles: The Team That They Said Had Nothing but a Championship*. Champaign, IL: Sports Publishing, 2001.

Graves, Ray. *Ray Graves' Guide to Modern Football Defense*. West Nyack, NY: Parker Publishing, 1966.

Grosshandler, Stan. "The Brooklyn Dodgers." *Coffin Corner,* Vol. XII, No. 3 (1990).

Grosshandler, Stan. "Fifty Years Ago: The Nadir (1943)." *Coffin Corner,* Vol. XV, No. 2 (1993).

Grosshandler, Stan, et al. "Coach Steve Owen: The Great Innovator." *Coffin Corner,* Vol. XVIII, No. 4 (1996).

Halas, George. *Halas by Halas: The Autobiography of George Halas*. New York: McGraw-Hill, 1979.

Bibliography

Heisler, John, ed. *Echoes of Notre Dame Football: The Greatest Stories Ever Told.* Chicago: Triumph Books, 2005.

Hewitt, Bill (as told to Red Smith). "Don't Send My Boy to Halas." *Saturday Evening Post,* October 21, 1944: 22–25.

Holland, Gerald. "Greasy Neale: Nothing To Prove, Nothing To Ask." *Sports Illustrated,* August 24, 1964: 32–39.

Horrigan, Joe. "Iron Words." *Coffin Corner,* Vol. II, No. 9 (1980).

Infield, Tom. "When the Steagles Roamed the Gridiron." *Philadelphia Inquirer,* October 26, 1993: D1.

Jarvis, Christina S. *The Male Body at War: American Masculinity During World War II.* DeKalb, IL: Northern Illinois University Press, 2004.

Johnson, Gertrude G. "Manpower Selection and the Preventative Medicine Program." *Personal Health Measures and Immunization, Vol. III, Preventive Medicine in World War II.* John Boyd Coates, Jr., ed. Washington, DC: Office of the Surgeon General, Department of the Army, 1955.

Kauffman, Ross E. "Football a Hobby of Eagles' Prexy." *Philadelphia Evening Bulletin,* June 23, 1941.

Kays, Joe, and Arline Phillips-Han. "Gatorade: The Idea that Launched an Industry." *Explore: Research at the University of Florida,* Vol. 8, Issue 1 (Spring 2003).

Kram, Mark. "Neale People." *Philadelphia Daily News,* October 12, 2004.

Kuklick, Bruce. *To Every Thing a Season: Shibe Park and Urban Philadelphia, 1909–1976.* Princeton, NJ: Princeton University Press, 1991.

Lancaster, Marc. "Legends: Frank Sinkwich." *Athens* (GA) *Banner-Herald,* 2002. Retrieved from *http://www.onlineathens.com/dogbytes/legends/sinkwich_02 .shtml.*

Lanctot, Neil. *Negro League Baseball: The Rise and Ruin of a Black Institution.* Philadelphia: University of Pennsylvania Press, 2004.

Leuthner, Stuart. *Iron Men: Bucko, Crazylegs, and the Boys Recall the Golden Days of Professional Football.* New York: Doubleday, 1988.

Levy, Alan H. *Tackling Jim Crow: Racial Segregation in Professional Football.* Jefferson, NC: McFarland & Company, 2003.

Lingeman, Richard. *Don't You Know There's a War On?: The American Home Front 1941–1945.* New York: Thunder's Mouth Press/Nation Books, 1970.

Littlewood, Thomas B. *Arch: A Promoter, Not a Poet: The Story of Arch Ward.* Ames, IA: Iowa State University Press, 1990.

Liu, Randall, and Matt Marini, eds. *2005 NFL Record & Fact Book.* New York: Time Inc. Home Entertainment, 2005.

Longman, Jere. *If Football's a Religion, Why Don't We Have a Prayer?: Philadelphia, Its Faithful, and the Eternal Quest for Sports Salvation.* New York: HarperCollins, 2005.

Lynch, Etta. *Tender Tyrant: The Legend of Pete Cawthon.* Canyon, TX: Staked Plains Press, 1976.

MacCambridge, Michael. *America's Game: The Epic Story of How Pro Football Captured a Nation.* New York: Random House, 2004.

Maiorana, Sal. "Battle Cry: 'Infamy.' A Day to Remember." *NLF.com.* December 7, 2003. Retrieved from *http://www.nfl.com/news/story/6877185.*

Mann, Alan. "The Unique Career of 'Greasy' Neale." *Coffin Corner,* Vol. XXVI, No. 3 (2004).

Manning, Thomas G., ed. *The Office of Price Administration: A World War II Agency of Control.* New York: Holt, 1960.

McClellan, Keith. *The Sunday Game.* Akron, OH: The University of Akron Press, 1998.

"M-Day Is Right Around the Corner." *Time,* October 5, 1942.

Mead, William. *Even the Browns: The Zany, True Story of Baseball in the Early Forties.* Chicago: Contemporary Books, 1978.

Meanwell, Walter E., and Knute K. Rockne. *Training, Conditioning and the Care of Injuries.* Madison, WI: [publisher unknown], 1931.

Mendelson, Abby. *The Pittsburgh Steelers: The Official Team History.* Dallas, TX: Taylor, 1996.

Miller, Frederic M., Morris J. Vogel, and Allen F. Davis. *Philadelphia Stories: A Photographic History, 1920–1960.* Philadelphia: Temple University Press, 1988.

Neale, Greasy, and Tom Meany. "Football Is My Life." *Collier's,* November 3, 19, and 17, 1951.

Neft, David S., Richard M. Cohen, and Rick Korch. *The Football Encyclopedia: The Complete History of Professional Football from 1892 to the Present.* New York: St. Martin's Press, 1994.

Oates, Robert, Jr. *Pittsburgh's Steelers: The First Half Century.* Los Angeles: Rosebud Books, 1982.

Orozco, Ron. "Longtime Softball Pitching Guru 'Mr. Z' Dies." *Fresno Bee,* August 23, 1997: D1.

Patterson, Ted. *The Golden Voices of Football.* Champaign, IL: Sports Publishing, 2004.

Pennsylvania State Council of Defense. *A Manual: Consumer Education for Wartime Living.* Harrisburg, PA: Commonwealth of Pennsylvania, 1943.

Petersen, Howard C., and William T. Stewart, Jr. *Conscription Manual: A Manual of Conscription Laws and Regulations.* Albany, NY: M. Bender, 1940.

Peterson, Robert W. *Pigskin: The Early Years of Pro Football.* New York: Oxford University Press, 1997.

Polmar, Norman, and Thomas B. Allen. *World War II: The Encyclopedia of the War Years, 1941–1945.* New York: Random House, 1996.

Povich, Shirley. "At Redskins-Eagles Game, Crowd Was Kept Unaware That War Had Begun." *Washington Post,* December 7, 1991: A15.

Prange, Gordon W., Donald M. Goldstein, and Katherine V. Dillon. *December 7, 1941: The Day the Japanese Attacked Pearl Harbor.* New York: McGraw-Hill, 1988.

Bibliography

Pro Football Hall of Fame. "Bert Bell: The Commissioner." *Coffin Corner*, Vol. XVIII, No. 3 (1996).

Pro Football Hall of Fame. "Hall of Fame Profile: Walt Kiesling." *Pro!*, December 13, 1981: 97–98, 118.

Py-Lieberman, Beth. "Any Bonds Today?" *Smithsonian*. February 2002. Retrieved from *http://www.kidscastle.si.edu/issues/2002/february/bonds.php*.

Riffenburgh, Beau, ed. *The Official NFL Encyclopedia*. New York: New American Library, 1986.

Roberts, Howard. *The Chicago Bears*. New York: G.P. Putnam's Sons, 1947.

Roberts, Randy, and David Welky, eds. *The Steelers Reader*. Pittsburgh: University of Pittsburgh Press, 2001.

Roberts, Ron E. *John L. Lewis: Hard Labor and Wild Justice*. Dubuque, IA: Kendall/Hunt, 1994.

Robinson, Alan. "Remembering When the Eagles and Steelers Were Teammates." *Associated Press*, December 5, 1993.

Ross, Alan. "The White, Night Football." *Coffin Corner*, Vol. XXI, No. 2 (1999).

Shaughnessy, Clark. *Football in War & Peace*. Clinton, SC: Jacobs Press, 1943.

Sherman, Allie. *Book of Football*. Garden City, NY: Doubleday, 1963.

Smith, David Andrew. *George S. Patton: A Biography*. Westport, CT: Greenwood Press, 2003.

Soskis, Benjamin. "Tale of Two Cities." *New Republic*, October 9, 2000: 23–25.

Spadaro, Dave. "Remembering the 'Steagles.'" *Gameday*, November 23, 1997: 4–5.

Spoelstra, Watson. "The Michigan Tackle That Time Forgot." *Sport*, November 1949: 46–48, 82.

Stephenson, Hugh. *The Kicks That Count*. Columbia, MO: Prolate Spheroid Press, 1981.

Strege, John. *When War Played Through: Golf During World War II*. New York: Gotham Books, 2005.

Stump, Al. "Get Smart—or Go Bust?" *Sport*, November 1948: 11–12, 74–76.

Thornley, Stew. *Land of the Giants: New York's Polo Grounds*. Philadelphia: Temple University Press, 2000.

"Three Americans." *Life*, September 20, 1943.

Tucker, Joe. *Steelers' Victory After Forty*. New York: Exposition Press, 1973.

United States Selective Service System. *Regulations for Third Registration*. Washington, DC: U.S. Government Printing Office, 1942.

United States Selective Service System. *Selective Service as the Tide of War Turns: The 3rd Report of the Director of Selective Service, 1943–1944*. Washington, DC: U.S. Government Printing Office, 1945.

United States Selective Service System. *Selective Service Regulations*. Washington, DC: U.S. Government Printing Office, 1941.

Warrington, Bob. "The Fight for Sunday Baseball in Philadelphia." The

Philadelphia Athletics Historical Society, 2001. Retrieved from *http:// philadelphiaathletics.org/history/sundaybaseball.html.*

Wechsler, James A. *Labor Baron: A Portrait of John L. Lewis.* New York: Morrow, 1944.

Westcott, Rich. *Philadelphia's Old Ballparks.* Philadelphia: Temple University Press, 1996.

Wexell, Jim. "Steagles 60th Anniversary." *Gameday,* August 16, 2003: S1–S8.

Whittingham, Richard. *What a Game They Played: An Inside Look at the Golden Era of Pro Football.* New York: Simon & Schuster, 1987.

Withington, Paul, ed. *The Book of Athletics.* Boston: Lothrop, Lee & Shepard, 1922.

Index

∎ ∣ ∣ ∣ ∣ ∎

Index

Cope, Myron, 39
Cosgrove, Randy, 222
Cotton, Russell, 41
Cowan, Percy, 31
Crain, Milt, 41
Crisler, Herbert "Fritz," 1, 2, 3, 100
Cullen, Bill, 123, 126, 199
Cururin, James W., 142

D

Daley, Arthur, 80
Daley, Bill, 100
Daugherity, Russ, 57
Davis, Bette, 98
Davis, Bill, 104
December 7, 1941, ix–xvi
DeGroot, Dudley, 84
Dent, Jim, 131
Detroit Lions, 54
  history of, 167–170
  Steagles versus, 170–172, 174–175
Dilweg, LaVern "Lavvie," 26
Dix, Dorothy, 76
Dodd, Bobby, 223
Donelli, Aldo "Buff," 65
Dorias, Charles "Gus," 168–169
Doyle, Eddie, 179
Doyle, Harriet, 25, 122–123, 124
Doyle, Ted, vii, xvi, 24–28, 33, 71–72, 83, 92, 107, 111, 113, 116, 123, 126, 135, 141, 156, 193, 197, 204, 209, 222
Draft
  Father, 43–45, 71, 86, 102–104, 205
  4-F status, xvi, 86–88, 181–183, 211
  military, 8–11, 43–45, 72–73,

86, 181–183, 211
  player, 33–34
Driscoll, Paddy, 131–132
Dropkick, 173
Dubofsky, Melvyn, 148
Dudley, "Bullet Bill," 41, 83
Duluth Eskimos. *See* Ernie Nevers Eskimos
Duluth Kelleys, 62

E

Effrat, Louis, 107
Eibner, John, 213–214
Eisenhower, Dwight D., 178
Elizande, Joaquin, xiii
Ennis, Al, 21, 71, 91–92
Ernie Nevers Eskimos, 62, 63
Espey, Jack, xiii

F

Farkas, Andy, 155, 190, 191, 194
Farley, Jim, x
Farman, Dick, 155
Father Draft, 43–45, 71, 86, 102–104, 205
Film review
  origin of, 69–70
  by Steagles, 117
Flaherty, Ray, 151, 152
Flaherty, Vincent, 155
Flutie, Doug, 173
Flynn, George Q., 8, 103
Football
  dimensions of, 173
  white, 114
Forbes, John, 93, 142, 221
Forbes Field, 93
Fordice, Kirk, 186–187
Formations
  Notre Dame box, 152
  T, 68–70, 79, 83, 84, 131

261

Index